Listening to Women on the Right

Listening to Women on the Right
Communication Strategies of Today's Female Republican Politicians

RACHEL FRIEDMAN, NICHELLE D. MCNABB
and KRISTEN L. MCCAULIFF

McFarland & Company, Inc., Publishers
Jefferson, North Carolina

LIBRARY OF CONGRESS CATALOGUING-IN-PUBLICATION DATA

Names: Friedman, Rachel B., author. | McNabb, Nichelle D. | McCauliff, Kristen L., 1979– author.
Title: Listening to women on the right : communication strategies of today's female Republican politicians / Rachel Friedman, Nichelle D. McNabb and Kristen L. McCauliff.
Description: Jefferson, North Carolina : McFarland & Company, Inc., Publishers, 2017 | Includes bibliographical references and index.
Identifiers: LCCN 2017020885 | ISBN 9781476667614 (softcover : acid free paper) ∞
Subjects: LCSH: Communication in politics—United States. | Women conservatives—United States—Language. | Women politicians—United States—Language. | Republican Party (U.S. : 1854–)—Platforms. | United States—Politics and government—1989–
Classification: LCC JA85.2.U6 F75 2017 | DDC 324.273401/4—dc23
LC record available at https://lccn.loc.gov/2017020885

BRITISH LIBRARY CATALOGUING DATA ARE AVAILABLE

ISBN (print) 978-1-4766-6761-4
ISBN (ebook) 978-1-4766-2947-6

© 2017 Rachel Friedman, Nichelle D. McNabb and Kristen L. McCauliff. All rights reserved

No part of this book may be reproduced or transmitted in any form or by any means, electronic or mechanical, including photocopying or recording, or by any information storage and retrieval system, without permission in writing from the publisher.

On the cover: Governor Nikki Haley at the 49th Annual Silver Elephant Dinner, May 6, 2016 (photograph by Sam Holland)

Printed in the United States of America

McFarland & Company, Inc., Publishers
  Box 611, Jefferson, North Carolina 28640
  www.mcfarlandpub.com

Table of Contents

Acknowledgments	vi
Prologue	1
Introduction: The "War on Women"	7
ONE • Terri Lynn Land	27
TWO • Joni Ernst	44
THREE • Carly Fiorina	58
FOUR • Nikki Haley	81
FIVE • Susana Martinez	101
SIX • Condoleezza Rice	116
SEVEN • Senate Sisters	130
Concluding Thoughts and Ideas	144
References	157
Index	181

Acknowledgments

Writing this book has been an exercise in patience and perseverance. The problem with timely research is that it is ever-changing and in need of constant attention.

Of course, time intensive and lengthy projects are often harder on those in our lives than they are on us. We feel fortunate to have had the support of our family, friends and animals. There are too many people and fuzzy companions to thank individually but we're eternally grateful for the times they listened to us think through ideas, allowed us to turn on televised speeches, and curled up at our feet as we typed.

Our colleagues in the departments at our respective universities were also amazingly supportive and patient. In particular, we'd like to extend our gratitude to Emily Rodriguez of Ball State University and Sarah Fogle of Embry-Riddle Aeronautical University. Both women provided exceptional research and editing skills during the process.

Finally, as women, we thank the female orators that we have written about as we know the challenges they face are many. The world is changing—sometimes for the good, sometimes for the bad—but we know that female political figures face challenges that their male counterparts typically do not. We thank them for their efforts and appreciate the opportunity to learn from them.

Prologue

It should not be a surprise that the three of us, who wrote this book about politics, watched the 2016 election from our separate locations around the country. We text messaged throughout the night. Like so many, we were surprised by the results. We feel comfortable disclosing that not only did the results not line up with the way we voted but they did not line up with our expectations given our knowledge of political communication, rhetoric, and the Republican Party's relationship with women. Indeed, as readers will see in the following pages, we have spent the last several years of our lives documenting, analyzing, and writing about the Republican Party's complicated relationship with women in its own party, female voters, and women's issues more generally. The genesis for this book began in 2013, on the heels of female voters soundly rejecting the GOP presidential candidate, Mitt Romney. Indeed, many politicos argued that after 2012, the party "ordered a full autopsy of the party to diagnose its image problems" with women (Bassett, 2016, n.p.). We spend the entirety of the Introduction documenting this context through the 2016 election cycle. And, truthfully, we conclude that the party has not done enough to repair its image with women. We, as scholars, truly believed that in the beginning of November 2016. In fact, in many respects, it seemed, when we wrapped up the first manuscript at the beginning of 2016, that the nomination of Trump and the primary election of 2016 did the exact opposite of help it attract more female voters. Katie Packer, a strategist the GOP enlisted to help repair the party's image, argued before the general election that she thought the party was "seeing the difference now between real attacks on women and what was very much fabricated in 2012" (Bassett,

Prologue

2016, n.p.). Packer believed that the GOP could repair its image with women but that it needed to "take a very strong stance" against Trump's rhetoric. She said, "I believe Trump's going to lose and it's going to take a little while to wash the stench of him from our party" (Bassett, 2016, n.p.). Indeed, Packer was not misguided in her thinking. A Gallup poll before the 2016 election showed that more than 70 percent of women had an unfavorable opinion of Donald Trump—the largest gender gap pollsters had seen for a presidential candidate (Illing, 2016). Pollster Stanley Greenberg wrote in May of 2016 that "there is something really basic, elemental, going on here with women reacting to Trump ... every signal he's sent that has built up his support with men and Republicans has had the opposite effect with women" (Brownstein, 2016, n.p.). In early and mid–2016, it was largely believed that Trump could not beat Hillary Rodham Clinton, or even stay competitive, without growing his lead with white, college-educated women—a voting block that traditionally leans Democrat. But it seemed, at least in early polls, that Trump faced unusually large deficits with them (Brownstein, 2016). And as one clearly partisan political commentator wrote:

> It is tempting to think of Trump as an outlier, as some foreign pathogen infecting the Republican Party. But that's not the case. His chauvinism finds a happy audience among conservatives. The more offensive and crass he is, the more appealing Republican men find him. This is a party that has worked hard to alienate women. Pushing intrusive and unconstitutional anti-abortion laws, threatening to defund Planned Parenthood, resisting equal pay measures—it's a mystery Republicans retain any women voters at all [Illing, 2016, n.p.].

But, as we know now, Trump did retain female voters in 2016. In fact, he retained many of them. The gender gap—the difference in the share of men and women who vote for a candidate—was 11 percentage points *for* Donald Trump (Miller, 2016). Moreover, 53 percent of white women voted for Donald Trump (Miller, 2016). Considering that national and state election polls from before the election had consistently put Clinton's chance of winning anywhere from 70 percent to as high as 90 percent, this data is surprising (Mercer, Deane & McGeeney, 2016). Kathleen Dolan, professor of political science at the University of Wisconsin, Milwaukee, who studies women in politics, argues that often gender does not play as big a role as pollsters and academics

Prologue

assume. Dolan says, "It does not change things at all. What matters 99.9 percent of the time is their political party" (Miller, 2016, n.p.), and we may conclude remarks that many deemed sexist did not turn large numbers of women away from Donald Trump. In exit polls, 70 percent of voters said that they thought his behavior toward women was a problem, but 30 percent of the people said they voted for him anyway. Dolan again writes, "People can have attitudes about these sorts of gendered things, and they still very rarely rise to the level of importance in their calculations. There's no better test than this election" (Miller, 2016, n.p.). So, clearly, the polls got the 2016 election very wrong. And as this book goes to press, we still do not fully understand the post-election results or the full support for Donald Trump. Yes, Hillary Clinton won the popular vote by nearly three million votes but the electoral data was clearly lopsided and complicated. As the American Association for Public Opinion Research wrote after the election, "As final results continue to be tabulated it would be inappropriate for us to participate in conjecture ... 'post-hoc analysis' will take six months" (Stelter, 2016, n.p.). As a result, this book will not speculate much about the results of 2016. We will not guess or offer speculation about how or why millions of women voted for Donald Trump and other down ballot Republicans.

So, who or what is this book for, then? Perhaps you are someone who, like us, was surprised and even dismayed by the election results. Perhaps you want answers on how a party that has such a complicated relationship with women and women's issues could be elected—in part because of female voters. Perhaps you are someone who was excited by the possibility of change in Washington and voted for Donald Trump not because you support his comments or policies as they related to women but because you think he can get things done. Perhaps you are a registered Independent who falls somewhere in the middle. We argue that this book is for you. This book is part playbook, with seven different case studies that are designed to provide a variety of glimpses into the Republican Party. These case studies, each from a different theoretical lens, examine how these women use, misuse, and (re)appropriate feminist messages. But they also seek to highlight key themes in issues and contexts that are often emphasized or overlooked within

Prologue

the Republican Party. These lasting lessons, as we call them, are helpful for someone who is both skeptical and supportive of the party. Regardless of your voter affiliation, understanding these complicated times is important. Election results do not happen in a vacuum. Nor do they happen without consequence. This closer look at the Republican Party and its relationship with female candidates and policies typically associated with women is necessary for us all to move forward. Now, more than ever, it is important for rhetorical critics, talking heads, political consultants, and candidates of all political persuasions to attune to gender and voting demographics. There are two primary reasons. First, pragmatism for the Republican Party. Trump has to work with women from both sides of the aisle who denounced his candidacy. Second, Trump and the party at large have to account for the millions of female (and other) voters who do feel scorned and isolated from the results. This prologue will detail these reasons before getting to the actual case studies. We hope that this set up will provide a lens through which to make best use of the information and case studies.

In the early days of October 2016, shortly after the release of a 2005 *Access Hollywood* video of Donald Trump making lewd comments about women, several GOP women rescinded their support of Donald Trump. For example, Virginia representative Barbara Comstock told voters that she could not support her party's nominee and urged Trump to drop out of the race. GOP senators Lisa Murkowski and Susan Collins, who are both featured in this book, denounced his remarks and said they would not endorse him. Martha McSally, Ileana Ros-Lehtinen and Mia Love did the same. And there were even more women, many of whom we discuss in the book, who slammed him for his rhetoric but extended a tepid endorsement citing belief in the party. So, where does President Trump go from here? He will have to work with a Congress that includes many women from his own party who repudiated his rhetoric and, in some cases, disowned him (King, 2016). Of course there are women who did support Trump and are eager to work with him. But Debbie Walsh, who directs the Center for American Women and Politics at Rutgers University, said the jury is still out on whether Trump can rebuild, or build for the first time, bridges with women of both parties who make up roughly one of every five lawmakers

Prologue

in Congress. She states, "We're going to see how this goes because he clearly alienated women in the course of this race (including) some of the very women he's going to need to work with on the Hill.... He's going to need to prove himself" (King, 2016, n.p.). It is too soon to know how many women will make it into a Trump cabinet but such appointments will serve as an olive branch of sorts. Walsh, again, writes, "During the campaign, Trump talked about how he valued women. Well, this will be a moment to see, does he want them in the room?" (Cohn, 2016, n.p.). Some of the women featured in this book have been invited to join his cabinet or have had their names floated as potential cabinet members. Therefore, we offer this book as an important first step to introducing these women and the strategies they have used to connect with voters and balance their identity as women within a party that often falls shorts of treating them respectfully.

Second, the voter landscape is complicated. As we stated, women did vote for Trump in the 2016 election but many of them did not. In fact, the majority of women voted in favor of Clinton. Her support was largely bolstered by minority women as 94 percent of black female voters cast their ballots for her and 68 percent of Latina women did the same (Fox, 2016). So, millions of women feel let down, disappointed, perplexed, and angry that more voters did not vote against Donald Trump. As Emily Jane Fox writes for *Vanity Fair*: "This election has been riddled with sexism. One candidate, over the years, has repeatedly referred to women as 'pigs' and 'dogs,' commented on women's weight and breasts and rated their attractiveness.... To have that language normalized in a campaign that was supposed to a historic, ceiling-shattering campaign for women was a kick in the stomach followed by a punch to the gut" (2016, n.p.).

Even people who were not turned off by Trump's comments or did not see his behavior as an indicator of sexism may be curious how Trump moves forward amidst this mistrust. Further, women's organizations seem dedicated to a close surveillance of his presidency. Stephanie Schriock, president of EMILY's List, which backs pro-choice candidates, emailed supporters the day after the election sounding a call that many women echoed: "I'm shocked and disappointed by the results of this election as you are.... After the dust settles, we'll find the

Prologue

resolve to come back and fight harder than ever against Donald Trump and the things he stands for" (King, 2016, n.p.). To put it bluntly, President Trump faces an incredibly complicated political landscape. Women do not like him. And if we are to take him at his word—that "no one respects women" more than him—we can assume that he is looking for ways to connect with women and overcome his reputation as sexist (Landsbaum, 2016). Thus, this book is particularly timely. It focuses on the party and how other candidates and elected officials have made this transition and balanced their identity as people who care about women but are perceived not to. Not only will the book introduce women who will be very important to the Trump cabinet but it introduces strategies that we may see Trump and his surrogates use as they attempt to connect with women. As you read this book, we invite you to see the aftermath of the 2016 campaign as the ultimate context. What can Trump learn from the experiences of others in his party? What can he use to help overcome this unprecedented landscape? As you do so, we leave you with Debbie Walsh again who argues that "we're going to have to see how this goes because he clearly alienated women in the course of this race including some of the very women he's going to need to work with on the Hill ... he's going to need to prove himself" (King, 2016, n.p.).

Introduction:
The "War on Women"

In 1990, Barbara Bush was asked to be the commencement speaker at Wellesley College when Alice Walker, author of *The Color Purple*, had to cancel her commitment to deliver the speech. When Barbara Bush was selected, 150 students from the 600-person class signed a petition protesting the selection of the first lady (Butterfield, 1990). Because Mrs. Bush dropped out of college after two years to marry George H.W. Bush, and because she was best known for her roles as wife and mother, the Wellesley students said she was not an appropriate speaker. Quite simply, she did not represent the type of career-driven woman that Wellesley is known to produce. Not only did Mrs. Bush show up and give the speech, but she was also friendly, complimentary and well spoken, and she brought Soviet president Mikhail Gorbachev's wife Raisa with her. Bringing Raisa Gorbachev seemed to indicate that she was not merely a simple housewife. Rather, she was involved with and knowledgeable of foreign policy and diplomacy.

Barbara Bush used the speech as an opportunity to lecture to the progressive elites who had rejected her because she worked in her home, raising children and supporting her spouse, *and* to speak to members of her own political party—she argued that feminism was about letting women be women. In a masterful piece of rhetoric, Barbara Bush (1990) said,

> Wellesley, you see, is not just a place but an idea—an experiment in excellence in which diversity is not just tolerated, but is embraced. The essence of this spirit was captured in a moving speech about tolerance given last year by a student body president of one of your sister colleges. She related the story by Robert

Introduction

Fulghum about a young pastor, finding himself in charge of some very energetic children, hits upon the game called "Giants, Wizards, and Dwarfs."

"You have to decide now," the pastor instructed the children, "which you are—a giant, a wizard, or a dwarf?" At that, a small girl, tugging at his pants leg, asked, "But where do the mermaids stand?" And the pastor tells her there are no mermaids. And she says, "Oh yes there are. I am a mermaid."

At the end of her speech, Mrs. Bush (1990) concluded,

For over fifty years, it was said that the winner of Wellesley's annual hoop race would be the first to get married. Now they say the winner will be the first to become a C.E.O. Both of those stereotypes show too little tolerance for those who want to know where the mermaids stand. So I want to offer a new legend: the winner of the hoop race will be the first to realize her dream—not society's dreams—her own personal dream.

Despite the fact that Barbara Bush lived a conservative life and was part of a traditionally conservative administration, her message was, perhaps, the most radical of all. Barbara Bush's message was very clear. Just as expecting women to get married and start families right out of college showed little tolerance for diversity, so did expecting women to be CEOs or career women. Real empowerment means being free to pursue whatever one chooses.

Barbara Bush was responding to a particular group of feminists on that Massachusetts spring day, but she was early to identify and address a more enduring problem that would plague conservative women and, more importantly, feminism for years to come. The *Washington Post* did a full historical retrospective regarding the state and inclusivity of feminism. This piece ran in January of 2016—25 years after Bush wondered what "counts" as feminism—but the enduring question stays the same, especially for conservative women. Elizabeth Velez, a Georgetown professor featured in the article, asked her class about Carly Fiorina, former CEO of Hewlett-Packard running for the Republican nomination. Fiorina identifies as a feminist and argued during the 2016 race that "a feminist is a woman who lives the life she chooses." But, when faced with the question if Fiorina, who opposes abortion rights and favors defunding Planned Parenthood, could "legitimately" claim to be a feminist, the majority of the students argued that she could not. One student did claim, however, that "we have this weird and often damaging tendency to divide people, where you're either one thing or you're not ... you're either a feminist or you're not ... and I think there is a gray area, and I think being a feminist takes all different forms" (Sheinin, Thompson & McDonald, 2016, online).

This question—about what counts as feminism and who gets to claim the label—is at the heart of this book. More than answering what a feminist is and who gets to be a feminist, this book will address how particular members of the Republican Party have negotiated that gray area. The book should be read as a series of seven case studies that provide readers insight into a variety of feminist strategies used in various ways. You will not find a monolithic argument that says "if politicians use this rhetorical strategy they are feminists." In fact, within each case study there are discussions about particular rhetorical strategies and whether, in a 21st century, postmodern landscape, those strategies are (or could be) considered feminist by the political electorate, so there is no overarching theory chapter. There is no guiding methodology or lens. Instead, we hope to provide a robust discussion about feminist strategies, political identity and the gender gap. (We define the gender gap as "the growing difference in voting behavior between men and women, particularly the higher propensity for women to vote Democratic" [Trevor, 1999, p. 67].)

Our aim in this book is not to offer up, as Bonnie Dow (1996) calls it, "the holy grail of truth" (p. 4). Rather, we want to argue for the possibility and the usefulness of understanding a rhetorical strategy in a particular fashion. We hope this volume reaches its capacity to engage a reader's thinking about the political implications of discursive practices (p. 5). In order to get this thinking started, this introduction will note the long existence of the gender gap, describe the way it has been fueled by politicians' comments in the last decade, and describe the ways Democrats have sought to exploit those comments and frame an agenda that excludes Republican politicians. This exclusion is key because it allows us to argue that now is a unique moment for the Republican Party to amp up its efforts to show that its members are the mermaids—the people who get to define their worldview. We look at several possible, instructive examples that are not all from any one specific year.

Introduction

The Gender Gap Historically

According to Gallup (Jones, 2012), "The gender gap has been evident in presidential voting since at least 1952, though it tended to be somewhat muted in the 1960–1972 elections, averaging just four points" (para. 4). It has not always been the case that the gender gap led women in a more liberal direction. "There was a relative Republican preference among women until 1960; they preferred Dewey, Eisenhower, and Nixon slightly more than did the men in each of these elections" (Whitaker, 2008, p. 3). Chappell (2012) states that a new phenomenon was noted by Reagan administration officials in the 1980s: "While women had supported the 'less radical' and/or more 'caring' candidate since the 1950s, in 1980, 'the gender gap began to manifest itself along ideological and partisan lines.' Women, an administration report warned, 'are now emerging as considerably more liberal and Democratic than men'" (p. 116). Ultimately, the gender gap has come to impact party identification. Kaufmann (2002) explains, "Beginning in 1992, however, the partisan movement of white men and white women begin[s] to diverge, with women turning toward the Democratic Party while men continue to grow more Republican" (p. 285).

The gender gap has come to be seen not only in presidential elections, but in congressional races as well (Clark & Clark, 2008; Manza & Brooks, 1998). Clark and Clark (2008) report: "Subsequently, it marked all presidential contests during the last two decades of the twentieth century, with the largest gaps of eleven to twelve percentage points occurring during the 1996 and 2000 presidential elections. The gender gap in congressional voting was somewhat slower to develop, but by the late 1990s, it had reached the level of presidential returns" (p. 50). In the 21st century this trend continued as the 2012 election proved no different. According to Decker (2014), "Republicans seeking a change in the party's approach have noted that unmarried women—who are the future, demographically—went for President Obama by a better than 2–1 ratio in the 2012 election. Among all women, Obama received 55 percent of the vote to Republican Mitt Romney's 44 percent" (para. 9).

The gender gap is important because it forces candidates to pay more attention to female voters in order to win their elections (Whitaker, 2008, p. 2). According to Whitaker (2008), "Race and social class differences are more prominent, but after these two factors, only religion and religiosity rival the ability of gender to predict party preference and voting. All other social differences, such as region, union membership, age, size and place of residence, are measurably less significant predictors of party preference and voting" (p. 1). Finally, Manza and Brooks (1998) explain, "The size of this 'gender gap' has often been larger than the margin of victory for Democratic candidates in congressional races as well as the 1992 and 1996 presidential elections" (p. 1236).

Scholars, politicians, and pundits have long posed the question of what explains the gender gap. Is there a gender gap because of candidates' positions on issues? Is the gender gap explainable because of stylistic differences between candidates? These types of rhetorical strategies may never be completely knowable. But research has offered some information. Manza and Brooks (1998) argue, "We have identified at least 23 analyses that date the origins of the gap to the 1980 election. In that election, Republican candidate Ronald Reagan ran a campaign emphasizing his opposition to the Equal Rights Amendment (ERA) and abortion and his support for 'traditional' family values and for an aggressive policy of military containment of Soviet-style communism" (p. 1237). Norrander (2008) suggests that "women's issues" do not explain the gap. "Women's issues such as abortion, support for the Equal Rights Amendment and women's role in public life were the first to be analyzed as a cause of the gender gaps discovered in the 1980s. Yet few gender differences were found on these attitudes" (p. 13). But Kaufmann (2002) offers a more nuanced explanation. She argues that presidential candidate Bill Clinton was more moderate and more fiscally conservative than previous candidates, and, consequently, Republicans could not just apply traditional labels like "tax and spend liberal" to Clinton as they had to Dukakis and others before him. Kaufmann (2002) concludes, "For the first time since the New Deal realignment, the most significant and defining differences between the Democrats and the Republicans were their social policy positions, in particular on abortion rights and gays in the military" (pp. 289–90).

Introduction

In general, men and women differ in their positions on "compassion issues." Norrander (2008) writes, "Women are more likely than men to favor government actions to assist individuals suffering economic difficulties or inequalities" (p. 11). This difference could be because women have long expressed a greater religious influence than men have (Norrander, 2008, p. 20). Pratto, Stallworth and Sidanius (1997) elaborate on what the compassion issues might be: "More women than men supported the enactment of gun control laws and increased government spending on social welfare, education and health. Women also supported programmes that aid the poor, blacks and the elderly, and policies that serve to equalize wealth (such as student loan programmes, wage and price controls, and minimum wage laws) more than men" (pp. 49–50).

Women may relate to these "compassion issues" more than men because they rely more on the public sector for education and other programs that help with caregiving responsibilities as well as function as a potential source of employment (Manza & Brooks, 1998; Whitaker, 2008). Clark and Clark (2008) state, "More recently, the 'feminization of poverty' has also pushed women in a liberal direction on these issues from self-interest arising from gender-specific cost bearing" (p. 54).

A final "compassion issue" that seems particularly relevant to the gender gap is defense. Women are less inclined than men to support military involvement in international affairs (Norrander, 2008), but in 2002, the gender gap almost disappeared in congressional voting and in presidential approval ratings. It has been suggested that the tragedy of September 11, 2001, resulted in more women being concerned about security and thus favoring the Republican party more for a time. The gender gap reemerged in 2004, when John Kerry won 51 percent of the female vote and only 44 percent of the male vote (Clark & Clark, 2008).

More recently, leading up to the 2012 election, Democrats and members of the media came to speak of a "war on women" by Republican candidates. This impression was, in part, shaped by a series of unfortunate statements Republican candidates made that appeared uniquely anti-women.

The "War on Women"

Unfortunate Comments

In February of 2012, Congress was debating the Affordable Care Act and "government rules requiring employers to offer insurance coverage for contraception" (*The Week*, 2012). The Democrats submitted the name of Georgetown University law student Sandra Fluke to testify that a close friend of hers had been denied coverage for the birth control pills she needed to treat polycystic ovary syndrome (Gibson, 2012). Representative Darrell Issa denied Fluke the ability to testify, claiming her name was submitted too late (*The Week*, 2012). The Democrats disagreed and claimed that the Republicans were attempting to silence women's voices (Fard, 2012; *The Week*, 2012). In response, Nancy Pelosi convened an unofficial hearing before the Democrats on February 23, 2012, in which Fluke disclosed that she had used contraceptives and that birth control cost as much as $1,000 a year because it was not covered by campus insurance (Fard, 2012).

On February 29, 2012, conservative radio host Rush Limbaugh slammed Fluke on his show, claiming that she was asking the government to subsidize her sex life: "What does that make her?" he asked. "It makes her a slut, right? It makes her a prostitute. She wants to be paid to have sex. She's having so much sex she can't afford contraception. She wants you and me and the taxpayers to pay her to have sex" (Reeve, 2013, para. 4). There were several obvious problems with Limbaugh's statement, in addition to the fact that he was referring to a third-year Georgetown law student as a "slut" and a "prostitute." First, women take the pill at regularly prescribed intervals. They do not take it every time they have sex. So there's no indication that a woman taking the pill is "having so much sex" that "she can't afford contraception." Second, women do not take the pill only to enable sexual intercourse. There are medically sound reasons to take the pill that have nothing at all to do with having sex. Finally, Rush Limbaugh was not objecting to insurance coverage for Viagra. He was not positioning himself as anti-*sex*. There appeared to be something uniquely objectionable to Mr. Limbaugh about female contraceptives.

The next day, March 1, 2012, "amid a chorus of criticism, Rush Limbaugh doubled down: 'If we are going to pay for your contraceptives,

Introduction

thus pay for you to have sex, we want something for it, and I'll tell you what it is: We want you to post the videos online so we can all watch'" (*The Week*, 2012, para. 7). Limbaugh, a conservative talk show host, was actually suggesting that the taxpayers ought to be able to watch sex videos of women who used their insurance coverage to help pay for their contraceptives. He did end up issuing an apology after John Boehner and Mitt Romney both publicly rebuked (*The Week*, 2012) his thrashing of Sandra Fluke. Ultimately, 45 advertisers pulled their advertisements from his show (*The Week*, 2012, para. 8) and "at least two stations dropped the show altogether" (Gibson, 2012, para. 4). But the damage was done. Davis (2012) reported the results of a Bloomberg poll that found more than half of the people it surveyed thought that Rush Limbaugh should be fired exclusively for his comments about Sandra Fluke (para. 6). The poll also showed a larger reflection on the candidates. Davis (2012) reported, "The results suggest the Republican candidates' focus on contraception is out of sync with the U.S. public. Seventy-seven percent of poll respondents say birth control shouldn't be a topic of the political debate, while twenty percent say it should" (para. 4). It is likely that Limbaugh's diatribe, while it may have appealed to some, created a further sense that Republicans were not the party of women's rights.

A second event occurred in August of 2012. Todd Akin, Tea Party-backed candidate for the U.S. Senate from Missouri, was asked about his unconditional opposition to abortion on a local St. Louis television show (Schlesinger, 2012). According to Schlesinger (2012), Akin explained, "First of all, from what I understand from doctors [pregnancy from rape] is really rare." Akin continued, "If it's a legitimate rape, the female body has ways to try to shut that whole thing down" (para. 4). He concluded by noting that even when a woman's "natural protections" fail, abortion should still not be legal for the rape victim. His word choice is particularly problematic. What does *legitimate* rape mean? Are some rapes illegitimate? That is, do women regularly accuse innocent men of raping them?

Then, in September of 2012, Akin compounded his problems by characterizing Claire McCaskill's assertiveness in debates as behavior that was not ladylike. Liptak (2012) quoted Akin: "'I think we have a very clear path to victory, and apparently Claire McCaskill thinks we do, too, because she was very aggressive at the debate, which was quite different than it was when she ran against Jim Talent,' Akin said. 'She had a confidence and was much more ladylike [in 2006], but in the debate on Friday she came out swinging, and I think that's because she feels threatened'" (para. 3). The idea that a woman cannot be assertive and be ladylike suggests that there is something unnatural about a female leader. The combination of these comments suggested that Todd Akin had some views about women that were clearly not politically correct. Akin had been ahead of McCaskill in the polls up until his legitimate rape statement in August (Bassett, 2012). Todd Akin went on to lose a winnable election to a "weakened" Senator Claire McCaskill "by a landslide" (Clement, 2014).

On October 23, 2012, Indiana state treasurer and Republican senatorial candidate Richard Mourdock made a gaffe during a debate against Democratic candidate Joe Donnelly and Libertarian candidate Andrew Horning (McAuliff, 2012; Saleton, 2013). All three candidates said they were anti-abortion. In explaining his position that the only instance in which abortion should be legal was when a mother's life was in danger, Mourdock said, "I struggled with it myself for a long time, but I came to realize life is that gift from God. And I think even when life begins in that horrible situation of rape, that it is something that God intended to happen" (Vorhees, 2013, para. 2). While Mourdock was not attempting to say that God intended for women to be raped, his word choice was poor. While he likely meant that even children conceived in rape are children of God, his comments were picked up by the mainstream media and liberal pundits, and he was blasted for the rest of the election.

During the 2012 election, a great deal of media attention was devoted to the Virginia gubernatorial campaign. Former chair of the Democratic National Committee and Clinton family friend Terry McAuliffe was running against Ken Cuccinelli, who was the attorney general in the outgoing McDonnell administration. "Republican Bob McDonnell had won women overall in 2009 by eight points in a race in which reproductive rights barely registered. (The exit polls didn't even ask about it)," according to Carmon (2013, para. 10). McDonnell

Introduction

was a dedicated opponent of legal abortion. During his administration, the Virginia state congress passed a series of laws designed to shut down abortion clinics (Carmon, 2013). Among them was a law requiring women to have vaginal ultrasounds and see the ultrasound images before she be allowed to have an abortion. Anti-abortion advocates supported such legislation because they hoped the laws would "persuade some women not to go through with an abortion" (Eckholm & Severson, 2012; McVeigh, 2012). This legislation was unpopular, to say the least. Lithwick (2012) described the procedure as one "in which a probe is inserted into the vagina, and then moved around until an ultrasound image is produced" (para. 1). Because of the invasive nature of the procedure, critics referred to it as "state rape" (Eckholm & Severson, 2012).

In response, Lithwick (2012) argued, "the law provides that women seeking an abortion in Virginia will be forcibly penetrated for no medical reason. I am not the first person to note that under any other set of facts, that would constitute rape under the federal definition" (para. 1). Though Virginia was not the first state to pass such legislation, it did generate a great deal of media attention. Perhaps greater media coverage was due in part to the fact that McDonnell had aspirations of being the Republican candidate for vice president, or that protestors gathered at the state capital. Comedians began to include references to the vaginal ultrasound legislation in their routines (Kumar & Vozella, 2012) and references to vaginal probes began to abound. In short, Virginia's law and the Republican officials who supported it became the punch line of jokes on late night talk shows.

McAuliffe's campaign "made sure that Virginians heard incessantly" that Cuccinelli was an "enthusiastic steward" of abortion restrictions (Carmon, 2013, para. 11). Carmon (2013) stated, "Messaging on access to birth control and abortion even made its way into ads put out by climate change and gun safety groups. In the end, McAuliffe won women overall by an 8–10 point margin" (para. 11). Moreover, 20 percent of voters in that race ranked abortion as the most important issue to them. Among those voters McAuliffe won by 25 points, according to exit polls (Feldmon, 2014).

More recently, in January of 2014, former Arkansas governor Mike Huckabee spoke at a luncheon for the Republican National Committee's winter meeting in Washington, D.C. (Miller, 2014). He spoke of what Democrats have come to term the Republicans' "war on women." Huckabee said that the Republicans were not waging a war on women, but, rather, a war *for* women. According to Parker (2014), Huckabee continued:

> And if the Democrats want to insult the women of America by making them believe that they are helpless without Uncle Sugar coming in and providing for them a prescription each month for birth control because they cannot control their libido or their reproductive system without the help of the government, then so be it, let us take that discussion all across America because women are far more than the Democrats have played them to be [para. 5].

This comment is reminiscent of Rush Limbaugh's rhetoric regarding law student Sandra Fluke because Huckabee suggested that women need government to help them control their libido. In addition to that, Huckabee referred to a provision in Obamacare as making women dependent on "Uncle Sugar." This would appear to make Barack Obama, the nation's first black president, "Uncle Sugar." Huckabee's reference seems to fit in with the larger, more mainstream Republican narrative about women's libidos and the tendency for women to rely on government to help them "have sex."

Is the Republicans' "war on women" primarily a rhetorical construct, brought on by voters' distaste for what Republicans have said? "Vaginal probes" and "state rape" do not have an appealing ring. Similarly, making statements like "legitimate rape," calling law school students "sluts," or saying that if a child was conceived in rape then it was God's will do not make Republicans seem like they are empathetic to women's issues or that they endorse female empowerment. Or is the "war on women" primarily a matter of the *policies* Republicans endorse? The Democrats began trying to exploit these unfortunate statements the press and late night comics had made so much of by presenting policies uniquely aimed at appealing to female voters.

Women's Economic Agenda

Nancy Pelosi, who served as both the minority leader of the House of Representatives and as the Speaker of the House, worked to shape

Introduction

a new "women's economic agenda" that the Democrats were promoting in the run-up to the 2014 midterm election that included "raising the minimum wage, guaranteeing workers the opportunity to earn paid sick leave, expanding affordable child care programs and passing the Paycheck Fairness Act" (Bassett & Jamieson, 2013, para. 3). According to Bassett and Jamieson (2013), Democratic support for these "worker friendly" reforms is not new. What is new is that Democrats are framing these issues not in terms of "economic fairness," as they normally would, but as essential to "gender equality and family stability" (para. 4). The "economic agenda for women" plays uniquely into the war on women rhetoric because it serves as a way of focusing voter attention on conservative comments by way of comparison.

The first economic issue Democrats reached out to women with was the minimum wage. Bassett and Jamieson (2013) explain that the framing of these economic issues as women's issues works because, as a Pew study found, "women are increasingly the sole or primary breadwinners in their families" (para. 9). Two-thirds of the minimum wage workers in America today are women (Bassett & Jamieson, 2013; Reston, 2014; Walsh, 2013). Women make up three out of five adults living in poverty, and they are twice as likely as men to rely on food stamps at some point in their lives (Walsh, 2013).

Bassett and Jamieson (2013) argue that "a woman working full-time, year-round, at the federal minimum wage of \$7.25 an hour, earns about \$14,500 a year. For a family of three, that's \$4,000 below the federal poverty line" (para. 19). Moreover, they went on to report that according to the Bureau of Labor Statistics in 2012, "almost twice as many women over age 16 earned minimum wage than men earning minimum wage," and "they are the majority of workers in the ten largest, lowest-paying occupations, according to the National Women's Law Center" (Bassett & Jamieson, 2013, para. 19). The lowest paying jobs include cashiers, food service workers, childcare providers, maids/housekeepers, restaurant servers, and home health aids, among others.

The Minimum Wage Fairness Act would raise the minimum wage nationally to \$10.10 per hour. Barbara Boxer said the increase in minimum wage from \$7.25 an hour to \$10.10 an hour "would lift the wages of 15 million women nationwide" (Reston, 2014, para. 3). The Minimum Wage Fairness Act faced strong opposition by House Republicans leading up to the 2014 midterm election. Republicans claimed that a minimum wage increase would lead to job losses nationwide (Reston, 2014). As businesses incur more labor costs, Republicans have argued, they will be less able to hire workers (Harris, 2014). Consequently, the very people a minimum wage increase was designed to help would be threatened by such a policy.

The second piece of legislation was the Paycheck Fairness Act. The Paycheck Fairness Act would close "some of the loopholes enabling pay inequities" (Walsh, 2013, para. 8) that results in women still earning only "77 cents for every dollar men earn" (Bassett & Jamieson, 2013). The bill would also prevent employers from retaliating against employees who disclose or ask for each other's salary information, and it would require employers to be able to show a justification other than gender for paying employees differently for the same work. This legislation was designed to make it illegal for men and women to receive different pay for similar work if they have the same qualifications. Senate Republicans filibustered the act in 2012 and House Republicans blocked a vote on the Paycheck Fairness Act in 2013 (Wicks, 2013). Benen (2014c) noted,

> Representative Cathy McMorris Rodgers (R–Wash.), the House Republican Conference chair, was asked yesterday whether she agrees with the president's position on laws mandating equal pay for equal work. "Yes, absolutely," she responded. "Republicans and I support equal pay for equal work." Rodgers failed to explain, however, why she, "like nearly every other congressional Republican," voted against the Lily Ledbetter Fair Pay Act and the Paycheck Fairness Act [para. 3].

We see Republicans have also been on the record as opposing legislation that requires equal pay for men and women who do comparable work.

The third piece of legislation Democrats claimed as related to women's financial issues was the Family Medical Insurance Leave Act. In 1993, the Clinton Administration passed the original legislation, which protected workers who needed to care for themselves or family members for an extended period of time from being fired. The act provided workers with 12 weeks of unpaid leave each year (Freedman, 2012). Currently, "only 11 percent of all private industry workers have access to paid family leave" (Zornick, 2013, para. 18). According to Freedman (2012), "America has no federal law mandating paid maternity leave. There are only a handful of other countries that also do not guarantee new mothers paid leave. Republicans, however, have opposed offering paid family medical leave." Zornick (2013) explains, "They blocked a proposal from President Obama in 2011 that would have created a $1.5 billion fund to push paid family and medical leave programs at the state level, and several similar efforts to enact such laws at the federal level" (para. 17).

A fourth issue that Democrats framed as a woman's issue was paid sick days. The National Partnership for Women and Families reported that "more than four in ten private sector workers—and more than eighty percent of low-wage workers—do not have paid sick days at all" (Koba, 2013, para. 2). Democrats argue that the need for sick leave disproportionately impacts women because more than 70 percent of women with children under age 18 are employed. In fact, most families need for both parents to be employed full-time in order to maintain a middle-class lifestyle (Feldman, 2012). What has not changed, however, is the tendency for the female head of family to assume the primary caretaker role when a child or other family member is sick (Bassett & Jamieson, 2013). Democratic senator Tom Harkin proposed legislation that would have allowed both full-time and part-time workers to earn up to seven days each year of paid leave for the worker's own illness or to care for a relative (Koba, 2013). Republicans opposed the legislation (Jamieson, 2014) because it would cost employers too much to offer paid sick leave.

A final piece of legislation that Democrats claimed was relevant to women and women's issues that was being debated leading up to the 2012 election was the Violence Against Women Act, originally passed in 1994 and reauthorized in 2000 and 2005 (Baucus, 2012). This legislation "increased federal penalties for domestic violence and provided funding for groups and services that aid victims of domestic abuse," according to Serwer (2012, para. 2). In April 2012, when it was time to renew the bill, the Senate passed a bipartisan bill that included new protections for Native American women; for gay, lesbian, bisexual and transgender women; and for undocumented immigrant women (Bendery, 2012). In May 2012, House Republicans put forward their own version of the Violence Against Women Act. Cohen (2013) explained, "The Republican proposal deleted provisions from the Senate measure that gave tribal authorities jurisdiction to prosecute cases on Indian reservations, specifically targeted discrimination of LGBT victims, and allowed undocumented immigrant survivors of domestic violence to seek legal status" (para. 11). Bendery (2012) cited Barbara Boxer's reaction: "Eric Cantor is going to put forward a bill that leaves 30 million people out? He should be ashamed of himself" (para. 19). Unfortunately, this issue was not resolved before the 2012 election, and though the law expired, Congress continued to fund it, but there is no guarantee that they will do so in the future.

These policies, and the Democrats' support of them, have come together to constitute an alternative to the war on women—at least in the rhetorical sense. At the very least, they draw attention to conservative statements and policies that came to be framed as the war on women. It seems that Democrats have been successful in creating the perception that Republicans are out of touch with female voters. Or perhaps the Republicans have helped the Democrats to create this impression. In the 2012 presidential election, Barack Obama won the female vote by 11 percent (Parker, 2013). In part, this may have had something to do with the unfortunate language Republicans used to talk about abortion and rape, as was discussed earlier. While people may argue over the GOP's policy positions on women's issues, it is hard to disagree on its (lack of) success at courting female voters. To be sure, the Republican Party is challenged in its appeal to female voters. According to Edwards-Levy (2014), "Fifty-five percent of Americans, including 59 percent of women, say the GOP generally does not understand the problems and concerns of women" (para. 2). Comparatively, a third of Americans, and 35 percent of women, said Democrats failed to understand women's concerns (Edwards-Levy, 2014).

Since the 2012 presidential election, GOP leaders have sought to coach party members on how to be more sensitive when talking about women's issues (Blake, 2014; Reinhard & Peterson, 2014; Shen, 2014;

Introduction

Zremski, 2014). Republican attempts to reach female voters included coaching candidates to avoid comments that might appear anti-women (Murphy, 2014), recruiting more female candidates (Zremski, 2014), and having candidates hold forums to listen to female business leaders (Reinhard & Peterson, 2014). Finally, following the 2012 presidential election, Mitt Romney's deputy campaign manager, Katie Gage, and his director of advertising, Ashley O'Connor, established Burning Glass Consulting, an all-female consulting firm that advises Republican candidates "solely on refining their message to women voters" (Murphy, 2014, para. 5). While it is too soon to argue that the Republican strategies are working, it is worth noting that the GOP ran only 4 percentage points behind Democrats in the 2014 midterm elections. And, at the very least, none of the Republican candidates committed the kind of gaffes that stoked the "war on women" narrative and put them on the defensive in 2012.

However, while many women won in several 2014 midterm elections, the gender gap remained (Blake, 2014; Kiley, 2014). Jocelyn Kiley (2014), an associate director of research at Pew Research Center, reported on November 5, 2014, "And the gender gap in elections is at least as wide today as at any point over the last 15 years." Blake (2014) explained that while Republicans won male voters by 20 points in the midterm elections of 2014, the Democrats still won female voters by 4 points. Yet, as we will document in this book, the party has a record-breaking number of female candidates and elected officials. Therefore, assessing the rhetorical strategies of female Republicans may inform future strategic choices by the Republican Party and any other candidates who have to navigate a political world in which their very identity seems to run counter to their identity politics.

Why offer a book analyzing conservative female speakers at this point in American history? There are many reasons to analyze the rhetoric of conservative women. First, a record number of Republican women were sworn into the 114th Congress (Tumulty, 2014). In addition, as we wrote this book, the Republican Party had a viable female candidate running for its presidential nomination. And, as the *New York Times* argued in 2015, Carly Fiorina has emerged as a GOP weapon against the "war on women" charges (Chozick & Gabriel, 2015, para.

1). These women, who are seemingly changing the face of the party and, perhaps, the discourse, are worthy of analysis. We argue that the texts and politicians analyzed in this book help underscore the changing nature of the Republican Party. While all the case studies are not from the 2016 election cycle, they provide helpful understanding of how the Republican Party has negotiated and will continue negotiate the voter gender gap. A comprehensive analysis of current and former GOP leaders allows us to speculate about whether the strategies used by conservative women, both successful and unsuccessful, are instructive of rhetorical strategies for future candidates. Finally, this book addresses a gap in the field's literature. While there have been notable essays covering prominent and controversial Republican women such as Sarah Palin, socially conservative feminism has been largely overlooked by scholars within the field of communication. As such, we do not have a wealth of literature helping scholars or candidates understand the public consciousness about women's issues and women in the Republican Party. While we cannot analyze every notable female conservative in this book, we argue this is a start and we urge other critics to heed our call and offer us more analysis of pertinent women and policies. For our purposes, we attempted to be both timely and historical. Ball (2014) argued: "Republicans championed [Terri Lyn] Land and Iowan senate nominee Joni Ernst, as walking refutations of Democrats' contention that the GOP is unfriendly to women" (para. 4). This is why we consider their inclusion, and Carly Fiorina's, essential. In addition, we include Nikki Haley who also rose to prominence during the 2016 election cycle when she was selected to give the GOP response to the State of the Union address. The women received much publicity in 2016 and drew upon common feminist tropes and illustrated new strategies that are both instructive and concerning. In Chapter 2, we examine a strategy that is often suggested for reaching women: encouraging more female candidates. In the Land versus Peters contest for retiring Michigan senator Carl Levin's seat, Terri Lynn Land made the argument that because she is a woman, she would be the best candidate to represent women's interests. We argue that Terri Lynn Land's disingenuous performance of womanhood fails as a strategy to connect with female voters in Michigan. Similarly, we argue in Chapter 3 that

Introduction

Joni Ernst's performance during the 2014 Iowa senate campaign is rooted in faux maternalism. This chapter affords us an opportunity look at an incredibly popular female candidate turned senator. By drawing on her uncommon, interesting personal story as an Iowa farm girl and Army National Guard combat veteran, Ernst related to her fellow Iowans and captured one of the most reliably liberal Senate seats in the country. The seat had been held by now-retired Democratic senator Tom Harkin for 30 years (Rogers, 2015, n.p.). While Ernst never calls herself a feminist, we argue that there is a "mama grizzly" appeal to traditional, male voters that relies on a particular, palatable brand of feminist discourse.

In chapters 4 and 5 we continue our analysis of women who were offered by the party as anecdotes to the war on women. We examine Nikki Haley and Carly Fiorina. Haley was the governor of South Carolina in 2016 when she was selected by the GOP to give the response to the State of the Union address by President Barack Obama. Her identity as both a child of immigrants and also a Southern woman allows her a particular charm and political moderation that is changing the face of the Republican Party—both literally and figuratively. Her rhetorical motives are best understood as a drama as she received various responses from the different conservative pundits throughout her career. Finally, she attempts to move the rhetoric to a more central place perhaps hoping to bring Democrats and Republicans together. Her rhetoric gained such traction in 2016 that her name was also touted as a potential vice presidential candidate.

The second woman particularly relevant on a national scale during 2016 was former Hewlett-Packard CEO Carly Fiorina. As we stated above, Fiorina ran for president in 2016 as part of the large pool of GOP nominees. In addition, she was selected during the primary to be running mates with one of the GOP frontrunners, Ted Cruz. In her debate performances during the 2016 GOP primary season, Fiorina actively denied others the power to define her feminism as unfeminine. Drawing upon Kathleen Hall Jamieson and other communications scholars, we argue that her ability to use both qualities allow her to break the double bind.

In addition to these recent women, we feel that it is also useful to explore the rhetoric of conservative women who have long been successful in navigating the challenges we have outlined throughout this introduction. Therefore, we then shift and apply an explicitly feminist lens in chapters 6 and 7 to examine Susana Martinez and Condoleezza Rice, respectively. One of the reasons we chose to conduct rhetorical analyses of both Susana Martinez and Condoleezza Rice is that they are both racial minorities and women in the conservative political party. It is interesting to examine how and where the rhetoric intersects for them. In other words, race is not most likely a "separate issue" for them. They cannot just choose to speak as women or speak as persons of Hispanic or African American origin. They must speak as a Latina Republican governor or an African American secretary of state as well as women. Their subject positions are interesting for so many reasons, especially since the GOP has had challenges in reaching the very demographics that these women represent.

In addition to their intersecting racial and gender identities, both Martinez and Rice represent many firsts in America and are thus trailblazing in ways some may not realize. In 2010, Susana Martinez was elected governor of the State of New Mexico. She became New Mexico's first female governor and the first Hispanic female elected governor in the history of the United States. She was named by *Time* magazine one of the 100 Most Influential People in the World in 2013, one of only two governors who made the list. In April 2011, *Hispanic Business Magazine* named Martinez "Woman of the Year" for her efforts to reduce the tax burden on New Mexicans, get the state's fiscal house in order, and promote a friendlier business environment allowing employers to create jobs and hire New Mexico workers. Therefore, she represents the role of a powerful conservative woman who has done some important things for the country.

In 2000, Condoleezza Rice was dubbed the "warrior princess" as she was George W. Bush's national security advisor. She was the first woman to occupy this role. She was also the first African American woman to serve as secretary of state (2005–2009). In August 2012, Rice also became the first woman (in addition to another businesswoman) to earn membership to the Augusta National Golf Club in Georgia. This club had been all male since 1933. There is also continuous

Introduction

speculation and support for Rice to run for president of the Unites States; there are many websites devoted to her for this purpose, but she seemingly has no interest. The way these women discuss issues pertaining to women and minorities is so important because ultimately they have or have had the ability to support legislation that could potentially benefit so many marginalized people. Furthermore, the strategies they use could inform us as to what works best when managing one's role as woman of color in the conservative political party. Certainly, political and legislative challenges exist with respect to their gender and racial identities.

Finally, we turn our attention away from individual candidates to larger political campaigns. We argue in Chapter 8 that the rhetoric of compromise may provide a good playbook for Republican women hoping to maintain or attain national attention. In this chapter, we examine the 2013 budget shutdown. More specifically, we examine media coverage of the "Senate Sisterhood" that worked to find accord and prevent a shutdown. The sheer amount of attention paid to these female senators make the case an interesting site of analysis. The situation provides an opportunity to tie in more feminist theory and argue that the political strategy of compromise, pragmatism and collaboration, which we call "Maternal Thinking," can be a useful rhetorical strategy in national politics. These case study chapters allow us to argue for some lasting lessons and advice in the conclusion.

• ONE •

Terri Lynn Land

The 2014 midterm election was thought to be capable of determining control of the Senate for the final two years of the Obama administration. The Republicans needed to regain just six seats in order to control the Senate (Gearan, 2014). A political analyst at the nonpartisan Cook Political Report, Jennifer Duffy, put the Republicans' chances of winning the Senate in the 2014 midterm election at 50–50 (Weisman, 2014). Consequently, *both* parties were focusing on the importance of winning over female voters (Batley, 2014; Gearan, 2014; Soltis-Anderson, 2014). For example, "Andrea Bozek, communications director for the NRCC, told NPR, 'Women are 54 percent of the electorate.... They aren't a coalition, they are the majority, and if you aren't actively engaging with women voters, you're going to lose'" (Batley, 2014, para. 9). Therefore, the war on women, outlined in the introduction, continued to be a major focus because campaigns have often been won or lost based upon which party turned out more women voters (Rosin, 2014).

An important race in which gender became a central issue was the competition for retiring Michigan senator Carl Levin's seat. Democratic representative Gary Peters, a relative unknown outside of suburban Detroit, ran against Republican Terri Lynn Land, who had twice been elected in large majorities and served as Michigan's secretary of state (Ball, 2014). Because this race was considered "one of the hottest midterm campaigns," it attracted big money from national sources (Woods, 2014a, para. 6). According to Egan (2014), "national pundits have said control of the U.S. Senate could largely hinge on the battle to fill the vacancy being created by the pending retirement of U.S. Sen.

Carl Levin, a Detroit Democrat" (para. 5). This Senate race was so significant that President Obama followed it and commented on it. In 2010, Land made the statement that the gender pay gap was deceiving, asserting that women earn less because women make choices that family is more important than work. According to Woods (2014a), "'the reality is that women have a different lifestyle,' Land said at the 2010 Senior Women's Club event. 'They have kids. They have to take them to get dentist appointments, doctor's appointments, all those kinds of things. And they're more interested in flexibility in a job than pay'" (para. 4). Shepardson (2014) reported on President Obama's response to Land:

> Obama commented for the first time on Michigan's race pitting Land against U.S. Rep. Gary Peters, D–Bloomfield Township, that could decide control of the U.S. Senate. The president grouped Land with Republicans whom he claims "just think that this idea there's a gender pay gap is a fantasy, it's not real.... [I]n fact, I think there was a candidate for the Senate, a Republican in Michigan, who voiced the opinion that women make other choices. And I think that's certainly true; every individual makes other choices. Very rarely do you meet people who make the choice to be paid less for doing the same job" [para. 2–3].

Republicans insist that the war on women is a fictional creation of the Democrats (Peters, 2014). While it may have been a fictional creation by Democrats, the Republicans helped to bring the war on women to life, in part, by addressing it as though it were a real threat. "More than a dozen female Republican lawmakers gathered ... with GOP operatives to hold a broad discussion on conservative ideas to empower female voters" (Palmer, 2014, para. 2). In fact, in 2013, "Republican candidates were subject to sensitivity training by the National Republican Congressional Committee because, as one staffer put it, they have 'a lot to learn'" (Rosin, 2014, para. 2). We may conclude that the Republican war on women is real because (1) the political parties are strategizing about how to win female voters over, (2) the parties are treating it as though it is real, (3) female voters may determine which party controls Congress, and (4) even the president is responding to the rhetoric related to the "war on women." A final rationale for including Land's rhetoric in an analysis of Republicans' "war on women" responses is that Terri Lynn Land's candidacy was heralded as an example

One • *Terri Lynn Land*

the right wing used to demonstrate that they were not waging a war on women. Their position justifies assessing the rhetoric in order to see how it appeals to likely female voters.

As a candidate, Land demonstrated many strategies for winning what the Democrats charged was the Republicans' war on women. This chapter will identify and analyze some of those strategies, beginning with a commercial the Land campaign aired starting in mid–April and continuing through May. This advertisement was entitled "Really?" Booker (2014) described Terri Lynn Land's commercial on National Public Radio:

> "I'm Terri Lynn Land. Congressman Gary Peters and his buddies want you to believe that I'm waging a war on women. Really? Think about that for a moment," she says. For the next 12 seconds of the ad, Land stops speaking and a campy musical interlude plays. Land stares briefly into the camera, reaches for and takes a sip from a blue mug, looks back at the camera and shakes her head in disbelief and then looks at her watch [para. 4–5].

The commercial closes with Land stating that she approved the commercial: "I approve this message because, as a woman, I might know a little bit more about being a woman than (Rep.) Gary Peters."

In our analysis of this commercial, we explore the advertisement and its tone, and we extend the analysis to include some of Land's positions on issues concerning women. This text allows us to draw conclusions about the authenticity of Land's "pro woman" campaign. On June 2, 2014, Dickerson (2014) wrote, "Land is widely acknowledged to have a problem with female voters" (para. 14). Three months later, it appeared that this advertisement was not a silver bullet for appealing to female voters. In fact, "Republican messaging guru Frank Luntz later said on FOX News that Land's ad tested worse with focus groups than any other he had seen this election cycle" (Marcotte, 2014, para. 4). Nia-Malika Henderson wrote an article in the July 15, 2014, *Washington Post* entitled "Land's clever anti-'war on women' ad didn't do much to close the gender gap in Michigan." This advertisement was not the complete answer to winning the battle for Michigan's female voters. In order to understand why, this chapter opens with a close examination of the advertisement.

In the advertisement, the visuals tie her to the domestic, private sphere as if to further solidify her identity as a woman. Terri Lynn Land is seated in what appears to be a nicely decorated living room with a white fireplace. Wearing a navy blue suit jacket and glasses and drinking from a coffee mug, she looks like an attorney or a banker or any other professional. Her haircut is simple and sensible. She is feminine, maternal. She could be someone's mom. What she does not look like is an evil villain popping off a movie screen brought to life by Disney. Cruella de Vil she is not. It is difficult to believe that she would be mean spirited or purposely attack women.

Republican pollster Frank Luntz immediately attacked the advertisement, calling it "the worst ad of the year" (Ball, 2014, para. 6). Indeed, as the advertisement aired, it appeared that the gender gap among voters expanded in Peters' favor. Marcotte (2014) explained, "Pollsters credited a surge in Peters' position to a widening gender gap" (para. 4) after voters had viewed Land's "Really?" advertisement for about six weeks. Frank Luntz developed his critique of the ad in greater detail on Electablog (2014): "That ad, it doesn't give any message, it doesn't tell you anything about her, and it doesn't communicate any sense of substance. She's a challenger, she has to prove where she stands, she doesn't do it" (para. 3). Since neither Peters nor Land had been elected to an office as high as that of state senator, Land needed to make a better argument. In effect, it seemed the argument she advanced was "I cannot be waging a war on women because I am a woman."

The advertisement depicts Land wearing a suit and glasses—seemingly performing congressional—but when Land had her first opportunity to answer questions as a candidate, she appeared to have trouble. Dickerson (2014) explained her debut opportunity as a candidate to answer questions at the Mackinac Institute on Mackinac Island in the spring of 2014:

> In one of her first unscripted appearances since declaring her candidacy last June, Land looked as if she were auditioning for a remake of "Bambi Meets Godzilla." She fumbled an audience question about Internet neutrality, responded to a query about her position on the auto industry rescue with a stream of non sequiturs, and at one point, during a scrum with reporters, threw up her hands in frustration, exclaiming, "I can't do this!" [para. 6].

One • Terri Lynn Land

This gaffe had great impact because Land did not interact with the press much after that incident. As Ball (2014) reported, "It's a single substanceless gaffe from several months ago, but it has come to symbolize Land's campaign, in part because she hasn't given the media mush else to report" (para. 7).

One would think that Land would have had to answer reporters' questions in her role as Michigan's secretary of state. Moreover, as a senatorial candidate representing a state such as Michigan, where the auto industry is central to both the economy and the state's culture, one would think she might have a clear position on the auto bailout. Although women may support female candidates, there is no reason to believe that female voters do not care about the issues or do not insist that the candidates they vote for prove themselves competent by being able take a position and make arguments in favor of their positions. Gizzi (2014) reported that Bill Ballenger, editor of *Inside Michigan Politics*, explained, "But people—and this includes many Republicans—are still apprehensive about when and if she sits down to debate Peters on television. They want to know if she is ready to step up to the plate" (para. 8). Although Peters emerged with a large and consistent lead over Land, and although candidates who are behind typically want to debate in hopes that it might help them catch up, Land never did agree to debate Peters (Ball, 2014). In fact, as time passed, Land appeared more and more difficult for people following the election to find. According to Brian Dickerson of the *Detroit Free Press*, Land "has been about as accessible to this point in her campaign as a music video diva recovering from plastic surgery" (para. 3). Ball (2014) reported, "Land held some campaign events when I visited last week, but they were not announced to the press or to the public in advance" (para. 11). It seems counterintuitive that a candidate would campaign in secret because the point of campaigning is to become known.

At first blush, this advertisement could be effective because it was amusing. It showed Land as human and authentic. It would seem obvious to voters that Land would know more about being a woman than her male opponent. The advertisement seems to be arguing that women should vote for Land because, as a woman, she has to be pursuing their best interests. She would also appear to be sympathetic to the struggles women face. Even though she may, obviously, be female, she may simply be out of touch with *other* women's issues or realities. The idea that one woman can be a spokesperson for all women is problematic. Not all women have the same needs or want the same things. Land may have no idea what it means to be pregnant at 15 or to try to support one's family on a minimum wage job. With a net worth of $32.8 million, Land was one of the wealthiest Senate candidates in the 2014 cycle (Lazar, 2014), so it is safe to say that she may have a different set of worries or concerns than the average contemporary American woman. We now take a closer look at Land's positions on women's issues, beginning with equal pay.

It is not our argument that all feminists have to take the same positions on issues or that Republican women cannot be feminists. It is possible that women can be against pro-choice policies due to their religious beliefs, but certain policies do tend to be associated with feminists and feminist organizations. The National Organization for Women lists the following as its primary issues of concern: "(1) NOW fully supports access to safe and legal abortion, to effective birth control and emergency contraception ... (2) Ending Violence Against Women, (3) Economic Justice, (4) LGBT Rights, (5) Racial Justice, and (6) Constitutional Equality Amendment." Feminists are not required to agree with each of these issues. If one appeals to women and advocates positions in opposition to these policies, however, one would need to devote time and attention to developing a rhetorical strategy in justification of feminists' support. Land does not. Remember, as Republican pollster Frank Luntz argued, her advertisement provided no argument at all. We now turn our attention to uncovering what Land's positions were on issues that women care about.

Equal Pay

A comical advertisement about how she was more in tune with being a woman than her male opponent was not likely to convince voters. Her positions on issues and the policies she supports were likely what mattered to informed female voters. Land opposed "the current congressional bill to raise the minimum wage, which disproportionately affects women" and "came out against the equal pay bill that would have made it easier for women to figure out whether they were getting the same wages as their male peers" (Collins, 2014, para. 8). Equal pay may not matter to all women because women deal with different life challenges and women possess different values. One might recall Land's 2010 statement that because women have kids and they have to get to "dentist appointments, doctors' appointments, all those kinds of things" (Woods, 2014a, para. 3), they care less about pay then they do flexibility in their jobs. This very statement implied a role for women to appropriately fulfill in their personal relationships and in society. Land's vision of modern marriage appeared to be one where the woman still assumes the *primary* responsibility for the home and offspring, and presumably the man assumes the primary responsibility for the family's economic survival. This is not a vision that represents reality for most women. In most contemporary American families, the woman's wage is needed for the family's economic survival. Jarrett (2010) argued, "Women are the sole or co-breadwinners in two thirds of American families. For them and their families, equal pay is not only a matter of principle; it's a matter of survival" (para. 4). In these families, survival likely trumps flexibility. Moreover, even in families where the woman is not an essential breadwinner, couples may choose to share responsibility for taking children to their various appointments. So, while Terri Lynn Land is biologically a woman, her vision of what is important to other women may not reflect the reality of millions of other women.

Moreover, stating that women care more about flexibility in work time than they do equal pay implies a certain social class bias. It is not every woman who is empowered enough to care about flexibility of time because one cannot buy milk, bread, and other basic grocery items with flexible time. For many women, meeting their children's basic financial needs has to be their primary financial concern. Land discussed her opposition to the Paycheck Fairness Act by "noting that the secretary of state's office had more female managers when she left than when she started" (Clawson, 2014b, para. 4). But not every woman has a boss who will give her the chance to move ahead. The Paycheck Fairness

Act is designed to help fight discrimination when it occurs. Moreover, as Clawson (2014b) noted, "it doesn't mean a whole lot, as a politician, to say you support equal pay for equal work if you would vote against a bill meant to ensure it" (para. 6).

Perhaps, like Laura Trueman of the Heritage Foundation, Terri Lynn Land believes that we live in a post-masculine world, because women earn more undergraduate and graduate degrees than men. But, as Messina-Dysert (2014) argued, "men continue to earn higher wages than women, and hold more than 80 percent of leadership positions in U.S. Despite women's educational success, they continue to be forced into roles with lower salaries or refused equal pay for equal work" (para. 7). Moreover, single mothers struggle most with poverty because of what Messina-Dysert (2014) termed "low wages and poor social policy.... While more than 80 percent of single mothers work 30 hours per week or more, they are disproportionately likely to be employed in low income positions" (para. 7). It is difficult to see how a female candidate could support women by arguing that they do not need provisions to ensure that they are paid what men earn.

On Land's (2014) blog, she attempted to appeal to female voters by portraying herself as the common woman: "Born in Grand Rapids, Michigan, Terri's early years were spent living at the family's La'Grande Grandville Motel and Trailer Park, which was started by her grandfather and grandmother. As both the business and Terri grew, Terri worked alongside her family at the motel, cleaning rooms, changing the beds, and working various jobs around the property" (para. 5). This post draws upon common tropes to imply that Terri Lynn Land's family was lower middle class, that she grew up in a trailer park and worked cleaning rooms. These details make her seem very much in touch with the struggles of the common person, but readers/listeners have no idea how often she cleaned rooms or worked odd jobs at the motel. Moreover, her grandparents did *own* the motel and trailer park. According to the Eeggert (2013), Land and her family have "assets worth tens of millions of dollars" (para. 1). Gray and Helms (2014) noted that although Land talked about her grandparents immigrating from the Netherlands and starting a hotel and trailer park, she did not talk about how her husband took over the park and got the residents to move out so the company could pursue redevelopment. In other words, she emphasized the part of her family narrative where her grandparents served as an example of the American dream. Although Land's family pulled themselves up by the bootstraps with hard work, she omitted the part of the family's story where she and her husband inherited the family business and forced common people out of their trailers in order to make way for more profitable development (Lazar, 2014). The second women's issue that we explore in greater detail is Land's position on abortion and birth control.

Abortion and Birth Control

According to Sargent (2014), Land received the Michigan Right to Life PAC's endorsement. The executive director of that PAC, David Malone, reportedly told Sargent that "no legislative candidate gets this endorsement unless he or she is 'pro-life with no exceptions other than the life of the mother,' and unless he or she agrees to a 'Human Life Amendment to the U.S. Constitution, effectively establishing personhood from the moment of conception'" (Sargent, 2014, para. 5). Campaign spokeswoman Heather Swift confirmed that Land is against abortion even in cases of rape and/or incest (Schultz, 2014). She does, however, support exceptions to save the mother's life. And she is also supportive of women "having access to mammograms and the pill" (Electablog, 2014, para. 23).

Perhaps what is most concerning about this is that Land supports a personhood amendment to the Constitution. According to Eckholm (2011), the amendment "would declare a fertilized human egg to be a legal person, effectively branding abortion and some forms of birth control as murder" (para. 1). This would mean that women would have considerably less control over whether or not they give birth. They could effectively not plan births around school completion, job security, or marital stability. Personhood amendments have failed in conservative states such as Montana, North Dakota, Oklahoma, and Mississippi (Clawson, 2014).

According to Clawson (2014), "This is something Land should be made to talk about. A lot.... Voters should know where Terri Lynn Land stands on this issue" (para. 4). It is the mystery surrounding Land's positions not just on women's issues, but on several issues, that is most concerning. We had to really search to find out what Land's positions on issues were. Apparently, so did Clawson (2014):

> There are all of two issues on Land's website: "health care reform" and "stronger Michigan manufacturing." Health care reform, of course, means repealing Obamacare and moving to Health Savings Accounts and deregulation. Land's blog indicated that stronger Michigan manufacturing should include "deregulation" and the keystone pipeline. Why doesn't Land clearly state her positions on a whole host of issues? One would think she would want the public to know what she stands for. If Land, as a woman, knows a little bit more about women than Gary Peters, maybe she knows that Obamacare prohibited being a woman from being a pre-existing condition. But if she knows, she apparently doesn't care enough to put it on her website. And where are issues of concern to women like the minimum wage or fair pay? They don't even rank a mention [para. 6].

Perhaps Land is way behind Peters in female voter support precisely because she is so ambiguous about issues women care about. It is possible that saying, "trust me, I'm a woman" is not enough for female voters.

Finally, at the end of 2013, Michigan's Republicans supported and passed a law banning private insurance companies from covering abortion. If women wanted abortion care, they needed to purchase additional coverage, according to the law. The bill was dubbed "rape insurance" since many women who would otherwise not want an abortion might want one if they were raped and because the law made no exception for cases of rape or incest. According to Rankin (2014), "So where was Land on this anti-woman bill? Nowhere. Silent. She said absolutely nothing other than 'government shouldn't pay for abortions" (para. 5). Land did devote some space on her blog to explaining to readers what women really consider important. We now turn our attention to that material.

Land's Blog

In an article on her blog entitled "The Real War on Women," Land identified the issues that are *really* important to women:

One • Terri Lynn Land

> When an entrepreneur is struggling to keep the doors to her coffee shop open because of high taxes and regulatory burdens, due to Congressman Peters' unpopular policies like Obamacare, that's a war on women. When a young woman who just graduated college faces student loan default because she can't find a good-paying job and struggles under the weight of unaffordable insurance, that's a war on women. When a grandmother living on a fixed income sees her Medicare benefits cut, to pay for ObamaCare, that's a war on women. When a single mom who saw her hours cut from full-time to part-time has to decide between buying gas and putting food on the table, that's a war on women [Land, 2014, para. 4].

It likely surprises no one that a Republican candidate declared Obamacare the number one threat to women in America today. Not coincidentally, the solution to empowering women is also the prescription Republicans offer for dealing with virtually every other crisis America faces: getting rid of Obamacare, cutting regulations and taxes, and eliminating "wasteful spending" (though it is unclear what this wasteful spending is). Earlier, we noted that Land argued the way to improve manufacturing in Michigan was also by de-regulating and reducing taxes. Schow (2014) also argued that the solutions Republicans suggest are pretty simple to recall: "It appears Land ... is saying that the problems women are facing in America are the same problems men are now facing—high taxes, regulatory burdens, and lack of jobs" (para. 9). It seems counterintuitive that there are no issues that women care about more than male voters. Moreover, one might think that if the main concern for women is that they face unemployment, then Terri Lynn Land might have wanted to support President Obama's bailout of the auto industry, but this was not her position. As we discussed earlier, when she was given a chance to explain her position, she did not do this effectively.

Gray (2014) explained how Terri Lynn Land dealt with questions related to the bailout when reporters asked her about it at the Mackinac conference in May of 2014: "when confronted with several questions, regarding whether she would have voted for the federal bailout for General Motors and Chrysler (she has said she didn't support the bailout), she repeated a rote answer: 'I support the autoworkers. I'm glad the autos are doing well'" (para. 6). Once again, according to Land, the solution is de-regulation and reduced taxes: "I support the autos, and what I want to do is go down to Washington D.C. and make sure we have a competitive environment here in Michigan and that you don't over-regulate, you don't over-tax and you don't over-burden Michigan families" (Clawson, 2014b, para. 3). Although Land said she was glad that the auto industry was doing well, she did not make a point of noting that she would not have saved it. Moreover, she appeared to make no argument as to why the position she took, that of the mainstream Republican Party, was correct.

Indeed, Land indicated that she cares *more* about women and shows *more* respect for women by *not* offering them government assistance such as fair pay, legal abortion, or birth control. Land concluded the blog post:

> Women know best how to manage their *own* money, without the interference of Washington politicians like Congressman Peters. As your Senator, I will continue to protect your paycheck by cutting wasteful spending, supporting tax relief, and reducing job-killing regulations. All women deserve opportunity and less interference from Washington so they can chart their own path. That is my vision, one that I believe women across Michigan share [Land, 2014, para. 7].

This trope of tough love is one Republicans often make. George W. Bush used to argue that he trusted the American people to invest in their own retirement instead of relying on Social Security. Now we are left wondering if anyone believes that. After all, Social Security was developed precisely because people did not have sufficient reserves on their own to provide for themselves.

Lessons Learned

In Land's (2014) advertisement, she says, "Congressman Gary Peters and his buddies want you to believe that I'm waging a war on women." Yet Sarlin (2014) quoted Congressman Gary Peters: "'I've never used the term "war on women" ever,' Peters told MSNBC. 'What I am doing is standing up for issues that women care about'" (para. 36). This seems to indicate that the concept of a war on women has resonated so much with the Republicans that he does not even have to say the phrase in order for Land to prepare an advertisement answering it. Moreover, the Republicans take this "war" seriously enough to prepare ads designed to answer it specifically. What is less clear, however, is whether or not they see a connection between people who wage war on women and the issues those candidates support.

Second, Peters may appear to be more of a feminist based upon his positions on issues than Land is. Peters (2014) wrote a letter to the *Detroit Free Press* that began:

> One of the first things I did in Washington remains one of my proudest: helping to ensure that women earn equal pay for equal work. It was five years ago this week that I supported the Lilly Ledbetter Fair Pay Act, an important step forward for women who deserve to earn the same pay as their male counterparts for doing the same job. This bill makes it easier for workers to seek a legal remedy for lost wages caused by pay discrimination [para. 1–2].

Peters went on to explain that short-changing women's pay constituted a drag on the entire economy because it reduced a family's ability to purchase groceries and other basic necessities. He then continued,

> I helped introduce another important initiative, the Paycheck Fairness Act, because I believe that paycheck fairness is a key component of continuing to improve our economy. This bill takes the next step to ensure equal pay by allowing employees to share salary information, so that when wage disparity exists, women have the necessary information to fight it. The bill requires employers to show that if wage disparities exist, they are a result of job related factors, not gender. I urge Congress to address the issue of paycheck fairness and vote on this important measure to address wage disparity. Michigan has always been a place of innovation and opportunity, but we must do better to keep that promise and build a stronger middle class. Hard work should pay off, and contributions should be based on merit, not gender [para. 7–8].

When one compares this letter to Michigan voters to Land's relative silence or positions that represent the standard Republican responses, Peters appears to be more supportive of women's needs.

Third, simply putting forth female candidates who support the same old policies that conservatives have long taken on, issues such as abortion and equal pay, is not enough to win over female voters. According to George Will (2014), "Land represents Republicans' most effective response to Democrats' hyperventilating about the 'war on women'—female candidates" (para. 10). Nocera (2014) noted, "The Republican establishment would love to have more women candidates—

particularly the kind like Land who campaign well and do not have plans to rock the boat on any subject whatsoever. But they've failed to deliver. Only four of the 20 women in the Senate are Republicans, and only 19 of the 79 women in the House" (para. 9). Female Republican candidates definitely create a visual image that seems to contradict the notion that the party is waging a war on women. This image might help the party to win a campaign of competing 30-second advertisements where image reigns supreme, but McDonough (2014) made a vital point: "the 'young guns' being scouted by the National Republican Congressional Committee may make for some more demographically representative campaign ads, [but] the policies they have built their careers on are pretty indistinguishable from the sea of white men who have been driving the GOP into the ground" (para. 2). If one looks below the surface, beyond appearances and examines policies, the young demographically-varied Republican candidates may prove less appealing. And it goes without saying that "being a female" is not a useful strategy for all Republican candidates.

So, do women's issues matter? Do women vote based upon those issues? Charen (2014) argued that Pew surveyed women regarding the issues we value, and found "abortion was named less often than health care, education, jobs, Medicare, the economy, terrorism, taxes, foreign policy, and the budget deficit. The only issues that ranked lower for women voters were immigration and energy. A post-election Kaiser poll found only 7 percent of those who voted for President Obama cited women's issues as most important to their vote" (para. 3). Perhaps these results occurred because abortion is currently legal and because being pro-choice does not mean that one is pro-abortion. While many women never plan to have an abortion themselves, they also see it as a necessary option to prevent other women and girls from dying during back-alley abortions performed by unqualified and unregulated providers. It is not an issue they perceive as a primary voting concern, but it is still important. Moreover, most women probably believe they deserve equal pay for equal work.

It is clear that pundits like George Will believe that female candidates are insulated from or immune to attacks that they are waging war against other women, but Reinhard (2014) cited "Democratic pollster

Celinda Lake, who has studied women voters, said it's unclear whether female Republicans are insulated from 'war on women' campaigns or are even more vulnerable because they are held to a higher standard" (para. 14). In other words, women are expected to perceive women's issues differently than their male counterparts. For example, former Supreme Court Justice Sandra Day O'Connor frequently broke with the other conservatives on the court when they were deciding women's issues. Hayes (2005) explained that "her vote upheld the right to privacy and reproductive choice, affirmative action, and disability rights" (para. 7). For a woman not to empathize with other women might be perceived as worse than a man's indifference; it might be seen as betrayal.

Moreover, if Land is correct on issues such as equal pay being the result of factors other than gender discrimination, it might come across as cold or indifferent for a wealthy white Republican woman to say so. As both political parties increasingly strive to win over a more demographically diverse electorate, it may appear to those very voters that a rich white female politician, who achieved her wealth by inheriting the family business, is not in touch with the struggles voters face. In the case of Terri Lynn Land, her campaign financing issues may have exacerbated this appearance that the candidate is out of touch. Kilgore (2014a) argued that part of Land's appeal as a candidate was that she was a "self-funder." That is, she was independently wealthy and could contribute to her campaign. Spangler (2014) noted that Land gave her own campaign $3 million over two years, but she did not list any accounts or assets in her name that were worth $3 million in her federal financial disclosure forms. Her campaign claimed it was an oversight because she neglected to disclose a joint account she had with her husband. This coverage was problematic in many ways. First, it meant repeated coverage that she donated $3 million to her own campaign. Second, not many people could simply forget having a joint account with one's spouse that is well in excess of $3 million. That amount of money would seem unforgettable. Third, the incident made it more difficult for Land to distance herself from the running of the family business and the removal of residents from their trailers. Clearly, she benefitted financially from her husband's business decisions. Finally, in her role as Michigan's secretary of state, it was Land's job to enforce campaign laws. As a candidate, it would seem like she would be very careful to follow those rules herself since a plea of ignorance would seem unbelievable.

Given all of this, our response to Republicans like George Will who argue that having more female candidates with the same old positions on issues is the solution to winning over female voters is that not only is this answer incorrect, as Land lost to Peters in 2014, but it is demeaning to women. It says that women do not care about the policies candidates support. It says that image is more important than substance. Perhaps more than anything else, Land's support for the same positions as typical mainstream male Republican candidates explains why female voters have failed to be drawn to Terri Lynn Land in spite of the fact that she clearly knows more about being a woman then Democrat Gary Peters. And it is this disregard for female voters as interested and knowledgeable about policies that makes Land and her party seem so out of touch.

Some have suggested that Land may have lost because she was not conservative enough and the Koch brothers withheld financial support from her campaign. We believe this is wrong for the following reasons. First, the National Republican Senate Committee did decline to buy the ad time they had reserved for the Land campaign in the last month before the election, but this was because they were "cutting their losses" since Peters had maintained a "consistent lead" over her "since early summer" and the state already leaned Democratic (Kilgore, para 4, 2014a). Second, there's no reason to believe that Land was short on funds. As Kilgore reported, "To listen to the quotes the group (NRSC) offered to Joseph, they're pulling out because Land has more money than she can possibly spend" (para 4, 2014a). Rather than Land losing the election because the NRSC reduced funding available to her, she lost funding because she was losing the election.

Why, then, did Land lose female voters to a white male politician? Our argument is that she lost because she was too polished and not out talking to voters and letting them feel like they knew the genuine, authentic person. We talk about authenticity with Joni Ernest in the next chapter. What we hope readers see is that Land's campaign was devoid of substance and the "Really?" advertisement served as a metaphor of her entire campaign. She took positions that were inconsistent with feminist ideologies, and she failed to explain why they were logical or compelling positions for women to embrace. In fact, when she did talk about women's issues, such as equal pay, she seemed to reveal that she was out of step with the problems most women face. That is, keeping appointments was the primary concern and not supporting the family financially. We do not think that she was not conservative enough. She seemed dedicated to the party line. As Ball (2014) explained, "In our interview, I found Land to be well-stocked with talking points but evasive when it came to explaining herself" (para. 13). For whatever reason, Terri Lynn Land seems to have been incapable of letting Michigan voters feel like they knew and liked her.

• Two •

Joni Ernst

The 2014 midterm elections brought the count of women in Congress to more than 100 for the first time in history. Given the success of female candidates during the previous election cycle in 2012, the high number was not surprising to political pundits and analysts. What may have been surprising to a number of people, however, was that it was Republicans who helped raise the number of women in the Senate, in particular, over the current record of 20. As Jessica Valenti (2014) reported, "six new Republican women were elected to the US Congress this week as part of the Democrats' staggering midterm defeat—including the youngest woman ever elected and the first black Republican woman in Congress" (n.p.). Indeed, it was a win for Republican women. In many ways, the surprise was just a continuation of the 2008 presidential election that saw traditional meanings of Democrat or Republican turned on their heads with the vice-presidential candidacy of Sarah Palin (McCarver, 2012, p. 59). Just because the trend is predictable does not mean it is not baffling. Writing in *Newsweek*, Anna Quindlen (2008) summarized her own confusion in regard to the upside-down Republican Party in 2008: "I never thought I would live long enough to see the day when the Republican presidential candidate would cite membership in the PTA as evidence of executive experience, when the far right would laud the full-time working mothers of newborns, when social conservatives would stare down teenage pregnancy and replace their pursed-lip accusations of promiscuity with hosannas about choosing life" (para. 1). While many feminist commentators were not as quick to note the progress in 2014, opting instead to claim that the election was not a win for women at all, the trend is worthy of study.

Two • Joni Ernst

This surge in Republican women can be personified by Joni Ernst's campaign. On the night of the 2014 election, the soon-to-be freshman U.S. senator from Iowa stood in front of a crowd of supporters and claimed, "It's a long way from Red Oak to Washington, from the biscuit line at Hardee's to the United States Senate." She then delivered her trademark line, the one she delivered in a campaign advertisement that focused on her early-life profession of hog castration: "Thanks to all of you, we are heading to Washington. And we are going to make 'em squeal" (Voorhees, n.p.).

More shocking than the line—or the childhood profession—was the fact that Ernst was giving a victory speech at all. Indeed, Ernst may have been the most surprising victory of the 2014 midterm elections. The three-year state senator became the first female senator of a state that President Obama took in 2012 by 6 points (Voorhees, n.p.). Ernst campaigned in small towns across Iowa and introduced herself to voters as a "southwest Iowa farm girl" (Solberg, 2014, n.p.). That "farm girl" stood in front of a tour bus covered with an American flag, her picture and the tag line "Mother. Soldier. Independent Leader." And while the *New York Times* argued that throughout the election Ernst never appealed to Iowans to help her break the glass ceiling and insisted that she was not running on her gender, she nevertheless provided a new "playbook for Republican female candidates" (Stolberg, 2014, n.p.). Although it may be a playbook of sorts, we argue that it is nothing new. In fact, when Ernst does talk about gender or, more rarely, feminism, it is in a way that is similar to what scholars have noticed about former Alaska governor and vice-presidential nominee Sarah Palin. Palin herself seemed to see the connection. While stumping for Ernst, Palin cried that she had not "been this excited about a candidate in quite a while" (Jacobs, 2014b, n.p.). New or not, it is this "playbook" that we discuss in this chapter. To do so, we look at Ernst's commercials, her performance in the three debates against challenger Bruce Braley, and her victory speech following her successful bid for the U.S. senate. We argue that Ernst exhibits some aspects of a maternal style but that, in large part, any traditionally feminine values were overshadowed by Ernst's masculine style. Drawing upon her military service and small town upbringing, she was viewed as authentic by the Iowa electorate.

This authenticity seemed to trump gender issues in the 2014 Iowa senate debate. In order to make this argument, the chapter is laid out in three major sections. First, we introduce Joni Ernst and her personality. We then turn our attention to close textual analysis of her campaign texts using Gibson and Heyse's (2014) idea of faux maternal personal and performance of hegemonic masculinity as our lens. We then draw conclusions regarding authenticity and personality as they played in Iowa. We use the Iowan experience to draw national conclusions given Ernst's visibility during the 2016 election cycle. We stress that her success in 2016 has been directly linked to her "authentic" personality. While she is a bright spot for the GOP, her strategies may be hard to replicate by others.

Joni "makes 'em squeal"

Ernst broke out of the Iowa primary in 2014 with 56 percent of the vote despite being outspent by retired businessman Marc Jacobs (Newton-Small, 2014, n.p.). She is outspoken against the affordable health care act, believes life begins at conception and is enthusiastically pro-gun. Her candidacy was deemed by many as "2014's most extreme" and "more conservative than most Republicans" (see MacGillis, 2014; Newton-Small, 2014). Her conservatism won her the support of prominent Republicans, including New Jersey governor Chris Christie and Senator Marco Rubio from Florida. But Ernst's campaign really came together in early November 2014 when retiring Iowa senator Tom Harkin was caught on video calling the Iowa Republican state senator "really attractive" (Alter, 2014, n.p.). Harkin, whose seat Ernst was seeking, commented that she's "as good looking as Taylor Swift but votes like Michele Bachmann"—comments that, not surprisingly, were denounced by Ernst herself. She stated, "I think it's unfortunate that he and many in their party believe that you can't be a real woman if you're conservative and female…. I believe if my name had been John Ernst on my resume, then Senator Harkin would not have said those things" (Alter, 2014, n.d.). And, indeed, Ernst may have been right, but her direct attention to gender was startling given that, for most of the

Two • Joni Ernst

race, Ernst denied the election was about gender. It was reported that Kellyanne Conway, a Republican pollster who went on to advise Donald Trump in 2016, advised Ernst against running "overtly as a woman" (Stolberg, 2014, n.p.). And on the night of her primary election victory Ernst said that a war on women was phony: "First, I am a woman and second, I have been to war. I am a combat veteran. This is not a war on women. Anytime Democrats are using the word war they need to do it to honor our service men and women" (Schwartz, 2014, n.p.). Of course, issues in politics are rarely that black and white. The gray area in this race found lots of examples of gender featuring prominently in stump speeches. Ernst herself, when questioned about her record on women's issues, once responded, "I think it's laughable that Congressman Braley is the one that's lecturing me on this. I'm a woman, and I have three beautiful daughters, and I just think when it comes to women's issues, I have an edge on women's issues" (Bassett, 2014, n.p.). Ernst and her advisors also reported during her primary race that "Joni is a mom, a grandmother who has volunteered at a crisis hotline, and that part of her bio will told" (Rucker & Baltz, 2014, n.p.). Her website reiterated that with the first word on her "about" page: "Mother."

If you ask any casual voter, however, the image of Ernst most widely circulated was not that of matriarch and family woman. Instead, two provocative advertisements transformed Iowa's senate race and her image. In March of 2014, Ernst spent $9,000 to air a commercial about her personal testimonial of castrating hogs on an Iowa farm and her promise to apply those same skills to Washington. Her second advertisement ran two months later and showed Ernst stepping off a Harley-Davidson in a leather jacket and firing multiple shots at a shooting-range target. The advertisement promised to take expert aim at President Obama's health care law. The advertisements, which Ernst herself admitted were edgy, were viewed more than 400,000 times in just three days and became the talk of cable news (Rucker & Baltz, 2014). In the general election, Ernst ran softer advertisements in which she was seated at a kitchen table talking about the "Iowa we leave our children" and the key to a good biscuit (Marcotte, 2014). All this is to say that despite the claim that Ernst's gender was not a focal point of her campaign, her rhetoric often offered a playful twist on masculine endeavors or reinforced long-held stereotypes of femininity. It is also to say that Ernst appeared to be providing proof for Ronnee Shreiber's (2008) argument that conservative women have often seen the value of playing around with the meanings and enactments of feminism for quite some time. In her book *Righting Feminism: Conservative Women and American Politics*, Shrieber illustrated that a growing number of conservative women are successfully using the language of women's empowerment to achieve conservative ends. Gibson and Heyse (2014) claimed that Sarah Palin's rhetoric during the 2008 campaign legitimized a conservative feminism by drawing upon the myth of the American frontier to revise the women's rights movement (p. 100). Palin romanticized an idea that it is not feminism that allows women to succeed but a type of womanhood predicated upon individualism and toughness. To be sure, during the primary and general election, Ernst never publically denounced or declared a feminist identity. But her willingness to show herself as someone feminine yet rugged, maternal yet tough, shows that she was willing to be a mascot for a type of conservative womanhood that was "aggressive and explicitly gendered" (Gibson & Heyse, 2014, p. 102). This narrative, made famous by Sarah Palin, has been dubbed "the Rise of the Mama Grizzlies" by academics due to Palin's description of a mama grizzly bear in her book *America By Heart*:

> In Alaska, the only thing we take more seriously than a grizzly bear is a mama grizzly bear with cubs to protect. Some misguided souls—particularly in the Lower 48—are determined to portray these bears as cute and cuddly.... Grizzly bears—mama or otherwise—are beautiful, ferocious, serious-as-a-heart-attack creatures. When you come upon one, you don't give her a hug. You tread lightly. Because when the ones she loves are threatened, she rises up [p. 127].

Palin trumpeted the Mama Grizzly as a collective political identity comprised of conservative women throughout the 2008 election (Rodino-Colocina, 2014). And, indeed, it appears Ernst was accepted into the club in 2014. While stumping in Iowa, Palin told an energized crowd, "Joni Ernst, she's a mama grizzly ready to take a stand ... she's pro-life, pro-second Amendment, pro–Constitution" (Jacobs, 2014b). Palin may be the most famous Mama Grizzly but she is certainly not the only one. This is a strategy that both parties use. Diane Feinstein was highly successful with a campaign that rhetorical critic David B. Sullivan (1998) called "tough but caring" (p. 22). Additionally, her counterpart, Barbara Boxer, played on her name as someone who would fight for what she believed in—"Barbara Boxer Gives a Damn" was the slogan of her first congressional campaign (Heller, 2015, n.d.).

We hope to show, like other scholars before, that the Mama Grizzly narrative seeks to depoliticize gender and nullify any challenges to patriarchy that can come with a female's candidacy like Ernst's (Gibson & Heyse, 2014, p. 100). The remainder of this chapter will examine Ernst's rhetoric as it appropriates and rejects the Mama Grizzly script.

"Give me a shot"

When Democrats began calling Ernst the new Sarah Palin in 2014, they meant it as an insult. Neither woman seemed to understand the criticism. During a May 2014 rally, Palin said that Ernst is a candidate "we can have faith in … liberals won't talk down to her about a 'war on women' … liberals try to characterize women as being defenseless, just little chicks who need big sugar daddy big government to take care of us" (Jacobs, 2014a, n.p.). Ernst responded that she was ready to fight and to be the candidate to go forward (Jacobs, 2014a, n.p.). This section investigates Ernst's rhetoric while drawing upon the important work that has been done by communication scholars analyzing Sarah Palin's political rhetoric.

In particular, we draw heavily on Gibson and Heyse's (2010) idea of "Faux Maternal Persona and Hegemonic Masculinity" (p. 235). Gibson and Heyse (2010) argued that Palin engaged in maternal rhetoric—no matter how inauthentic—but that she also followed traditional hegemonic scripts that celebrated John McCain's masculinity while emasculating President Obama. Similarly, the *National Journal* argued that Ernst ran on her compelling biography, "including her down-home Iowa farm upbringing and National Guard service … while working to portray Rep. Bruce Braley, her Democratic opponent, as an out-of-touch elitist" (n.p.).

Listening to Women on the Right

Faux Maternal Persona

Scholars have noted that to engage in maternal rhetoric is to potentially introduce feminine values into public life. Contemporary speakers have used motherhood tropes on a political stage to drum up support for a variety of ideological positions such as supporting nuclear disarmament, advocating for environmental justice, and pursuing peace politics (Mehan & Wills, 1998; Peeples & DeLuca, 2006; Ruddick, 1989). Hayden (2003) contends that maternal appeals have the potential to challenge dominant political values and advance a politics of care that values nurturance, community and empathy as political values.

On the surface, Ernst seems to be openly and unabashedly maternal. The tagline "Mother. Soldier. Independent Leader" could be found everywhere on her campaign—her tour bus, stump speeches, debate introductions, and website. She would often bring her 15-year-old daughter on the trail with her—serving as living proof of the "mother" line (Stolberg, 2014, n.p.). But in the wrong hands, Hayden (2003) argued that the maternal persona can likely only reaffirm prevailing hegemonic beliefs that the feminine is subordinate. Indeed, as George Lakoff (1996) has argued, within some conservative contexts it is possible that the maternal role is likely to possess very little clout and that values such as nurturance, empathy and care will not be embraced to the same degree as protection, independence and moral righteousness. While it is well-known that Ernst is a mother, very little of her political philosophy seems to come from mothering. *Mother Jones*'s Patrick Caldwell (2014), an expert on Iowa politics, wrote that the GOP establishment urged her to run and bet that her "biography and folksy political charm would matter far more than her extreme political positions ... and if she wins on Tuesday, she'll set an example that Republican candidates will emulate for years to come" (n.p.). While he does not specify, we suspect Caldwell is guessing that Republican candidates will emulate Ernst's individualism.

Ernst often implies that her role as mother and maternal thinker is guiding her policy choices, but it is hard to find examples of that reasoning. In one interview she said, while defending the personhood bill she proposed in the Iowa senate that would have outlawed all abortion and many forms of birth control, "I'm a woman and I have three beautiful daughters, and I just think when it comes to women's issues, I have an edge on women's issues." Instead of elaborating on what her edge would provide, she followed up her statement with "When's the last time somebody came up to you and asked you about men's issues? I mean, truly. Has anybody ever asked you that?" And instead of arguing how this personhood bill is good for women, she continued, "but we try and scare women by stating, this is a woman's issue, and this woman is going to take away your access to contraception, which is completely untrue" (Sioux City Journal, 2014, n.p.). This was a common campaign trail quip from Ernst in an effort to discount the war on women. She was known to repeat, as evidenced by the repetition of this phrase already in the chapter, "I am a woman, and I have been to war and this is not war" (Will, 2014, n.p.) or "First, I am a woman and second, I have been to war. I am a combat veteran. This is not a war on women" (Schwartz, 2014, n.p.).

Despite her reminders that she is, in fact, a woman, in the three hours of Iowa debate coverage she only ever mentioned "women" or "children" when talking about herself or her own. In fact, her opponent, Bruce Braley, routinely brought up maternal issues and logic. When speaking about the minimum wage, Braley argued in the debate that of "60 percent of Iowans who would get a pay raise by raising the minimum wage, 50 percent of them are over the age of 30, many of them have children and are depending on the jobs." Ernst followed up the conversation by bringing up taxes and paychecks. She stated, "My family worked very hard. I know many families work very hard. Let's allow them to make decisions on how they're spending their paychecks." For Ernst, progress and success are individually oriented. She claimed that the federal minimum wage increase was unnecessary, as $7.25 an hour suffices for Iowans, and she would often claim that she missed the days before food stamps when "wonderful food pantries" took care of the poor (MacGillis, 2014, n.p.). Indeed, when she gave the Weekly Republican Address in July 2014, she sounded Reganesque as she talked about her family's ability to "teach us the lessons of not spending what you don't have. In our small town, we relied on each other—our neighbors lent us a helping hand when we needed it ... today, to get America back on track, it is going to teach each of us to advance solutions to our problems" (Weekly Republican Address, 2014). This compassionate conservatism seems to argue that the small town is the hero. It calls forth an image of shop owners, or even the Walton family, sitting on their porch eager to help their neighbor.

And while her "Take Aim" advertisement alludes to the fact that she is "not your typical candidate," the advertisement is not referring to her gender. It implies, instead, with a close up of a handgun, that "she carries more than just lipstick in her purse." And Ernst herself often claimed that she was not your "typical" politician. But, again, instead of drawing on her maternal role, she turned to what she often called "The Iowa Way," which was a blend of "honesty, service, and hard work" (Voorhees, 2014, n.p.). The "Iowa Way," it seems, is a reliance on individualism, which Harter (2012) argued is an embodiment of a "masculine subjectivity" (p. 93). While not completely in line with the popular mythic depictions of the cowboy myth, Ernst's rhetoric reflects an intense value of independence and implicitly argues against governmental action, favoring instead an optimistic belief that confident, tough individuals can prevail over circumstance. A video put together by the National Republican Senatorial Committee in support of Ernst narrated that growing up in Iowa taught Ernst "anything can be accomplished with a little elbow grease and common sense" (Duty, Honor and Iowa). At its core, this notion of individual hard work and common sense is rooted in a logic of masculinity. Women are not the heroes of the story. Government does not have to work hard to hold up women and ensure they have access to health care, a living wage, or even regular meals. A consequence of this narrative is that rugged hard work and individualism ultimately produce a campaign playbook that undermines the need for policy to promote women's issues.

Performance of Hegemonic Masculinity

By all accounts, the above explication of Ernst's reliance on individualism can be seen as hegemonic masculinity. But a perhaps more overt breach of her traditional femininity was her reliance on working and middle class imagery to prove her folksy toughness. Further, her combat military service stood in sharp opposition to Bruce Braley's lack of the same. Both tropes allowed Ernst to subvert any type of maternal appeal she may have made to instead celebrate traditional, hegemonic masculinity. While Ernst ran advertisements showing her in a home setting or talking about "bringing people together," her campaign persona is decisive and direct and cites her military background and leadership (Keifer, 2014, n.p.).

In a political rally in Des Moines, Iowa, in the month leading up to the midterm election, Ernst told a cheering crowd that what she wanted to do was "compare and contrast [her] record when it comes to foreign policy and military affairs" with that of Congressman Bruce Braley and President Obama (Goldmacher, 2014, n.p.). Indeed, she highlighted her military background and criticized Braley's attendance record with the House Veterans' Affairs Committee: "He left 120,000 American veterans hanging out to dry without the health care not only that they deserved but they had earned through their honorable service." She went on to claim that Braley's absence meant he was too late to recognize serious security threats. When talking about the Islamic State, Ernst used the opportunity to minimize Braley, saying, "No kidding, Congressman Braley. Where were you two years ago?" (Goldmacher, 2014, n.d.). When talking about the Islamic State in the debates, Ernst repeated a similar line, saying, "I am someone who has served in the military for 22 years. I am a combat veteran. My boots have been on the ground in Iraq. I will stand with our troops and make sure that we think through our actions carefully." Her self-description as someone who is tough, present and experienced suggests that Ernst views herself as what Rodino-Colocino (2012) has termed "a mama grizzly taking care of business" (p. 84). To drive home the point, her campaign repeated that was why she was going to Washington. In both her squeal and shot advertisements, Ernst claims that once she gets to Washington, D.C., she will "make them squeal" and "take aim" at the wasteful spending occurring inside the beltway. Her message in the Shot commercial was particularly resonate given her appearance—clad in a Carhartt vest or leather jacket inside a barn or at a shooting range. It was this persona that *Los Angeles Times* reporter Maeve Reston

(2014) called an Annie Oakley type of message: "Don't pen me in, don't hold me down, I can shoot better than you" (n.p.).

In the debates, Ernst was able to combine her time as a lieutenant colonel with her previous work on her family's farm to delegitimize Braley. She repeatedly called attention to Braley's background as an attorney and said, "I grew up on a southwest Iowa farm and my father is a farmer. One in six jobs are created by the Iowa farmer." And "I still am a normal Iowan," she said. "He is a very wealthy man. I live in a home that I bought for $80,000. He lives in a home that most Iowans would never dream of owning" (Rubin, 2014, n.p.). This idea that she stands up for those against power, greed, and terrorists is recurring. In the debate in October of 2014, about a month before the election, Ernst said: "I will stand up and do what's right for Iowa.... Not President Obama. The Iowa people. I am someone that has stood up for my community, my state, and my nation. I have not left my rural roots but I think the congressman has left those behind in the beltway."

And if the public was ever confused about Ernst's strength, Sarah Palin, while referencing Ernst's hog advertisement, repeatedly told crowds, "It's like, whoa, nobody's going to push her around" (Rucker & Balz, 2014, n.p.). Indeed, Ernst's strong language proved her a force not only during the general election but also early on in the primary. During the primary race, Ernst's Republican opponent, Marc Jacobs, was forced to change his language. Advisors to Jacobs said that he needed to argue he was a "normal Iowan," emphasizing that he was the type of chief executive who "rolled up his sleeves and got his hands dirty traipsing around power plants in jeans and steel-toed boots" (Rucker & Balz, 2014, n.p.). As the *New York Times* argued, Ernst forced the four-term congressman Bruce Braley to "out bumpkin her." Late in the general election, he began to "assure voters that he grew up doing farm jobs and working a grain elevator" (Leibovich, 2014, p.11). While not degrading traditional feminine characteristics outright, coupled with her dismissal of the "war on women," she is certainly coming dangerously close to reinforcing a culturally constructed relationship between politics and masculinity. Tiffany Lewis (2011), who analyzed woman suffrage speeches in the American West, argues that women rhetors who demonstrate women's capability of participating in the rituals of manhood may make space for American women to live outside the restrictions of "true womanhood" (p. 144). Unfortunately, Lewis (2011) claims that only women who can "prove their manhood" are worthy of political equity (p. 144). By condemning traditional notions of a politics of care, Ernst instead glorified masculinity and masculine ideals. Her "corn-fed political charisma" proved so potent that it effectively gave her a $12 million lead over her democratic opponent and propelled her into office (Scher, 2015, n.d.).

Lessons Learned

It is tempting to assume that all voters, and female voters in particular, saw through the faux brand of feminism that Ernst offered. The idea that candidates can talk about maternity and motherhood without actually showing support for policies that help women has been well documented by scholars and pundits alike. But, as we know, Ernst was victorious in the 2014 general election. And it seems, in this case, that the victory was less about gender and more about authenticity.

Many feminists have pointed out that the 2014 election was a win *by* women but not *for* women. Jessica Valenti (2014) argues that just being a woman does not make Ernst's policy positions any less scary (n.p.). Indeed, the assumption by many was that Ernst and other Republican candidates were relying purely on the male vote. But, seemingly, that is not what happened. Marcotte (2014) wrote before the election that "Ernst is relying on the male vote to push her over the top" and Ernst did win more of the male electorate—58 percent to 40 percent (Reston, 2014, n.p.). But the race was not a slam dunk for Braley with the female electorate. Instead, women split their support evenly between the two candidates (Reston, 2014, n.p.). As a result of the female vote, in the aftermath of the election, GOP and Democratic strategists alike were commenting on Ernst's successes. Celinda Lake, a Democratic pollster, said, "She is a real role model for future Republican women…. She's a real right-winger, but she was able to use her gender and bracket—not just every faction of her party, which was remarkable, but frankly independent women in her state as well" (Reston, 2014, n.p.).

Certainly we do not want to suggest that we expect women voters to vote for the most traditionally feminine candidate, but it is curious that Ernst, who admittedly rejected not only a campaign about gender but also many female-friendly policies, was able to take 49 percent of the female vote. What is obvious is that instead of seeming like a woman—or even *for* women—Ernst seemed authentic, authentically masculine, independent, and fierce. David Axelrod, a former adviser to President Obama and a strategist with a long history in Iowa, argued that Ernst won because she "seemed like Iowa" (Jacobs, 2014a, n.p.). GOP consultant Robert Haus argued that the Iowa race focused more on personality than almost any other race in recent history and while issues were important, they took a backseat to personality. This discussion of Ernst's authenticity resonates with Louden and McCauliff's (2004) urging that scholars pay attention to a "candidate's fit with self" (p. 100). Further, Sullivan (1998) argued that a public can deal with dishonesty, but is unforgiving when it comes to politicians who are "faking it" (p. 9). An Ernst strategist said, "biography matters because we don't elect positions, we elect people" (Schultheis, 2014, n.p.). And what was shown in Ernst? "Iowans saw courage under fire, the kind that is forged in real battles that most of us will never endure" (Jacobs, 2014a, n.p.). We would be remiss if we did not return to the elephant in the room, the issue that Senator Harkin inappropriately took note of—Joni Ernst is attractive. At the very least, she upholds traditional notions of beauty. She is white, thin, and takes care in her dress. In an era in which television, YouTube and Internet memes dominate electoral politics, we have to at least speculate that her attractiveness helped build her personal image. At the very least, her willingness to conform to heteronormative standards of beauty allows her a particular freedom in advancing arguments. Sigelman et. al (1987) found that a female candidate's physical attractiveness has powerful indirect effects on her candidacy. She can be perceived as "feminine, dynamic and nice" even when exhibiting masculine or androgynous traits (p. 32). Of course, a message articulated by an attractive female candidate that is largely devoid of policy and ripe with themes of military service, farm work, and down home values might be a uniquely appropriate strategy for a state like Iowa.

The 2016 election cycle suggests that Ernst's Iowan charm plays well nationally. Ernst was part of a group of Republican women who backed Donald Trump's bid for president. It was widely rumored that Ernst was vetted as a possible running mate for Trump (Peters & Haberman, n.p.). Despite Trump's claim that she turned down his invitation because she "felt she needed a little more seasoning," Ernst remained committed to his campaign (Lynch, n.p.). Indeed, the first-term senator was a featured speaker at the Republican National Convention. She spoke under the banner "Make America Safe Again" and used her status as the first female combat veteran to serve in the Senate to argue that Trump "gave voice to a movement of millions of Americans who are tired of politics as usual" and that she knew that "as president he will work tirelessly to keep our nation safe" (Noble, n.p.). The convention appearance was the latest in a series of prominent speaking roles as she had also been chosen to give the Republican response to President Obama's last State of the Union in 2015—after only two weeks on the job in the Senate. As a candidate who often held herself as the antidote to traditional Washington politicians, her personality seems to square well with the Trump approach to politics. But the question remains whether Ernst's personality and rhetorical strategies would work for a candidate from any other state. One thing is clear—the Ernst case suggests that women should portray themselves as unafraid to talk about hard work and let the pundits talk about the historic nature of their election.

♦ THREE ♦

Carly Fiorina

Beginning with the 2004 election, American voters applied what has come to be known as the "beer test" to presidential candidates. That is, in 2004, voters said they would prefer to have a beer with George W. Bush rather than John Kerry. Presumably, this means that voters have often wanted candidates with whom they can identify. Americans want to vote for someone who shares their values and concerns, someone they believe is likeable. Consequently, the rapid rise of Carly Fiorina's stock in the Republican presidential primary during the fall of 2015 was puzzling because as a former CEO of a Fortune 500 company (Hennebergert, 2015), a divorcee (Fiorina, 2015), and a woman, she did *not* seem like someone with whom the Republican primary electorate would readily identify.

Furthermore, as a woman, her positions of power have been contrary to what many voters would expect. As we have mentioned, throughout American history, the public sphere has traditionally been dominated by masculine speech (Campbell, 1989; Jamieson, 1988). Dow and Tonn (1993) explain, "Because women's communicative patterns are associated with their roles in the private sphere of home and family, women have been perceived as ill-suited to the competitive, task oriented, or deliberative behavior of the public sphere" (p. 288). This chapter continues our conversation about masculine and feminine styles of speech. We document the long history of women being excluded from the dominant public sphere. This history allows us to argue that, to some extent, Carly Fiorina represents a break in that history. As one of the first women to legitimately run for president on the Republican ticket, Fiorina represents an interesting case study in how a woman negotiates the expectations, which are largely rooted in patriarchal, masculine standards. In this chapter, we argue that Fiorina's femininity allows her to make particular arguments about feminism, masculinity, and women's rights. In advancing this argument, we draw on ideas of storytelling and narrative, cultural myths, and ideological ideas regarding feminine roles and values.

The Masculine Public Sphere

Indeed, there has been an expectation of women's silence in matters that concerned the public good. According to Jamieson (1988), "In seventeenth century colonial America, the ducking stool held a place of honor near the Courthouse alongside the pillory and the stock" (p. 67). Women who spoke out "inappropriately" were bound to the stool. A woman receiving a lesson in the need for silence was then "submerged in the nearest body of water where she could choose between silence and drowning" (Jamieson, 1988, p. 67). If the woman promised to renounce her "verbal past," the "dunking would cease." Women who spoke out were silenced, and others who witnessed such events refused to speak out for fear of public sanction.

These ideas about rhetoric are, interestingly, tied to questions of women's sexuality and related perceptions about those who spoke out. As Jamieson (1988) explains, "Public speaking took women from the home, where, their opponents assumed, they should be bearing and raising children" (p. 71). By this logic, the family was threatened by a woman's refusal to be silent, and women who spoke out were labeled "harlots" or "whores." These epithets also had the effect of discouraging female speakers. Additionally, emotional speech by women was sometimes seen as evidence of a diseased mind, for which the prescribed cure was to control one's need for self-expression. According to Jamieson (1988), "Women whose speech defied such cures risked being labeled crazy and institutionalized" (p. 72). If society could not silence them by other means, asylums silenced them by removing them from society. Finally, women who spoke out were also frequently labeled witches. Again Jamieson explains, "In Essex County, Massachusetts, more 'witches' were convicted of 'assaultive speech' than any other crime including 'lying.' An inability to control one's tongue was a sign of witchcraft" (p. 75). Being labeled a witch or punished for being one also served to censor not just the speech of the women who spoke out of turn but also to silence others as well. Women who violated the expectation of silence have been known as "'scolds,' 'nags,' 'shrews,' 'fishwives,' 'harpies,' 'viragos,' 'bitches,' 'harridans,' 'magpies,' and 'termagants.' Unlike men, censored women 'hector,' 'bitch,' 'boss,' 'scold,' 'shriek,' and are 'strident' and 'shrill'" (Jamieson, 1995, p. 82). Labeling women who refuse to remain silent encourages other women to follow public norms or risk similar shame. Many of these adjectives and labels remain today because views of outspoken women have been slow to change.

Part of the reason it has taken so long for society and women to transition away from these perceptions is that, in many ways, the skills associated with being an effective public speaker have traditionally been at odds with the values Americans celebrate. Campbell (1999) argues, "The sex role requirements for women contradict the dominant values of American culture—self-reliance, achievement, and independence" (p. 126). Presenting "cogent argument(s), clarity of position, offering compelling evidence, and responding to competing views," according to Campbell (1999), are qualities that are "gender-coded as masculine" (p. 4). Thus, if a female speaker demonstrated public speaking competence, "she was likely to be judged as masculine, unwomanly, aggressive, and cold" (Campbell, 1989, p. 12). Women who demonstrated effective public speaking skills were often stereotyped as bitches or as lesbians (Jamieson, 1995). Examples of women labeled bitches in contemporary America include Hillary Rodham Clinton, Ruth Bader Ginsberg, Geraldine Ferraro, Elizabeth Warren, and Michelle Obama (Alter, 2014). These depictions have also served to censor women who do not wish to be perceived as either a bitch or a lesbian.

In 1989, Campbell wrote, "Quite simply, in nineteenth-century America, femininity and rhetorical action were seen as mutually exclusive. No 'true woman' could be a public persuader" (pp. 10–11). Women who attempted public advocacy were considered unlikeable, unwomanly, immoral, or mentally unbalanced. In 1995, Jamieson specifically articulated a few sets of double binds that women faced: (1) "women can exercise their wombs or their brains, but not both"; (2) "women who speak out are immodest and will be shamed, while women who are silent will be ignored or dismissed"; (3) "women are subordinate whether they claim to be different from men or the same"; (4) "women who are considered feminine will be judged as incompetent and women who are competent, unfeminine"; and (5) and "as men age they gain wisdom and power; as women age, they wrinkle and become superfluous" (p. 16).

Women did not historically make their voices heard by arguing that they had a right as citizens to influence public affairs. Because women's proper place was thought to be the private sphere, where they would care for family, raise moral children, and be sheltered from the public sphere, women were thought to be "pure and pious," according to Campbell (1998). These circumstances also "implied that they were particularly well equipped to advise on moral matters, and their earliest efforts at public advocacy arose in relation to issues closely related to what were seen as women's concerns—works of benevolence toward the poor and orphaned, the struggles against the moral evils of prostitution, slavery, and alcoholism" (Campbell, 1988, p. 4). Early female rhetors worked to merge the private and public spheres by fighting to speak and write publicly in order to correct moral wrongs.

As a result of such traditional and limiting views of gender, female speakers have developed a "feminine style" that allows them to "perform or enact femininity" (Campbell, 1998, p. 5) while participating in public advocacy. In Chapter Five, we discuss the feminine style, which includes using a personal tone that is intimate or indicative of caring, self-disclosing, using a female persona, using anecdotes or stories as evidence instead of facts and statistics, and using emotional appeals. Speakers using the feminine style might also avoid such "'macho' strategies as tough language, confrontation or direct refutation, and any appearance of debating one's opponents" (Campbell, 1998, p. 5). With this background in mind, we use both media accounts and her own words to reveal points of overlap and difference. But first, we explain what makes Fiorina's candidacy significant.

Fiorina's Significance

In pursuing the Republican nomination for the 2016 presidential election, Carly Fiorina dealt with the challenges of being a competent speaker while also attempting to seem likeable to potential voters. Her candidacy is worthy of examination for several reasons. First, she showed real potential to advance in or win an election. In August of 2015, she entered the "undercard" debate for the candidates who did not place among the top ten Republican primary candidates. According to Graham (2015), Fiorina "surged after dominating the undercard at the first Republican debate in August, and after winning a promotion to the main stage for the second debate, she was the consensus winner there, too" (para. 4). Sommers and Rosen (2015) report that after her appearance in the second debate, her first on the main stage, "her poll numbers shot up, and the internet was buzzing with analyses of her strong performance" (para. 1). Linda Chavez (2015), former director of public liaison in the Reagan White House, argues, "At the Republican debate she showed herself to be not just an equal to the 10 men on the stage but superior in performance to almost all of them" (para. 2). Finally, her impressive debate performances translated, for a time, into progress in national polls. Phillip (2015) explains, "At her peak, in early October, polls showed Fiorina in second place in New Hampshire, according to an average of polls compiled by *Real Clear Politics*. In Iowa and South Carolina, she placed third" (para. 10). In just a few months, she rose from running in relative obscurity to becoming really competitive.

In addition, Carly Fiorina showed potential to resonate with both conservative and liberal voters alike. Nate Silver (2016) states in a discussion on his *Five Thirty Eight* blog, regarding whether Fiorina could help save Ted Cruz's candidacy as his choice for vice president, "Gallup and most other places had her with reasonably good favorability ratings among Republicans" (para. 17). Przybyla (2015) shares the impressions Karlyn Bowman, a polling expert from the American Enterprise Institute, had of Carly Fiorina: "I thought, my God, this woman could possibly make it in the Republican Party. Republicans are enthusiastic and Republican women in particular." What was really impressive, however,

Three • Carly Fiorina

was how she piqued the interest of many liberal females. According to Sommers and Rosen (2015), "Elite liberal women found it easy to dismiss Republican candidates like Sarah Palin or Michele Bachmann—it's hard to imagine either giving a TED lecture or moderating a panel at Davos. Fiorina is another matter" (para. 19). Comedian Lori Chandler (2015) explains why, although she would not vote for Carly Fiorina, she admires her style:

> At the second G.O.P. debate she walked onto a stage with 10 men, most of whom were more politically experienced and one of whom is blatantly sexist, and walked out a winner.
> She doesn't apologize for her ambition, she doesn't back down to male aggression or dumb herself down so people will like her better. That's a feminist attitude. That's rarely seen on TV, where both real and fictional women are consistently modulating their behavior based on the men around them.
> It's true she's not Gloria Steinem or Betty Friedan, she's not even Mary Tyler Moore. But I admire this sister not because I want her to be president (I don't) but because she's herself. It's not cute. She has no desire to dot her letters with hearts, to talk with a baby accent or to defer to men via self-deprecation.
> There's no way I would ever vote for Carly Fiorina, but I wouldn't mind breaking as many glass ceilings as she has and doing it in heels [para. 4–7].

Some liberal feminists clearly admired Fiorina. Such crossover appeal would be powerful and necessary to win in a general election.

Finally, Carly Fiorina's candidacy is an opportunity to explore how well a conservative female candidate manages the simultaneous challenges associated with being a woman, speaking in a masculine style, and attempting to be the candidate with whom voters might choose to have a beer. Many scholars have written about how female speakers use a maternal persona (Dow and Tonn, 1993; Gibson and Heyse, 2010; Parry-Giles and Parry Giles, 1996; Vasby Anderson and Horn Sheeler). On the other hand, Foust (2004) examines the rhetoric of cultural icon Judge Judy, whose persona is embraceable, he argues, because she employs the myth of the *tough* mother: "Judge Judy is justified to castigate society with impatience, a loud voice, biting wit, and brutal judgment. Judge Judy can perform femininity and aggression simultaneously, because her rhetoric 'makes sense' with neo-conservative construction of a culture and government in moral chaos" (p. 284). It is worthwhile to explore whether a political candidate might employ the same mythological topoi in order to allow herself to better manage the double bind. We use Fiorina's rhetoric as a case study to explore these theoretical assumptions.

Use of the Masculine Style

As noted earlier, debates require speaking skills traditionally considered to be masculine, such as being direct, using refutations skillfully, making cogent arguments, expressing clear positions, offering compelling evidence, and responding to competing views. Fiorina indeed possesses many of these skills. In the debate moderated by Jake Tapper of CNN, on September 16, 2015, Fiorina demonstrates many of these qualities:

> Jake, I'll tell you—I'll tell you why people are supporting outsiders. It's because you know what happens if someone's been in the system their whole life, they don't know how broken the system is. A fish swims in water, it doesn't know it's water. It's not that politicians are bad people, it's that they've been in that system forever.
>
> The truth is 75 percent of the American people think the government is corrupt; 82 percent of the American people think these problems that have festered for 50 years in some cases, 25 years in other cases. The border's been insecure for 25 years; 307,000 veterans have died waiting for health care. These things have gone on for so long because no one will challenge the status quo.
>
> You know what a leader does? They challenge the status quo, they solve problems that have festered for a long time and they produce results. That is what my whole life has been about. People know this is about far more than replacing a D with an R [Beckwith, 2015, para 94–96].

As we stated before, directness is an element of masculine style. While we do not necessarily agree that masculinity is a stable identity—one that manifests itself in the same way with each person—we do assert that many critics and the general public code rhetoric of a certain type as masculine. One way we could argue that Fiorina uses masculine rhetoric is that she is very direct in her answers. People support outsiders because the status quo is broken. Her position is clear:

Three • Carly Fiorina

because you cannot fix problems from within, a leader who comes from outside of government, like herself, is best suited to the current American conditions. She uses the most masculine form of evidence here: statistics. As we argue in Chapter Five, a more feminine form of evidence would be narrative or stories. People can identify with, and relate to, stories. Statistics, however, stress authority over relatability; clearly, this is the more masculine choice. At the very least, it is a choice not rooted in the elements of feminine style.

Fiorina also gave what amounted to a masculine answer with respect to American foreign policy with Russia. In the same debate, on September 16, 2015, Jake Tapper asked Donald Trump, "Mr. Trump, you say you can do business with President Vladimir Putin, you say you will get along, quote, 'very well.' What would you do right now if you were president, to get the Russians out of Syria?" After Trump had an opportunity to answer, Fiorina jumped in:

> FIORINA: Having met Vladimir Putin, if I may...
> TAPPER: ...yeah, you've met Vladimir Putin. Yes.
> FIORINA: Having met Vladimir Putin, I wouldn't talk to him at all. We've talked way too much to him.
>
> What I would do, immediately, is begin rebuilding the Sixth Fleet, I would begin rebuilding the missile defense program in Poland, I would conduct regular, aggressive military exercises in the Baltic states. I'd probably send a few thousand more troops into Germany. Vladimir Putin would get the message. By the way, the reason it is so critically important that every one of us know General Suleimani's name is because Russia is in Syria right now, because the head of the Quds force traveled to Russia and talked Vladimir Putin into aligning themselves with Iran and Syria to prop up Bashar al-Assad.
> Russia is a bad actor, but Vladimir Putin is someone we should not talk to, because the only way he will stop is to sense strength and resolve on the other side, and we have all of that within our control.
> We could rebuild the Sixth Fleet. I will. We haven't. We could rebuild the missile defense program. We haven't. I will. We could also, to Senator Rubio's point, give the Egyptians what they've asked for, which is intelligence.
> We could give the Jordanians what they've asked for...
>
> TAPPER: Thank you, Ms. Fiorina.
> FIORINA: ...bombs and materiel. We have not supplied it...
> TAPPER: Thank you.
> FIORINA: ...I will. We could arm the Kurds. They've been asking us for three years. All of this is within our control [Beckwith, 2015, para 167–175].

Listening to Women on the Right

In this answer she does not allow Tapper to cut her off; she is direct and to the point and, not coincidentally, also pro-military—potentially a masculine response. Certainly, the military and the idea of valuing the military may have long been documented as masculine. Fiorina's answer is effective for several additional reasons. First, because she is a woman with no elected political experience, one who has not dealt with foreign policy, it is important that she appear to have already considered this issue and know what she would do. Fiorina takes a clear and direct position on Russia, saying that Russia is a bad actor and our actions should do the talking for us. She then spells out what she would specifically do differently from the status quo: "We could rebuild the Sixth Fleet. I will. We haven't. We could rebuild the missile defense program. We haven't. I will." Although these specific, seemingly aggressive answers are often not thought of as feminine, when we see and hear Carly Fiorina using these strategies, it is clear that they can be effective.

The two previous examples illustrate how Fiorina can "out-macho" the men. Some women are clearly cheering her perceived competence, her ability to be in control, and her assertiveness. But how does she do this without appearing to be unlikeable? How does she manage the double bind? In one of her most notable debate moments, Jake Tapper turned to Carly Fiorina: "Before we end this block, Ms. Fiorina, I do want to ask you about this. In an interview last week in *Rolling Stone Magazine*, Donald Trump said the following about you. Quote, 'Look at that face. Would anyone vote for that? Can you imagine that, the face of our next president?' Mr. Trump later said he was talking about your persona, not your appearance. Please feel free to respond what you think about his persona" (Beckwith, 2015, para. 188).

This is a tough moment for a female candidate. If Carly Fiorina says something nasty about Donald Trump or his appearance, then she risks being perceived as poorly as he is. She might look mean or "bitchy"; if she is too conciliatory, however, she might look weak or incapable of being a strong leader. Either way, the stereotypical assumptions of women are at work. Fiorina instead navigates a middle ground, responding, "You know, it's interesting to me, Mr. Trump said that he heard Mr. Bush very clearly and what Mr. Bush said. I think women all over this country heard very clearly what Mr. Trump said" (Beckwith, 2015, para 189). In this way, she does not let him off the hook because she is saying to other women that his conduct is unacceptable and that they should hold him accountable. She also appears above the fray, because she is not personally attacking him. She is simply saying that the voters will judge him for themselves. In addition, she links herself to other women—making the answer forceful and masculine and rooted in the collective strategy of feminine style. This strategy is truly brilliant, one that really works only for a woman; it both minimizes and evokes her femininity and enables her to appeal to multiple audiences.

Carly Fiorina's appearance also helps her in dealing with the double bind. She is an older woman (61) and she looks like a CEO. She typically dresses in business suits with skirts or in professional-looking dresses, usually one solid color, often a shade of red. Her hair is conservatively and neatly styled suitably for her age, and her makeup is generally minimally applied. In public photos, Fiorina wears conservative, rather than ornamental, jewelry. She appears well put together, and her professional appearance also keeps her from seeming like an intellectual lightweight. She dresses the way a CEO, a college professor, or a female senator might dress. Carly Fiorina's conservative skirts and dresses, her makeup and hairstyle, and her jewelry convey a feminine, almost classy, look about her. In addition, it must be said that her appearance is corporate, mainstream, and white; overall, it allows her particular amounts of readability and forgiveness with the audience.

The Tough Mother Metaphor

Another way in which Carly Fiorina may cope with the double bind is by benefiting from the tough mother metaphor or persona. Foust (2004) argues that the tough mother myth evolved from the virtuous woman myth of Campbell's work (discussed earlier) in which virtuous women gave way to strong, reform-minded women who could speak out. As Foust (2004) explains, "Yet, unlike the Virtuous Woman, the tough mother who embarks on a journey of public advocacy does not have to hold her tongue in a 'feminine way.' Rather, as women of the temperance movement proved, the tough mother may speak in a publicly aggressive style because society respects her moral authority and fears her Christian power" (p. 275).

Cultural myths are stories or shared visions that McGee says are "dangled before people" from a culture's past, representing longings that remain dormant in the culture unless a speaker calls on the audience to resume those longings. According to McGee (1975), "The duty of a champion is to find 'an old longing' and 'help it to victory.' This duty necessarily involves a search of the nation's history with a constant sensitivity toward the characterization of the 'people' who executed it" (p. 240). In the case of Carly Fiorina, the longing is for a strong female authority figure who is at the same time strict and demanding in order to help us achieve our best and also to nurture us.

Myths appeal to people because we are narrative beings; consequently, myths rely on narrative logic. Fisher (1984) argues that narrative rationality is an ability all human beings possess, precisely because we are storytelling beings. The myth's appeal needs to make sense in the current context in which the rhetor is speaking. This means that the circumstances of the myth do not have to fit exactly with the current context of the rhetor's story. To the extent that the story type is a familiar one, the audience sees the archetypes and relates the people in the culturally embedded narrative to the rhetor's present story. Fisher (1984) explains that "the operative principle of narrative rationality is identification rather than deliberation" (p. 9). Because myths are so embedded in the culture, audiences relate to those stories and the archetypal characters without having to deliberate over every detail. We do not have to obsess about whether Carly Fiorina is indeed a tough mother. We merely have to know that she fits into the archetype of women who have been tough mothers, such as women who fought to end slavery or public drunkenness. Moreover, Americans have likely all known a strict but loving grandmother, school teacher, or Sunday school teacher.

Foust (2004) identifies the tough mother as the ideological counterpart to the "Strict Father" myth that Lakoff (2002) writes about:

This model posits a traditional nuclear family, with the father having primary responsibility for supporting and protecting the family as well as the authority to set overall policy, to set strict rules for the behavior of children, and to enforce the rules. The mother has the day-to-day responsibility for the care of the house, raising the children, and upholding the father's authority. Love and nurturance are, of course, a vital part of family life but can never outweigh parental authority, which is itself an expression of love and nurturance—tough love. Self- discipline, self-reliance, and respect for legitimate authority are the crucial things that children must learn. Once children are mature, they are on their own and must depend on their acquired self-discipline to survive. Their self-reliance gives them authority over their own destinies, and parents are not to meddle in their lives [p. 33].

Thus, the tough mother preaches self-discipline, self-reliance, and morality—in short, she advocates tough love. The government is not to provide for us; we are to be self-reliant.

Fiorina as Tough Mother

Fiorina is clearly using the myth of the tough mother. In the telling of her own story, for example, she stresses the value of pulling one's self up by one's bootstraps through the myth of the American Dream. In her book *Tough Choices,* Fiorina (2006) describes her own upbringing: "We were a modest, middle-class family. My mother was a full-time mother and homemaker, my father was an academic, and there were three children to raise. Success, was not, to my parents about fame and fortune. It was ultimately about the quality of one's mind and one's character" (p. 4). And because of her character, Carly was able ultimately to find fame and fortune. Fiorina (2015) explains, in her book *Rising to the Challenge,* as she has explained many times before and since, "I know that only in America is it possible for a young woman to start out as a secretary and become the CEO of the largest technology company in the world" (p. 10). Hers is the story of pulling one's self up by one's bootstraps; it is a celebration of rugged individualism. Except that it is not.

When Fiorina tells of her rags-to-riches rise through the corporate ranks, she exaggerates her struggle by omitting the fact "that her father, Joseph Tyree Sneed III, who died in 2008, whom she describes in her book as a simple academic, was a law professor at the University of Texas, Stanford, and Cornell, the dean of Duke Law School, a deputy attorney general under President Richard Nixon, and a longtime senior judge on the Ninth U.S. Circuit Court of Appeals in San Francisco" (Hennebergert, 2015, para. 20). Also, as she relays her personal story, Carly Fiorina started out as a simple secretary, but she had a degree from Stanford, and her father was a prominent man. While she did work hard to advance in a context that many women found overwhelming, her story was not exactly the stuff of Horatio Alger dime novels about immigrants coming to America and making it on their own with hard work alone (Hee Lee, 2015).

Carly Fiorina also displays her tough mother persona both in the issues she chooses to address and in referencing her role as a mother. We will first discuss how Fiorina's discussing the issues that might uniquely concern a woman affected her perceived tough mother persona.

Criticizing Planned Parenthood

In the second Republican primary debate, the first debate in which she appeared on the main stage, Fiorina states,

> As regards Planned Parenthood, anyone who has watched this videotape, I dare Hillary Clinton, Barack Obama to watch these tapes. Watch a fully formed fetus on the table, its heart beating, its legs kicking while someone says we have to keep it alive to harvest its brain. This is about the character of our nation, and if we will not stand up and force President Obama to veto this bill, shame on us [Beckwith, 2015, para. 148].

If true, this description would certainly be a moral cause worthy of the early suffragists' attention. Following this debate, Fiorina's polling numbers climbed to 15 percent and vaulted her to second place behind Donald Trump (Bradner, 2015).

Unfortunately, following the debates, the *Washington Post* rated these statements "3 Pinocchios" (Phillip, 2015). Phillip (2015) explains, "Fiorina has also attracted negative attention for statements that proved to be untrue. She came under fire after the Reagan Library debate for describing a video she saw of an aborted fetus lying on a table and kicking as doctors discussed harvesting its organs for fetal tissue research. No such video has surfaced" (para. 29). Fiorina responded to fact checkers by insisting, "I've seen the footage. And I find it amazing, actually, that all these supposed fact checkers in the mainstream media claim this doesn't exist. They're trying to attack the authenticity of the videotape" (Murray, 2015, para. 9).

For voters who stood strongly against Planned Parenthood, Fiorina's word that the videotapes existed may well have been evidence enough because they were predisposed to question the status quo. Standing up to fact checkers might have enhanced Fiorina's perceived strength and credibility among such voters. Regardless of whether one perceived her attack on Planned Parenthood as justified or not, the persona of a woman fighting to save unborn fetuses is reminiscent of the early suffragists fighting to correct moral wrongs like alcohol consumption and prostitution. If she believes she is correct, she is morally right to fight this fight. Moreover, Fiorina is arguing for the veto of funding for Planned Parenthood. Some might also perceive her paternalistic sense of knowing what is best for women as being indicative of the strict parent.

Toward the end of Fiorina's campaign, in January of 2016, she entered a pro life forum at the Greater Des Moines botanical garden. Levy (2016) states, "She reportedly steered more than a dozen preschoolers to sit around her on a small stage, then discussed her opposition to abortion." Pictures were then released of Fiorina speaking to the children, seated on the floor around her. This visual image, coupled with speculation of what she might have said, based upon what she actually said during the debate, was problematic. One could imagine some bizarre world nightmare in which a politician talks to children about harvesting babies' brains. This visual image, even though not real, would jolt almost any voter out of the mythical understanding of Fiorina as tough mother and right into a perception of her as creepy or unbalanced.

Although no one can say for certain what caused Fiorina's eventual fall from grace or failure to catch on as a national candidate, certainly this image undercut the notion of the tough mother persona.

Listening to Women on the Right

On Donald Trump

Like most tough mothers, Carly Fiorina stands for what is moral. In the August 2015 Republican primary debate hosted by Megyn Kelly, Kelly asked Donald Trump tough questions that he was not comfortable with and he became visibly irritated with her and said that she was "not nice." After the debate, he continued to tweet about the Fox News anchor, calling her a "lightweight" and claiming that she was personally attacking him, presumably because she was hormonal. Trump said, "there was blood coming out of her eyes, blood coming out of her wherever" (Flores, 2015, para. 3). The following weekend, Carly Fiorina appeared on *Face the Nation* and she told host John Dickerson, "Presidential campaigns are designed to reveal character under pressure and over time. It's why people like you ask tough questions, and it's up to candidates to answer those questions. So Mr. Trump got asked tough questions by a lot of people on Thursday night, but he chose to attack Megyn Kelly" (Flores, 2015, para 2). Fiorina then concluded, "I think women of all kinds are really sort of horrified by this" (Flores, 2015, para. 4). Fiorina called out Donald Trump's attack on a younger conservative woman as unacceptable character for a presidential candidate.

Carly Fiorina dropped out of the Republican primary in February of 2016. In March, she explained to voters why she was endorsing Ted Cruz and not Donald Trump. According to Manchester (2016), she explained, "There are people in our party who are actually kind of horrified by Donald Trump. I'm one of them. We're going to have to beat Donald Trump at the ballot box. And the only guy who can beat Donald Trump is Ted Cruz" (para. 6). Even once Trump clinched the nomination, Fiorina never endorsed him because she found his behavior unacceptable, horrifying.

Then, in early October 2016, the *Washington Post* released a 2005 video of Donald Trump bragging about making sexual advances toward a married woman (while he was also married) and touching women in inappropriate places on their bodies without their permission. In the video Trump proclaimed, "And when you're a star, they let you do it." Carly Fiorina was the first of Donald Trump's former primary opponents to call for him to step down from the ticket. According to Reilly (2016), Fiorina said, "Donald Trump does not represent me or my party. I understand the responsibility of Republicans to support their nominee. Our nominee has weighty responsibilities as well. Donald Trump has manifestly failed in these responsibilities. Today, I ask Donald Trump to step aside and for the RNC to replace him with Governor Mike Pence" (para. 2–4). Carly Fiorina was not afraid to speak out against Trump's inability to meet certain basic moral standards. In fact, while several conservative men insisted that the incident merely amounted to "locker room talk," Fiorina took the tough position of calling on Trump to resign.

Burying a Child

Another way in which Fiorina casts herself as the tough mother is by talking about how her stepdaughter died from drug abuse. Jake Tapper posed the following question, "Senator Paul, Governor Christie recently said, quote, 'if you're getting high in Colorado today,' where marijuana has been legalized, 'enjoy it until January 2017, because I will enforce the federal laws against marijuana.' Will you?" After other candidates took their turns, eventually Fiorina was able to address the question:

> FIORINA: I very much hope I am the only person on this stage who can say this, but I know there are millions of Americans out there who will say the same thing.
> My husband Frank and I buried a child to drug addiction. So, we must invest more in the treatment of drugs.
> FIORINA: I agree with Senator Paul. I agree with states' rights. But we are misleading young people when we tell them that marijuana is just like having a beer. It's not. And the marijuana that kids are smoking today is not the same as the marijuana that Jeb Bush smoked 40 years ago.
> (LAUGHTER)
> We do—sorry, Barbara. We do need—we do need criminal justice reform. We have the highest incarceration rates in the world. Two-thirds of the people in our prisons are there for non-violent offenses, mostly drug related. It's clearly not working.
> But we need to tell young people the truth. Drug addiction is an epidemic, and it is taking too many of our young people. I know this sadly from personal experience [Beckwith, 2015, para.759–763].

Listening to Women on the Right

Carly Fiorina wants America to learn from her personal experience. Moreover, she wants people to stop telling young people that smoking marijuana is like drinking beer. Clearly, it is worse. In true Nancy Reagan fashion, "just saying no" is the tough mother talking because, as Lakoff suggests, it emphasizes self-discipline, self-reliance, and respect for authority. Smoking marijuana is not like drinking beer. If it were, it would be legal. Some parents, however, might view experimentation with pot as a normal stage of adolescent growth. For example, in 1975, former first lady Betty Ford, who had previously admitted that her children had tried marijuana (Frum, 2011, para. 6), stated in a *60 Minutes* interview that had she been young in the 1970s she might have tried marijuana (Gerald R. Ford Presidential Foundation, n.d.). As tough mothers, Nancy Reagan and Carly Fiorina shared no similar interest in experimenting with marijuana use. Also, in talking about how her stepdaughter died, she is reminding Americans that she is more than a hard-edged CEO. She is also a mom.

Fiorina opened her book *Rising to the Challenge* with the police coming to report her stepdaughter's death to her and her husband, Frank. In sharing this experience with readers, she writes about having fallen in love with the child immediately upon meeting her. According to Fiorina, when she met Frank's children she was already "eager for a family," and "I fell in love with her and her big sister, Tracy, almost before I fell in love with their father, my husband, Frank. They were little angels, both to be with and to behold. Tracy was a brunette and looked like her father. Lori had long blond hair and sparkling eyes. We came into each other's lives just when we needed each other the most" (2005, p. 2). The way Fiorina words this account makes it seem as though she really wanted to be a mom and Lori was desperately in need of a mother, and in marrying their father, she stepped in to fill that void. Her account, however, raises some questions. Ridge (2015) reports that she married Frank Fiorina and helped him raise his two daughters. Another report is that once Carly became a CEO, Frank quit his high-powered job to travel with his wife and to care for his children from his previous marriage (Koplowitz, 2015). What seems peculiar is that, according to Kruse (2015), the girls' mother had custody of them. So why Lori desperately needed Carly or why Frank quit his job to raise children he did not have custody of seems puzzling. The myth seems more powerful than reality might be.

Carly Fiorina repeatedly reminds audiences that she is a mother to Frank's two daughters. In this way, she is maternal—a characteristic required of the tough mother. That audiences buy into the narrative and accept the persona, however, may mean it is less important that it be a storybook example of an ideal American family than that it basically appears to be true.

Helping Women

A final example that is indicative of Carly Fiorina's tough mother persona is her feminist prescription for helping other women. Quite simply, she feels that government can best help women by not helping women. This is the self-reliant, self-disciplined, pull-yourself-up-by-your-bootstraps-type prescription that one might expect from Lakoff's strict father or, in this case, the tough mother. In her manifesto entitled "Redefining Feminism: The State of Women in America," Fiorina (2015b) proclaims: "Lastly, we must tackle the webs of dependence that are trapping women today. We need a top-to-bottom review of every economic development and assistance program we have to ensure that they encourage women—and men—to strive instead of settle, because there is dignity in all work." This is the kind of tough love that comes straight out of Marvin Olasky's (1992) book *The Tragedy of American Compassion*, which influenced George W. Bush's "compassionate conservatism." Olasky argues that the best way to help Americans is for the government to step aside and allow religious institutions to serve people; with this approach, poor people have to change their lives in order to receive help.

But the tough mother has another side that makes her relatable: she is nurturing. Being seen as feminine, nurturing, and relatable is important because it allows the tough mother to be perceived as a worthy speaker instead of falling into the traditionally negative notions regarding female speakers. Carly Fiorina demonstrates that she relates to others, and she has a sense of humor. Although Fiorina is tough in debates, she is more feminine elsewhere, as the following two examples illustrate.

Listening to Women on the Right

First, her appearance on the *Tonight Show with Jimmy Fallon* (Vitali, 2015). Fallon told audience members that Fiorina sometimes sings made-up songs to her grandkids and her dogs, Max and Snickers. She offered to sing one of the four verses of the song that she sings to Snickers. The song was set to the tune of "Rock Around the Clock" but she had changed the lyrics to "My name's Snick, and I'm lazy. Please don't take a walk with me. I'd rather stay right here at home instead. I want to lie back down in my nice, warm bed. My name's Snick and you're gonna have to carry me" (Vitali, 2015). As she sang, the crowd clapped to the beat and cheered when she finished. Vitali (2015) then notes that candidates have used the *Tonight Show* to "soften their images" for years and likens her appearance to that of Bill Clinton playing the saxophone on the *Arsenio Hall Show* when he was a candidate. This performance helps with the tough mother persona by showing that tough mothers are also nurturing at times; they are the kind of people who would sing to children or pets.

Second, the YouTube *Buzzfeed* video called "If Men Were Treated Like Women in the Office with Carly Fiorina." In the video Fiorina shares her sense of humor with audiences.

> Carly is seated at a table with a man and a woman. The man says, "Here's an idea, maybe we could restructure?" The female co-worker says, "Here's an idea.... How 'bout we restructure?" Fiorina as the boss replies, "Yes. Great idea, Joanna."
> "BEING DEFINED BY FAMILY"
> Fiorina says to a male employee, "So how do you manage the work life balance?"
> "GETTING ASSIGNED DOMESTIC TASKS"
> Fiorina says to a male employee, "You like to bake—how about you handle the cake for Gina's birthday?"
> "BEING DEFINED BY FAMILY—(AGAIN)"
> Carly Fiorina asks a male employee, "Is work less of a priority for you now?"
> "(AND AGAIN)"
> She asks him, "Does your wife help? [pause] With the kids?"
> "COMMENTING ON YOUR FOOD"
> At lunch, Fiorina says to a male worker, "Wow, are you gonna eat all that yourself?" He appears to look down in sadness.
> "BEING TALKED DOWN TO"
> Carly Fiorina is meeting with two male workers. She says to them, "Well, we shouldn't have too many men on the project, you know how that can be, I'm assuming you two can work together without getting catty."

Three • Carly Fiorina

"BEING DEFINED BY YOUR GENDER"
The video closes with Fiorina saying to a male worker, "Look at you being funny, I didn't know men could be funny" [Fiorina, 2015b].

This video relays to other women the idea that Carly understands what all women know, that we are not treated with the same respect as men in the workplace. It conveys it in a humorous fashion so as to not offend men, but it makes Carly Fiorina relatable to other women. It serves as a signal that women, even liberal women, can identify with her. Lakoff (2002) might classify this as an example of Fiorina being a nurturing parent and thus, not tough. He lists the various kinds of business practices that count as nurturing, such as "humane treatment of employees," "fairness in hiring and promotion," "the building of a work community," and "development of excellent communication between employees and management." In admitting that women are often treated unfairly at work, Fiorina may be perceived as making an argument for management to promote better relationships with female employees. Or one might argue that she is merely calling for equality. If a boss would not talk to a male worker about his responsibilities and time demands brought on by his children, for example, then he or she should not talk to a woman about these time demands. And we know that Fiorina faced these challenges. She routinely talks about attending a business meeting at a strip club where all of the other people attending were men (Fiorina, 2006; Fiorina, 2015c). She also mentions being called "the token bimbo" by a boss once (Fiorina, 2006; Fiorina, 2015c). But she prevailed and, through hard work and self-discipline, so can other women. Indeed, unlike other conservative female politicians, she admits that we have not achieved equality. This acknowledgment may be part of what makes some liberal women embrace Carly Fiorina.

Lessons Learned

There are a number of lessons to be learned from examining the use of the tough mother metaphor in Carly Fiorina's rhetoric. First, from a political perspective, future candidates can learn from Fiorina's persona that, at least in 2016, people tend to embrace a woman using the tough mother persona. Moreover, future candidates might learn from Fiorina how to construct such a persona. Carly Fiorina does it by choosing to emphasize issues of moral concern, such as the ethics of Planned Parenthood and the importance of saying no to drugs. Second, her physical appearance helps to reinforce this persona and to contradict others as she appears distinguished and classy versus young, cheap, or stereotypically beautiful. Finally, she balances her ability to succeed in a forum that rewarded masculine communication skills such as a debate; other public appearances that reveal her relatability; her sense of humor; and her ability to be nurturing. Other candidates could follow similar formulas.

Communication scholars can learn from the appeal of Fiorina to both conservatives and to liberal women. It is an interesting phenomenon that we believe is based on identification, as public advocacy always has been. The tough mother persona allows conservatives to relate to her. She is tough and demanding because she wants to see the American people do well. Most people have known and loved a mother, a teacher, a Sunday school teacher, or other female authority figure like this who balances strictness and nurturance. This is an identifiable archetype. Her toughness, outspokenness, and tough style are acceptable because they are based upon tough love.

For conservatives, the identification may be with a cultural archetype. For liberals, the identification may be with a masculine style they wish they were empowered to enact, or they may relate to work challenges they have also faced. The myth means that audiences can deal with the ambiguities and not question every detail because the larger story has narrative coherence in American culture. That is, the story of what a woman can and should be fits with other story types for appropriate female behavior. Knowledge of the cultural stories that encompass the myth allows audiences to conceive of Fiorina's persona deductively. As Foust (2004) argues, "Because myths do not rely upon specific premises as logical reasoning does, their content is inherently ambiguous, allowing them to rhetorically bridge contradictions" (p. 273). Certain aspects of Carly Fiorina's persona do not need to be based in facts much as they needs to fit the archetype so that audiences can fill in the blanks in their own minds. In fact, the ambiguities might be a strength because they do not settle the idea of which camp Fiorina belongs to: liberal or conservative. People on both sides of the political aisle can identify with her.

What is interesting from a theoretical perspective is that the myth is used not to construct the persona of the audience as in Reagan's Challenger speech in which he called on the American people to be the heirs to the great pioneers or to be rugged individualists who pull themselves up by their bootstraps instead of relying on help from government but to create the persona of the speaker and to smooth over stylistic and substantive inconsistencies in her message. More often, we think rhetors use myth to relate what their proper role is to the audience. Fiorina's use of myth to address the double bind, therefore, is interesting.

The ability to create a relatable image is everything. Parry-Giles (2010) reminds us that governments are made up of people, not issues (p. 39). The ideals of "deliberative democracy, while compelling, are often limited as they ignore the realities and demands of contemporary life—a complicated life where citizens do not have the luxury of attending carefully to detailed matters of public policy at issues forums or study circles of community groups" according to Parry-Giles (2010). In short, people are too busy raising children, going to work, tending to the yard, etc., to follow closely every aspect of public policy. But they can, and do, evaluate a person's character. Such a focus explains why the electorate leading up to the 2016 election is so very negative about the prospect of an election featuring Donald Trump and Hillary Clinton. It also helps to explain why people can say with a straight face that they support either Donald Trump or Bernie Sanders even though they are reasonably far apart on many aspects of the political spectrum, such as immigration, statements regarding women, and defense policy. While they are not similar from a policy perspective, both candidates have tapped into an anger with the status quo.

While there are inconsistencies and factual inaccuracies in Carly Fiorina's rhetoric, they are noticed less because people do not follow minute details of politics closely. They do not have the time. What they *are* looking at is whether the candidates are intelligent, capable and kind. They want to know if the candidates share their values. As we have argued elsewhere in this book, voters assess candidates' authenticity; candidates do not appear to be required to have everything voters want. The electorate settles for what they think is the best available image.

At this point, it is still too early to say what the impact of Carly Fiorina's candidacy will be for the Republican Party and for America. It is, however, interesting because she challenges many of the stereotypes associated with conservative female candidates. She excites liberal women because she is strong, outgoing, and direct. At the same time, she is also nurturing, possesses a good sense of humor, and relates to the struggles women face. Carly Fiorina's candidacy may offer a blueprint for future women in coping with the double bind.

• FOUR •

Nikki Haley

Nikki Haley has been performing on the stage of American politics since 2005. Her role is important because she has represented a relatively new character in national political culture: a conservative woman seeking political power in a way that projects a particular image of feminine power. As is the case with most political figures, this image is a co-creation of Haley's rhetorical choices and the frames used by the mass media to report on her political activity. Born in 1973, Nikki Haley was the governor of South Carolina. Before she became governor, she was the Republican representative from Lexington County in the South Carolina House of Representatives (2005–2011). She is the second Indian-American governor in the United States but the first female governor in South Carolina. Re-elected in 2014, she was set to serve as governor until 2019 but she was selected by President Trump to be the U.S. ambassador to the United Nations. While Haley was a vocal critic of Trump during this election, she will be the first non-white and female official in his administration.

Nikki Haley was born Nimrata Nikki Randhawa in Bamberg, South Carolina, to Sikh parents. Her parents immigrated to Canada from India for education and then to the United States seeking better opportunities, although her parents' families were both considered to be upper-class in India. Her father earned his Ph.D. in Canada and then took a job at Voorhees College in South Carolina. According to Haley, in her autobiography entitled *Can't Is Not an Option*, her family did not exactly fit in small-town South Carolina. She tells stories of the police arriving at the local produce stand to make sure her father (who wore a Sikh turban) was not a criminal. People often asked what "that" was on her father's head. And people would refer to her brother Mitti as a girl because he had long hair (Sikhs do not usually cut their hair). When her mother went back to work, she tried to find childcare for the kids but was rejected until one woman living near their home agreed to watch them. She ended up beating them quite badly. Once, Nikki and her sister were dismissed from a beauty contest they had entered because the tradition was to choose one black girl and one white girl as the winners. Because the judges could not place the Indian-American girls' race, they were dismissed as they were neither black nor white. Haley has many of these stories that set the backdrop for what she has accomplished and what the South used to be. When she discusses these terrible incidents, she does not appear to dwell on these problems; rather, she seems to use them as a measurement for progress in the South. As she wrote in her autobiography, "In the end, my fellow South Carolinians loved that we [her family] knew the greatness of the American Dream just as much as anyone born here—and maybe more, because my parents had come from a place where they couldn't dream such dreams" (Haley, 2012, p. 19).

In this chapter, we will employ Kenneth Burke's theory of dramatism to better understand Haley's rhetorical motives. We will also examine various conservative responses she has received throughout her career thus far. Finally, we argue that her attempts to move the rhetoric to a more centered state results in quite controversial reactions from her own party.

Kenneth Burke's Theory of Dramatism

To understand dramatism, we must understand that language reveals motive, that language is a vehicle to understand how and why people do the things they do. Without language we could not function as a whole society, nor could we understand human motive. The method associated with the theory of dramatism, the pentad, comes from Kenneth Burke. According to Foss (2004),

> Two basic assumptions underlie dramatism. One is that language use constitutes action, not motion. Motion corresponds to the biological or animal aspect of the

Four • Nikki Haley

human being, which is concerned with bodily processes such as growth, digestion, respiration, and the requirements for the maintenance of these processes.... In contrast, action corresponds to the neurological aspect of the human being, which Burke defines as the ability of an organism to acquire language or a symbol system. This is the realm of action or the symbolic [p. 383].

Action must have certain conditions—there must be choice (there cannot be force), there must be purpose, and there must be motion. Humans engage in action, while animals engage in motion (doing something without a particularly critical motive). Dramatism is predicated upon the assumption that humans are actors and present themselves in a fashion similar to a play. As Hart (1997) writes, "By adopting the dramatistic model for criticism, Burke therefore seized on features of drama that had long been recognized but inadequately developed as a critical paradigm" (p. 263). We must be more systematic in how we approach this as a method. Some key ideas to seek out in the methods of dramatism are hierarchy, motive, and scapegoating. The most important idea here is motive. We can chart and derive peoples' motives by analyzing the basic elements of a drama—act, agent, agency, scene, and purpose—that form what is called the pentad. We explain each of the elements of the pentad in turn.

Scene

In *A Grammar of Motives*, Burke describes "scene" as "when or where it was done" (p. 139). In using "'scene' in the sense of setting, or background ... one could say that 'the scene contains the act'" (p. 146). How a speaker describes the scene is important because this description can make an action appropriate or inappropriate. A scene shapes action. Furthermore, the types of action a rhetor seeks defines his or her political style. We will examine the realist political style as it most clearly aligns with Haley's calls for action.

When Robert Hariman (1995) discusses the elements of realist style, using the text of Machiavelli's *The Prince* as illustration, he writes about it as dominated by a supposedly objective appraisal of scene. Hariman argues this realist style is the basis of the prince's success and that "at times the successful political leader has to act unethically" (p. 14). Such behavior would occur when the scene *requires* it. Perhaps

Nikki Haley's decision to remove the Confederate flag (which she had not been opposed to in the past) was dictated by the scene or background of the Emanuel African Methodist Episcopal Church shooting and the consequent marches in Charleston.

Hariman (1995) cites a current example of the same concept: "More recently, George W. Bush relied on this style when defending his 'inherent power to commit our forces to battle, namely, near complete usurpation of the Congress' power to declare war" (p. 29). In both the case of Machiavelli and George W. Bush, the scene is used to justify a style of decision-making. Haley does not have the power of the commander in chief, but we believe she acts to remove the Confederate flag because in many ways the scene (the Charleston shooting) dictated that act.

Another element of the realist style (Hariman 1955) "places politics in a cultural hegemony," thus allowing the politician to define and construct the politics of the culture as he or she sees fit. When Haley uses the examples of what the South used to be in her book, she places the horribly racist events she and her family experienced in a culture that was just acceptable in the past. Hence, these behaviors against her and her family were justified. In this case, the scene dominates political choice and constrains options, which in turn create this cultural hegemony. In many cases of political rhetoric, the scene is the dominant rhetorical constraint and this is very much true for an Indian-American female governor in the Deep South.

Agent

The agent is "who did it" (p. 139). Rhetorical critics look at how rhetoric describes political actors. According to Burke (1969), "Our term, 'agent' ... is a general heading that might, in a given case, require further subdivision, as an agent might have his act modified (hence partly motivated) by friends (co-agents) or enemies (counter-agents)" (p. 143).

Burke (1963) once indicated that a homeless person could be described as lazy, pathetic, drunk, etc., or maybe described as down on one's luck, unfortunate, etc. These descriptions or word choices are important because they reveal how a speaker thinks. They reveal his

Four • Nikki Haley

or her motivation. Under "agent," one could place any personal properties that are assigned a motivational value, such as "ideas," "the will," "fear," "malice," "intuition," or "the creative imagination" (p. 143).

Hariman (1995) suggests that political agents operate in a "distinctive mode of political consciousness, and call to political participation, is activated by these designs that equate politics with the social relations embodied in public address" (p. 131). In this sense, it is the job of the agent to use language to create the civic virtues of the given society. Because the key trope of civic republicanism is civic embodiment, the speaker then becomes a model of civic virtue. Ethos is critical in this orientation because rhetors are constructing their character as they deliberate, and thus creating the agent's political identity (as Hariman illustrates with Cicero's crafting of his civic republican persona).

Because the republican persona cultivates elitism to some extent, decorum is very important with this political style. We see Nikki Haley using a particular Southern decorum because she believes she acts with virtue. She values many of the same things the GOP values. She's pro-life, in favor of making concealed weapon permits easier to acquire, against Obamacare, for in flat tax, against welfare checks, for minorities and women as special interest groups, against gay marriage, and a supporter of the idea that people should invest in charter schools. So much of how she votes and legislates creates her political identity as a conservative, a woman, and a Southerner.

Act

Burke suggests the act is "what took place in thought or deed" (p. 139). In a drama, there is always an act. Yet sometimes the act can be constricted by a scene making the act more difficult. In other words, when a politician blames people of the inner city for their "situation," the politician is suggesting they can simply rise up and get out of the environment. Thus, the environment is not the problem, the people are the problem. Act is part of a political style that focuses on doing things (being a fighter, a doer, etc.); therefore, people should change their environment if it is not working to their advantage. Haley echoes some of these sentiments in her 2012 Republican National Convention speech when she talks about how her family arrived here with nothing and built their multimillion dollar business on their own. We will discuss this in further detail later in the chapter.

Agency

The agency is "how he did it" and "what means or instruments he used" (p. 139). Hariman (1995) uses agency to describe the bureaucratic style, exemplified by Kafka's *Castle*, as being impersonal; thus rules and policies are followed and are legitimate because they are the objective rules. Everything follows a rational procedure. While this may be an ideal approach for leaders, Hariman mocks this to some extent, (1995): "Much as we like to think of an organization having a human face, we expect people working in it to be fully dedicated to fulfilling their organizational functions. All Kafka has to do to suggest the illegitimacy of the system is portray its officials as incompetent, lazy, distracted by their desires, or otherwise living for themselves rather than for the organization" (p. 153).

As Hariman discusses Kafka's *Castle*, he seems to reveal that bureaucracy and hierarchy are problematic because they require so many steps. Similarly, Haley takes many steps in removing her race and gender from how she votes and how she manages her image as a Southern woman.

Purpose

"Purpose" is defined as why someone committed a given act. Purposes vary. Because so many pentadic elements overlap, there is a circumference that suggests "when 'defining by location,' one may place the object of one's definition in contexts of varying scope" (p. 161). The circumference is the scope of the scene or the act. Additionally, conservative politicians tend to emphasize *what* happened, while the liberals tend to examine *why* something happened. This difference can be evidenced in Haley's Republican National Convention address during which she again claims that she and her family were successful all by themselves. The purpose is also often part of other ratios, such as the agent-purpose ratio in civic republicanism, as seen with Cicero and exemplified by Hariman.

Four • Nikki Haley

Range of Ratios

Political styles can be explained by the features of the pentad. Hariman suggests that different political styles emphasize different elements of the pentad and the elements of emphasis provide the reader or viewer a better way to understand the rhetor's motives. For example, the realist political style features scene more often. A bureaucratic style features agency, while civic republicanism features agent and purpose. Hence, the pentad makes the most sense when we view its elements in pairs or ratios and analyze their implications in a certain context. With the five parts of the pentad, there are ten possible ratios that can overlap through the analytical process of applying them. According to Rountree (1998),

> The rhetorical power of such grammatical limitations is illustrated in Burke's observation that one's characterization of a given situation "prescribes the range of acts that will seem reasonable, implicit, or necessary in that situation" ("Dramatism," p. 14). Thus, the movie-goer who screams "Fire!" —a scenic description—implicitly recommends the act of quickly exiting the theater. That is not to say that a fire alert will send everyone scurrying. One's characterization of a room as "ablaze" is not deterministic in dictating the "reasonable" act of fleeing. However, such characterizations are terministic in suggesting how such actions are to be interpreted.

Actions are not dictated, but rather they are shaped by what we do and how we do it. But the *what* and the *how* must be taken together. Simply identifying them is not enough to provide good insight. According to Rountree (1998),

> Rhetors not only draw attention to particular terms (and away from others), and characterize those terms, they also characterize terministic relationships, suggesting how scenes relate (or should relate) to acts, agents to agencies, and so forth. The "direction" of terministic relationships can have significant implications for our interpretations of motives, as Barry Brummett shows in his analysis of two gay rights controversies. Pro-gay rights groups insist that people are born gay and this leads them to engage in homosexual acts; thus, agent determines act. Anti-gay rights groups reverse the equation, urging that the choice to engage in homosexual acts makes individuals homosexual (act determines agent).

If the audience accepts the premise already, then the rhetor can build on that. If the audience does not accept the premise, then it is the job of the rhetor to change the frames. We argue that Nikki Haley is changing the frames and adapting as necessary to meet the needs of her audience(s) and context. The first thing Haley tends to do in her speeches is tell a story about her background and her roots. This tactic encapsulates the agent, purpose, and scene. The second story she often tells is about the purpose of politics—that is, why she is doing what she is doing. This story requires the agent, agency, and purpose. Haley seemingly switches the ratios to adapt to her given audiences.

As mentioned, there are ten possible ratios: scene-act, scene-agent, scene-agency, scene-purpose, act-purpose, act-agent, act-agency, agent-purpose, agent-agency, and agency-purpose. Burke (1969) writes, "The ratios are principles of determination" (p. 52). The scene is the constant formula in the pentad and as a result "contains" the act and the agent; however, the act and the agent are different when it comes to the ratio. "The act-agent ratio is more clearly defined by time or sequence. The agent does not contain the act.... And the act does not 'synecdochically share' in the agent" (p. 153). So the scene contains the act and the scene contains the agent. Ratios are selected. That they are not intended for cause-effect arguments is what makes the ratios so powerful. Additionally, "if an agent acts in keeping with his nature as an agent (act-agent ratio), he may change the nature of a scene accordingly (scene-act ratio) and thereby establish a state of unity between himself and his world (scene-agent ratio)" (p. 156). The circumference of all terms moves us forward perhaps to understanding attitudes. Burke (1969) suggests,

> We cherish the behaviorist experiment precisely because it illustrates the relation between the circumference and the circumscribed in mechanistic terms; and because the sharpest instance of the way in which the altering of the scenic scope affects the interpretation of the act is to be found in the shift from teleological to mechanistic philosophies. Christian theology, in stressing the rational, personal, and purposive aspects of the Creation as the embodiment of the Creator's pervasive will, had treated such principles as scenic. That is, they were not merely traits of human beings, but extended to the outer circumference of the ultimate ground. Hence, by the logic of the scene-act ratio, they were taken as basic to the constitution of human motives, and could be "deduced" from the nature of God as an objective, extrinsic principle defining the nature of human acts. But when the circumference was narrowed to naturalistic limits, the "Creator" was left out of account, and only

the "Creation" remained (remained not as an "act," however, but as a concatenation of motions) [p. 79].

All elements of the pentad tell a dramatistic tale. Furthermore, the ratios are the windows to the discourse, telling a story to reveal motive. If the elements are taken separately, the results are an inoperable narrative. Therefore, it is our goal to determine what Haley's political style is by examining her use of reoccurring pentadic ratios.

We act and enact frames in many different contexts (i.e., historical, cultural, etc.). Kenneth Burke's book, *Attitude Towards History*, focuses on the "attitudes" or "frames" of acceptance and rejection. Based on how someone tells a story, we have some latitude in whether we are willing to say, yes, I accept this story, or no, I absolutely do not accept this as truth. These orientations are formed to respond to the pain, distress, and disarray of the human experience that help or hinder our identification with a certain story. According to Burke (1984),

> "Acceptance" and "rejection" ... start from the problem of evil. In the face of anguish, injustice, disease, and death one adopts policies. One constructs his [sic] notion of the universe or history, and shapes attitudes in keeping. Be he poet or scientist, one defines the "human situation" as amply as his imagination permits; then, with this ample definition in mind, he singles out certain functions or relationships as either friendly or unfriendly. If they are deemed friendly, he prepares himself to welcome them; if they are deemed unfriendly, he weighs objective resistances against his own resources, to decide how far he can effectively go in combating them [pp. 3–4].

Hence we create certain frames that we enact based upon how acceptable or unacceptable the given behavior is. Furthermore, Burke writes, "To act wisely, in concert, we must use many words. If we use the wrong words, words that divide up the field inadequately, we obey false cues. We must name the friendly or unfriendly functions and relationships in such a way that we are able to do something about them. In naming them, we form our characters, since the names embody attitudes; and implicit in the attitudes there are the cues of behavior" (p. 4). Humans develop ways of dealing with evil by constructing attitudes toward history—that is, orientations toward the changing social contexts over space and time and how people deal with the stability (permanence) and instability (change). The frames are thus the sociocultural attitudes toward evil (i.e., greed, discrimination, hierarchy, etc.). In other words, "by 'frames of acceptance' we mean the more or less organized system of meanings by which a thinking man gauges the historical situation and adopts a role with relation to it" (Burke, 1984, p. 5). Additionally, Rountree (1998) writes, "specific dimensions of terministic relations are normative, established by a discourse community's shared beliefs about 'what goes with what' at a given point in time, underlying expectations that one will or should find certain types of agents engaging in certain types of actions, using certain agencies, within certain scenes, for certain purposes, evincing certain attitudes." People expect individuals to act in certain predisposed ways; politicians bank on this predictability and use these terministic screens, or ways of seeing the world, to get voters to vote for them. Haley very much engages in this terministic screen as she uses the events of her childhood to measure the success of the South. She does not indict the Southern culture of the past; rather, she operates as though the progress that has been made does not require history to really be retold. This stance is an odd choice for her because she frequently mentions in her autobiography how hard it was to get elected as an Indian-American woman. So we know she is aware of these challenges, but she changes the social context to get voters to support her.

Who Is Nikki Haley?

Nikki Haley's identity as an American and as a patriot may be constructed in a way that demonstrates the relationship between "leader and people" (Burke, 1974, p. 27). Michael McGee (1975) argues "that a kind of rhetoric defines 'the people' at each stage in a 'collectivization process' of coming to be, being, and ceasing-to-be an objectively real entity" (p. 243). In a way, "the people" have been written into a history of their own culture and country, partially through a powerful political process. McGee suggests the discourse constitutes the audience similarly to Burke's notion of identification, which associates rhetoric with motives. As Charland (1987) points out, "As Burke recognizes, 'persuasion,' as rhetoric's key term, implies the existence of an agent who is free to be persuaded. However, rhetorical theory's privileging of an audience's freedom to judge is problematic, for it assumes that audiences with their prejudices, interests, and motives are *given* and so extra-rhetorical" (p. 133). In other words, peoples' identities have been rhetorically constructed. Nikki Haley's identity has been rhetorically constructed, and she is successful because, as McGee (1975) writes, "it should be possible to speak meaningfully, not of one's own, but of *the people's repertory* of convictions, not as they ought to be, but as they *are* (or have been)" (p. 219).

Given what texts are available, we begin this section by asking these questions: (1) What is the rhetorical persona Haley has constructed over 11 years of public service? (2) What consistent themes or elements does she discuss? (3) What variations or adaptations of these elements are evident in response to situational or positional expectations? (4) What political style does she articulate throughout her career? The best way to address these questions is to examine the various elements of her discourse, specifically from her two most famous speeches: her August 2012 Republican National Convention speech in Tampa, Florida, and her response to Obama's 2016 State of the Union address, broadcast on television from South Carolina.

Analysis of Her Speeches

Using the theoretical framework of dramatism, we will turn to Haley's 2012 Republican National Convention speech in which Romney's slogan, "We *did* build it," became the theme of the convention. In her approximately ten-minute address, the themes Haley discussed were how businesses are built, how the federal government is ruining the American Dream and how President Obama is destroying the country, and how the Romneys can fix the country because of Mitt's experience and Ann's faith. Through these themes, she succeeds in identifying with her political party in the audience, the GOP.

She begins her speech by discussing her immigrant parents and their success as owners of a business that only they built. She ties this accomplishment to the businesses built in South Carolina (planes, cars, tires) by South Carolinians. She receives praise from the audience as she embodies the American Dream myth, stating, "As I said, my parents loved that when they came to America, if you worked hard, the only things that could stop you were the limits you placed on yourself. Unfortunately, these past few years, you can work hard, try to be as successful as possible, follow the rules, and President Barack Obama will do everything he can to stand in your way." In this statement, Haley uses the scene to dominate political choice and constrain peoples' options. She claims it is impossible to be successful in the economy that Obama has created. She says this limitation is particularly true given the president's inability to "secure our border." This statement is interesting because *The Economist* (2014) reported, "America is expelling illegal immigrants at nine times the rate of 20 years ago; nearly 2 million so far under Barack Obama, easily outpacing any previous president." He has even been nicknamed the "deporter-in-chief." Haley's claims that Obama is soft on illegal immigrants and is killing the American Dream are false, yet her remarks are the perfect example of the scene containing the act: Obama's economy is bad because he does nothing about illegal immigrants. But Haley's tactic is effective because the scene is the Republican National Convention and her actions and words receive great applause, given the audience's disdain of Barack Obama. She makes this exact same claim in her 2016 rebuttal to Obama's State of the Union address when she says, "My story is really not much different from millions of other Americans. Immigrants have been coming to our shores for generations to live the dream that is America. They wanted better for their children than for themselves. That remains the dream of all of us, and in this country we have seen time and again that that dream is achievable." First, she enacts the American Dream myth, and then she says,

> At the same time, that does not mean we just flat out open our borders. We can't do that. We cannot continue to allow immigrants to come here illegally. And in this age of terrorism, we must not let in refugees whose intentions cannot be determined.
>
> We must fix our broken immigration system. That means stopping illegal immigration. And it means welcoming properly vetted legal immigrants, regardless of their race or religion. Just like we have for centuries.

Four • Nikki Haley

This is a slightly different message about immigrants than we heard in her convention speech, but this scene is depicted differently and thus requires a different act, one that was not well-received by some of her GOP colleagues because the action suggests we "welcome properly vetted legal immigrants." Well-known and controversial conservative pundit Ann Coulter tweeted the following after Haley's address: "@s@sF-ingChr@st—even GOP response to Obama's SOTU is a paean to immigrants. And GOP can't figure out why Trump is sweeping the country. 'Nikki Haley says "welcoming properly vetted legal immigrants, regardless of religion." Translation: let in all the Muslims. The only way to keep out Muslim terrorists, is to keep out Muslim immigrants.... Trump should deport Nikki Haley." As Burke explained, the "'scene' is basically the setting, or background, that contains the act. Nikki Haley's scene suggests that immigrants, perhaps Muslim Syrian immigrants, are coming from a horrible place ravaged by war, despair, and death. This scene sets the act of allowing properly vetted immigrants into the United States, regardless of his or her religion or race as Haley says. Thus, Haley flips the ratio to more a liberal perspective by asking why the immigrants are trying to come here to the United States instead of focusing on the "what," which perhaps for Ann Coulter is immigrant/Muslim terrorists. In fact, Ann Coulter went on Fox news after Haley called for the removal of the Confederate flag and said Haley cannot understand American history since she is an immigrant and is thus unqualified to make that decision. If one were to look at facts, Nikki Haley was born in America, in South Carolina. This contrast provides an interesting way to examine the scene-act ratio because it really shows the motives of not only Haley but also of some of the other members of the GOP.

Returning to the second theme we identified in Haley's 2012 address, we will look at how she discusses the role of the federal government. She argues that Obama and the National Labor Relations Board (NLRB) sued the state of South Carolina when Boeing brought production to her state. She says:

> In 2009, South Carolina was blessed to welcome a great American company that chose to stay in our country to continue to do business. That company was Boeing. Boeing started a new line for their 787 Dreamliner, creating 1,000 new jobs

in South Carolina, giving our state a shot in the arm when we truly needed it. At the same time, they expanded their job numbers in Washington state by 2,000. Not a single person was hurt by their decision. Not one.

What did President Obama and his National Labor Relations Board do? They sued this iconic American company. It was shameful. And not worthy of the promise of America.

Here is what actually happened. The major production plant is in the Puget Sound area in Washington. This unionized factory was building the 787 Dreamliner at the rate of seven planes a month. Boeing decided to have a second factory in South Carolina (a non-union state) and they built about three planes a month. According to Greenberg (2012) of politifact.com,

> The International Association of Machinists and Aerospace Workers complained. The NLRB's general counsel tried to bring the parties together, but failed. In April 2011, the general counsel's office formally started a hearing process against Boeing on the grounds that the company built its factory in South Carolina in order to punish the union. Retaliation of that sort, if proven, violates federal labor law.
>
> In December 2011, the union and Boeing struck a four-year deal that provided raises, job protections and a commitment to make more planes in the Puget Sound area. With the South Carolina plant no longer seen as a threat to jobs in Washington state, the union dropped its complaint and the NLRB general counsel ended the hearing process.

While the NLRB is an extension of the President of the United States, Barack Obama did not sue Boeing. In fact, no one was sued. Rather, the NLRB held a hearing. Furthermore, the President nominates members of this board who are confirmed through the Senate. And finally, William Gould, who chaired the NLRB under President Clinton, said, "It's an independent quasi-judicial administrative agency.... I am sure that the White House had absolutely nothing to do with this. During my 53-plus months, we never heard anything from the White House" (Greenberg, 2012). Nonetheless, Hailey's comments are couched in the scene of the Republican National Convention in Florida and in the act of a president whose goal it is to obstruct the American Dream. As Haley said, "Slighting American ingenuity and innovation, that's what this president has meant to South Carolina." The way Haley uses the American Dream myth is interesting because a myth lacks enthymeme—there is no need to prove there is an American Dream.

It just exists and it is good and possible. This use of myth is Haley's agency; it is how she gets people to believe what she says is true. It does not matter that the president is separate from the NLRB. It does not matter that there is no specific, clear definition of the American Dream. And it certainly does not matter that there is a history of the decline of the American economy in general. What matters here are the scene-act ratio and Haley's agency.

The third idea or theme in Haley's speech is the ability of the Romneys to repair all that's wrong with the country. She cites four reasons as to why Mitt is the man for the job: "He's taken broken companies and made them successful. He took a failing Olympics and made it a source of pride for our country. He went into a Democratic state, cut taxes, brought in jobs and improved education. Oh, and by the way, he actually balanced his budget." Now, it is obviously the nature of a convention speech to be brief and lend credibility to the candidate. Her statements, however, are not accompanied by evidence and they are all defined by action, which is a typical conservative strategy. A common conservative theme is if you dos not like living in poverty, just get out, just pull yourself up by your bootstraps.

Haley claims that Romney improved education. Well, this is neither true nor false: "The most important point to make with Gov. Romney's record is that the reform he initiated was part of a much larger and longer movement that existed in Massachusetts," said Chad d'Entremont, executive director of the Rennie Center, which provides independent, nonpartisan research to inform public education reform in Massachusetts. Furthermore, "Skinner, the expert with the teachers' union, added that Romney was "a somewhat absent 'education' governor. He was very agenda driven.'"

As far as his ability to balance budgets and turn failing companies around is concerned, the way Romney has conducted his business affairs is controversial. Romney's wealth was largely acquired through Bain Capital. According to Taibbi (2012), "A man makes a $250 million fortune loading up companies with debt and then extracting million-dollar fees from those same companies, in exchange for the generous service of telling them who needs to be fired in order to finance the debt payments he saddled them with in the first place." According to

Creamer (2012), "The point is not just that workers were laid off, or jobs were outsourced—though they were. The point is not whether some of the ventures Romney funded succeeded and others failed. The point is that the impact of Romney's business activity on the lives of ordinary people was incidental to his one and only goal: making huge sums of money for himself and a small group of his partners and investors." It is surprising that the average person of South Carolina would find these values appealing; if he or she did, Nikki Haley would have a much harder time proving the assertions she makes are true. But again, it does not matter because her statements use President Barack Obama as the scapegoat, blaming him for the entire economic crisis and praising Romney for his governing abilities in one of the wealthiest and most educated states in the United States, Massachusetts.

On January 12, 2016, President Obama gave his last State of the Union address. What followed was a nine-minute rebuttal from Nikki Haley in which she focused on the economy, the responsibility of both Republicans and Democrats for the current problems, the American Dream, immigration, and the church shooting at the Emanuel African Methodist Episcopal Church in Charleston just seven months before this speech. Her tone was a bit different as she discussed some of the more challenging ideological issues of race and religion, perhaps in an attempt at unifying the American people regardless of political party.

In *The Rhetoric of Hitler's Battle,* Burke (1975) explains that leaders create scapegoats which furthers the division from and unification to the people. Here, Burke cites Hitler's writing to explain:

> As a whole, and at all times, the efficiency of the truly national leader consists primarily in preventing the division of the attention of a people and always in concentrating it on a single enemy. The more uniformly the fighting will of a people is put into action, the greater will be the magnetic force of the movement.... It is part of the genius of a great leader to make adversaries of different fields appear as always belonging to one category only, because to weak and unstable characters the knowledge that there are various enemies will lead only too easily to incipient doubts as to their own cause.
>
> As soon as the wavering masses find themselves confronted with too many enemies, objectivity at once steps in, and the question is raised whether actually all the others are wrong and their own nation or their own movement alone is right [p. 193].

Four • Nikki Haley

In her rebuttal, Haley appears to be questioning her own movement and party. She creates unification with the less xenophobic members of the GOP and perhaps some liberals, and creates further division with the likes of Donald Trump, Laura Ingraham, and Ann Coulter and those that follow them. We already discussed Coulter's tweet about Haley and her supposed immigrant status. But in this rebuttal, Haley said, "during anxious times, it can be tempting to follow the siren call of the angriest voices. We must resist that temptation." She is clearly referring to the voice of Donald Trump and she confirmed this to NBC News the following day. Shortly after this speech and after Haley's endorsement of Marco Rubio, Trump tweeted, "The people of South Carolina are embarrassed by Nikki Haley," to which Haley replied, "Bless your heart." She used the proper Southern construction in order to mock him.

Nonetheless, Haley discusses allowing in "properly vett[ed] immigrants regardless of race or religion." She talks about the horrible mass murders of the nine innocent people that were praying in the Emanuel African Methodist Episcopal church. Haley says, "That night, someone new joined them. He didn't look like them, didn't act like them, didn't sound like them. They didn't throw him out. They didn't call the police. Instead, they pulled up a chair and prayed with him. For an hour." She continues, "We didn't turn against each other's race or religion. We turned toward God, and to the values that have long made our country the freest and greatest in the world. We removed a symbol that was being used to divide us, and we found a strength that united us against a domestic terrorist and the hate that filled him." She explains why the Charleston community and South Carolina came together, saying, "There's an important lesson in this. In many parts of society today, whether in popular culture, academia, the media, or politics, there's a tendency to falsely equate noise with results." She indicts the actions of the racism loudly spewed by people like Trump. She is saying that these behaviors are unacceptable, and she believes the media can be more responsible. These are concepts that should unify people against offensive ideas, people, and outlets. It is as though Haley is presenting herself as the "objective voice" to unify the people who do see and live these struggles each day. After all, the past is not the past for many people because many are still living in the realm of racism, discrimination by gender or sexual orientation, and overall injustice.

As she continues these acts of identification, she states,

> We need to be honest with each other, and with ourselves: while Democrats in Washington bear much responsibility for the problems facing America today, they do not bear it alone. There is more than enough blame to go around.
>
> We as Republicans need to own that truth. We need to recognize our contributions to the erosion of the public trust in America's leadership. We need to accept that we've played a role in how and why our government is broken.
>
> And then we need to fix it.
>
> The foundation that has made America that last, best hope on earth hasn't gone anywhere. It still exists. It is up to us to return to it.

She embraces the hope that Obama embraced during his initial presidential run. Hope is so powerful because it is a desire that everyone has—hope for a better education, for a place to live, for children to do better than the parents did, for health and a long life—the hope of achieving the American Dream. We all have hope. Haley begins telling her story as the child of Indian immigrants:

> Growing up in the rural South, my family didn't look like our neighbors, and we didn't have much. There were times that were tough, but we had each other, and we had the opportunity to do anything, to be anything, as long as we were willing to work for it.
>
> My story is really not much different from millions of other Americans. Immigrants have been coming to our shores for generations to live the dream that is America. They wanted better for their children than for themselves. That remains the dream of all of us, and in this country we have seen time and again that that dream is achievable.

She unified her vision with a vision that many liberals and conservatives could support. We all hope. We all dream.

Finally, she indicts Obama on his record, as he is always the scapegoat; she engages in "purification by disassociation" as Burke (1975, p. 202) called it. Taking a position similar to the one in her 2012 convention speech, she feels "the President's record has often fallen far short of his soaring words." She continues,

> As he enters his final year in office, many Americans are still feeling the squeeze of an economy too weak to raise income levels. We're feeling a crushing national debt, a health care plan that has made insurance less affordable and doctors less available, and chaotic unrest in many of our cities. Even worse, we are facing the

most dangerous terrorist threat our nation has seen since September 11th, and this president appears either unwilling or unable to deal with it.

In using Obama as the scapegoat, Haley garnered the praise of many of the more moderate GOP figures, such as Chris Christie and Jeb Bush.

Lessons Learned

Nikki Haley is an interesting woman to keep an eye on. Perhaps she is the changing face of the South that characterizes change and progress. Certainly, she has her own rhetorical strategies that work for her. She uses Burke's concepts of unification and division. She often focuses on the action rather than the scene as is a popular conservative tactic. She also employs a certain double-edged Southern charm, as seen in her tweet to Trump—"Bless your heart."

Haley seems more moderate in her political style perhaps because she is the daughter of Indian immigrants, perhaps because she grew up not fitting in in Bamberg, South Carolina, perhaps because she is a woman. Because she has only been in the national political arena since 2011 and in the local legislature from 2005 to 2011, she is not as experienced as a Condoleezza Rice or Elizabeth Dole, but she certainly is worthy of study—there was talk about her as a vice-presidential candidate for the 2016 election. *The Economist* (2016) cited "that combination—fiscal ferocity and a capacity for conciliation" as reasons she might be asked to join the Trump ticket. She has managed her rhetorical persona rather well over the last few years and can perhaps become a voice less loud than Donald Trump's but perhaps stronger and more unifying. The themes she has discussed more recently, after the Charleston church shooting, have certainly been more ideological and perhaps more challenging for her base. Because she has not had the lengthiest career, it is hard to address how well she adapts to situational or positional expectation, but her rise to becoming governor happened very quickly, especially given her lack of experience in national politics. She took over after a scandal involving former governor Mark Sanford, even earning the endorsement of Jenny Sanford, his ex-wife on whom he cheated and about which he lied. So, thus far, Haley has been able to manage the challenges of both situation and position. Finally, we asked, what political style does she articulate throughout her career? She articulates a Southern style that is both tough but likeable. According to Starr (2004), "Dixie is hardly a bastion of female empowerment, political or otherwise: state legislatures in the region have the lowest percentages of female members in the country. But by manipulating traditional perceptions of Southern womanhood, the Magnolias have been able to win powerful statewide offices" (p. 36). Haley is an example of such an achievement, especially since she will be the U.S. ambassador to the United Nations. After all, her autobiography isn't called *Can't Is Not an Option* for no good reason.

• FIVE •

Susana Martinez

Public address has traditionally been dominated by male rhetors, but over the past 30 years, we have seen an increase in female political figures and orators (Campbell, 1973, 1989, 1989; Griffin, 1993; Foss & Griffin, 1992; Foss & Griffin, 1995). In fact, in the most recent 2012 election, 20 women won U.S. Senate seats. Women also played a large role in who got elected as "55 percent of women and 45 percent of men voted for Obama and 44 percent of women and 52 percent of men voted for Romney" (Abdullah, 2012). Obama was considered to have the "gender advantage." This assumption, coupled with the examples in the introduction, shows there is a need for the Republican Party to use invitational rhetoric. Foss and Griffin (1995) argue the "rhetoric of patriarchy reflect[s] its values of change, competition, and domination" (pp. 3–4), so perhaps there is a need to create a rhetoric built on new values (Foss & Foss, 1994)—values that move women and women's issues to the forefront of the public forum. However, we argue we are seeing many of the female GOP speakers using much of the competitive and dominating rhetorical style as that used by their male counterparts. The focus of this chapter is nicknamed "Susana Barracuda." She is Susana Martinez, the first female governor of New Mexico and the first Hispanic female governor in the United States.

Susana Martinez grew up in El Paso, Texas, in a middle class family and earned her Juris Doctor degree from the University of Oklahoma. She and her first husband, a lawyer, moved to Las Cruces, New Mexico, and after their divorce, she married her current husband, Chuck Franco, who works in law enforcement. Martinez was the assistant district attorney and then the deputy district attorney. As stated in her

2012 Republican convention speech, she and her husband had been lifelong Democrats until 1995, when they switched parties after having lunch with some friends. As Martinez famously stated, "When we left that lunch, we got in the car and I looked over at Chuck and said, 'I'll be damned—we're Republicans.'" This became the key theme of her 2012 speech. We will use feminine style to better understand the force of Martinez's speech. This theoretical framework works well because she is a strong speaker with conservative values whose policies seem to enforce the "pull yourself up by the bootstraps" or the "tough love" approach. As a Hispanic American woman, she uses an interesting approach to helping the state of New Mexico. We will now consider the framework of feminine style and tie it to invitational rhetoric to understand Martinez's style and lessons that can be gleaned from her for other candidates.

Feminine Style

Karlyn Kohrs Campbell (1989) identified "feminine style" as the type of style in which the speaker adopts a personal tone; audience members are treated as peers, with an emphasis on identification, and arguments unfold inductively. Such a style has the advantage of making the speaker appear conventionally feminine; it appeals to women in audiences even as it encourages them to participate actively in reaching conclusions instead of accepting claims passively (p. xv). Because this style arose from the experiences women had, women had to develop certain approaches to public discourse because "the very act of speaking publicly violated concepts of womanhood" (p. 14). This argument alone calls for a feminist approach to understanding women's speech because, as most feminist scholars seem to agree, it is not biology that that causes people to view women as less important speakers. The arguments Campbell takes on, in studying women who fight for social justice and change, however, suggest that women should fulfill their roles as caregivers, mothers, wives, etc. To act outside of these roles is to be unwomanly. Additionally, her analyses demonstrate the types of creative and interesting stylistic devices drawn from the "feminine style" such as narrative, consciousness-raising, identification, etc., all of which was fostered by "common values and shared experience" (p. 14).

Campbell focused largely on female speakers from the mid–1800s to the early 1900s because these were the first known feminists, fighting to abolish slavery, to have rights to protect themselves from their husbands (who may have been alcoholic and/or physically abusive), and, later on, to achieve woman's suffrage. Scholars continue to study women's public address because "the obstacles early women persuaders faced persist, although in altered forms, in the present" (Campbell, 1989, p. 15).

Several scholars followed Campbell's inquiry on female reformers, most of whom agree on a few key things. First, there is tension between the norms of public political discourse, which is masculine, and the women speakers who wish to engage in political discourse. Second, the majority of these scholars discuss whether the discourse is compatible with women and found that, for whatever reasons, whether it is women's nature or the socialization of gender, women are not compatible with this form.

A number of scholars have looked at the rhetoric of several female speakers from this lens. For example, Gutgold (2001) examined how Elizabeth Dole's speech at the 1996 Republican National Convention shifted her from Bob Dole's wife to Elizabeth Dole, presidential candidate. Foss and Griffin (1995) would suggest that these types of studies reaffirm that persuasion and rhetoric are synonymous and the scholars would seemingly prefer to redefine rhetoric altogether. Foss and Griffin have argued that because rhetoric and persuasion are separate, there needs to be an entirely different system for understanding rhetoric, perhaps a new paradigm, one more compatible to women, one that challenges our theoretical home of classical rhetoric. They further believe that there is patriarchal bias in rhetorical theory (as most feminist scholars do) and this fact alone makes for a very limited understanding of rhetoric. To fully understand the scope of the feminist perspective and of women's public address, Foss (1989) demands formulating "new rules for the construction of knowledge. Adopting the feminist perspective does not mean just grafting women's concerns onto the theories of knowledge that already are in place; it demands a reconceptualization of knowledge" (p. 2). Foss admits there are several obstacles to legitimizing this type of scholarship and suggests as a solution of sorts to "acknowledge the existence of these obstacles and to see feminist inquiry not as a threat but as an opportunity to celebrate diversity of communication in all of its forms" (p. 8). Again, she is challenging (as have several scholars) the definition of rhetoric. Therefore, if rhetoric has traditionally been defined as the "available means of persuasion," and these means have generally been male-dominated means, why would we force women into this canon or speaking style?

Foss and Griffin's (1993) notion of invitational rhetoric more clearly "suggest[s] that the exclusive focus on persuasion in rhetorical scholarship has limited the scope of the discipline and has hindered efforts to understand forms of rhetoric that do not involve the intent to change the behavior or beliefs of others" (p. 1). In other words, they argue to reconceptualize rhetoric, since it does not always mean persuasion. In this sense, if it is women who function in ways of self-discovery and affirmation, it would be unlikely that a woman would adhere to the forcefulness of traditional persuasion (Foss & Foss, 1991). Yet Susana Martinez is interesting because we see her adhering to the traditional persuasive style, speaking about the exact same topics her male counterparts do but in narrative style. Perhaps some of these stylistic elements are due to the nature of convention speeches, but for a political party that has such challenges in reaching women and getting women to vote for them, it is surprising that there was no mention of women, women's issues, or any cultural issues one might expect from the first female Hispanic governor in the history of the United States.

Most of the research in the past ten to 15 years has sought to expand the study of female speakers and the "feminine style" beyond female social reformers. One study that does this is Blankenship and Robson's (1995) examination of the style as seen among 45 women "holding or seeking appointive office in a branch of federal or state government" (p. 357) between 1990 and 1994 because their texts were speeches from congressional hearings, their databases were the *Congressional Record* and C-SPAN. As a result, Blankenship and Robson found there are five clear characteristics of a "feminine style," which include "1. basing political judgments on concrete, lived experience; 2. valuing inclusivity and the relational nature of being; 3. conceptualizing power of the public office as a capacity to 'get things done' and to empower others; approaching policy formation holistically; and moving women's issues to the forefront of the public arena" (p. 359). Using Campbell's framework of "feminine style" as well as Blankenship and Robson's (1995) we begin the feminist rhetorical criticism of Susana Martinez's Republican National Convention speech in Tampa, Florida, on August 29, 2012.

2012 Republican National Convention

The national political conventions provide a good context for study because they are ritual performances, which seemingly have specific roles and scripts for all of the people involved, thus making them dramatizations to some extent. Also, previous research has examined the development of the conservative party and the success of it, but to date there is not much cultural criticism or analysis of the female orators at these events. Several issues tend to characterize the Republican National Convention, but the 2012 convention was centered on the concept "We built it." This notion was a direct response to or attack on the following comments Obama made while campaigning in Roanoke, Virginia, on July 13, 2012.

> If you were successful, somebody along the line gave you some help. There was a great teacher somewhere in your life. Somebody helped to create this unbelievable American system that we have that allowed you to thrive. Somebody invested in roads and bridges. If you've got a business—you didn't build that. Somebody else made that happen. The Internet didn't get invented on its own. Government research created the Internet so that all the companies could make money off the Internet.

Thus, a response to "You didn't build that," which was taken out of the context in which it was intended, resulted in Romney's slogan and convention theme "We built it."

Susana Martinez was no different, as the key things she spoke about were the American Dream, risk in business, guns and God. But she is a bit different from many of the other Republican women in that she embodies a feminine orientation and conservative ideology. She exemplifies the role of a mother (she has a stepson) and the role of political agent. She bridges some of the gender gap and some of the racial gaps we see in American voting history and "according to a poll last month by Survey USA and Albuquerque station KOB, Martinez enjoys the support of 66 percent of New Mexico's voters, including 70 percent of women, 64 percent of independents, and 44 percent of registered Democrats" (Sanchez, 2013). As a Republican woman, Martinez utilizes a certain type of rhetoric, perhaps uses the "feminine style," has a cultural charm speaking both Spanish and English on the campaign trail, and perpetuates certain masculine values like gun ownership. She manages to be feminine (at least in the way she dresses and looks) yet she is firm and assuring that business, capitalism, hard work, and religion are what Americans need—hence a vote for Mitt Romney is a vote for these American values.

At around ten on the night of the 29th, Susana Martinez was introduced as "the first Hispanic female governor in history of the United States." She wore a black and blue skirt suit, high heels and relatively simple jewelry (a necklace and earrings). Her light brown hair was coiffed around her face, and she appeared to be wearing a little makeup.

She began her speech by calling for prayers for the victims of Hurricane Isaac. Immediately after, she began a narrative based on the myth of the American Dream. Hargreaves (2013) stated that "the American Dream is supposed to mean that through hard work and perseverance, even the poorest people can make it to middle class or above. But it's actually harder to move up in America than it is in most other advanced nations." This myth is a large part of Martinez's speech as she said things like "Growing up I never imagined a little girl from a border town could one day become a governor. But this is America. Y en America, todo es posible." Twice in her speech, she spoke Spanish possibly to make her points stronger or to attempt to identify with other audiences. She continued to say her parents taught her that her "future could be whatever [she] dreamt it to be. Success they taught [her] is built on the foundation of courage, hard work and individual responsibility."

Five • Susana Martinez

As she tells these stories of America as she sees it through the eyes of a "little girl from a border town," she embraces the narrative style used by many feminine political speakers. These are her "concrete, lived experiences," as Blankenship and Robson (1995) described. These stories are also examples of the "personal tone" Campbell (1989) described in the "feminine style." But according to Frye (1957), "The romance is nearest of all literary forms to the wish-fulfillment dream, and for that reason it has socially a curiously paradoxical role. In every age the ruling social or intellectual class tends to project its ideals in some form of romance, where the virtuous heroes ... represent the ideals and the villains the threats to their ascendancy" (p. 186). As with the American Dream myth, there begins the discussion of how one becomes successful. Martinez was quick to say, "Despite what some would have us believe, success is not built on resentment and fear." This suggests a few things. First, she is of the ruling class in this context; therefore, she projects her ideal view of the world in direct relation to the "villains" that threaten it. She is really claiming that some people or parties fear success. This is her narrative to attack the president and his earlier comments regarding the role that government, teachers, and other things and people play in helping us become successful. Finally, her story suggests that less successful people are fearful and resentful of those with more accomplishments. Since Martinez is still discussing this American Dream myth, it is probably safe to suggest that she defines success as wealth. So, in this myth, would school teachers be successful? Would social workers be successful? Are homemakers successful? These are not typically the jobs associated with wealth in America.

Martinez's family moved up in social class. She shared a personal story about her family:

> We grew up on the border and truly lived paycheck to paycheck. My dad was a golden gloves boxer in the Marine Corps, then a deputy sheriff. My mom worked as an office assistant.
>
> One day, they decided to start a security guard business. I thought they were absolutely crazy—we literally had no savings, but they always believed in the American Dream. My parents grew that small business—from one 18-year-old guarding a bingo—to more than 125 people in three states. And sure, there was help along the way. But my parents took the risk. They stood up. And you better believe that they built it.

Listening to Women on the Right

This story brings the audience back to the theme of the convention: "We built it." Again, there is this "emphasis on identification" (Campbell, 1989) through the American Dream myth. This American Dream theme she carries throughout the speech is interesting because according to a 2013 Gallup Poll, "non–Hispanic whites accounted for 89 percent of Republican self-identifiers nationwide ... while accounting for 70 percent of independents and 60 percent of Democrats. Over one-fifth of Democrats (22 percent) were black, while 16 percent of independents were Hispanic" (Newport, 2013). Typically appealing to more marginalized people in an attempt to give them hope, the American Dream does not typically describe the people at the Republican national conventions. Again, the myth she discusses could be for the purpose of identifying with Hispanic voters or working- or middle-class voters. But this message would probably not resonate with wealthy white males. According to Fay (n.d.), "Financially, Republicans fare better than either Democrats or Independents, and tend to identify themselves as such. Republican candidates gain a significantly higher percentage of votes from individuals with incomes over $50,000 per year, and the advantage increases along with the income level, to a height of 63 percent of individuals earning $200,000 or more a year supporting Republicans." Essentially, many Republicans are not struggling economically. Martinez even concedes that she and Mitt Romney certainly had very different upbringings as she said, "In many ways Mitt Romney and I are very different. Different starts in life. Different paths to leadership. Different cultures." This is true. Mitt Romney and Susana Martinez are quite different.

Martinez further identified with her audience as she said, "So, my dad worked to grow the business. My mom did the books at night. And at 18, I guarded the parking lot at the Catholic church bingos." The audience chuckled at that. Then she said, "Now my dad made sure I could take care of myself. I carried a Smith & Wesson .357 Magnum." The crowd roared at this statement, the most popular one she made based on the audience applause. She continued, "Yes, that gun weighed more than I did." This garnered many laughs. It should be no surprise that many GOP lawmakers support lax gun laws in the United States. In fact, "if House Republicans have their way, District of Columbia residents won't be allowed to walk the streets with a joint in their pocket, but they will be allowed to carry a semi-automatic rifle. The GOP–controlled House approved a spending bill Wednesday that would undo the District's strict gun-control laws" (Associated Press, 2014). According to ontheissues.org (2014), which is a nonpartisan source, the Republican platform supports "no frivolous gun lawsuits," "no gun licensing," "more public land to hunt" and "the right to obtain and store ammunition without registration." It is obvious that Martinez's story about her .357 Magnum was a popular one. Mitt Romney was not guarding parking lots at 18 with such a weapon.

Martinez continues her narrative as she appeals to the myth of the triumphant individual, for "the parable has at its subject the humble person who works hard, takes risks but has faith in self, and eventually reaches or even exceeds goals of fame, honor, and financial success" (Larsen, 2001, p. 203). She claims not only did her parents take such risks, but these chances and risks were taken because "my parents also taught me about having the courage to stand for something. So I went to law school. And I became a prosecutor." She actually prosecuted cases of child abuse and child homicide. Protecting the children brings forth this motherly persona that allows her to fulfill her role as a caregiver in some way, thus perhaps appealing to women, specifically married women since they tend to vote Republican. Typically, because married women tend to have more financial stability than single women, their affluence influences how they vote. Also, because Martinez does not have biological children (she has a stepson), perhaps her job helps demonstrate that she is feminine enough yet aggressive enough. Nonetheless, Martinez's appeal here is that hard work and courage will mean success in America.

The final themes of Martinez's speech include economics and bipartisanship. She believes she is efficient and effective as a politician because she can work with others, unlike President Obama. Martinez said at the Republican National Convention in 2012, "I fear some of our leaders today have lost the courage to stand up. What we have now are politicians. They won't offer real plans, and only stand up when they want to blame someone else." But a few sentences later she says,

Listening to Women on the Right

> But that is not the kind of leadership that we are seeing from President Obama. He promised to bring us all together, to cut unemployment, to pass immigration reform in his first year, and even promised to cut the deficit in half, in his first term. Do you remember that? But he hasn't come close. They have not even passed a budget in Washington, D.C. in 3 years.
>
> If he can take credit for government building small businesses, then he can accept responsibility for breaking his promise and adding $5 trillion to the national debt. Because he did build that.

What she does here is hypocritical but placates the audience. When she asks, "Do you remember that?" everyone shouts, "Yesssssss!" When she blames Obama for the deficit and budget problems, the audience shouts, "Boooooooooo!" Their interaction with her as active members of the audience is part of feminine style, but the message is clearly blaming the president, a tactic she said is the wrong way for politicians to conduct themselves. She got huge applause after blaming Obama and asks him to take responsibility "because he did build that." She returns to the theme of the convention, which is about who built what and who is responsible for what, and so on. Bill Clinton really clarified this concept at the Democratic National Convention on August 5, 2012, in Charlotte, North Carolina, when he quoted Bob Strauss, who said, "every politician wants every voter to believe he was born in a log cabin he built himself." This concept of "I" is a very powerful part of the Republican narrative. Bill Clinton continues to explain in this speech that the country works better when it is "we." "We Democrats—we think the country works better with a strong middle class, with real opportunities for poor folks to work their way into it—with a relentless focus on the future, with business and government actually working together to promote growth and broadly share prosperity. You see, we believe that 'we're all in this together' is a far better philosophy than 'you're on your own.' It is."

The story Martinez is telling is really about what she believes she and her family accomplished on their own. She couches the point of help from the system or the government by saying, "And sure, there was help along the way." She does not specify what kind of help or in what capacity, but she says it nonchalantly as though she and her family really pulled themselves up by their bootstraps. She does not acknowledge any legislation that has enhanced Equal Opportunity Employment for her as a woman or a Hispanic woman. She does not reference any educational systems that helped her get to where she is today. In fact, according to Catanese (2014), she made the following comments about school teachers: "teachers ... already don't work, you know, two and a half months of the year, three months out of the year, but earn salaries at the same rate of people who do work 12 months a year." This is an interesting narrative because teachers are usually not wealthy. It is hard to believe they earn the same salaries as doctors or lawyers who work 12 months a year.

Martinez's comments regarding women's organizations are equally problematic. According to Andy Kroll (2014),

> During an October 2010 campaign conference call, Martinez said she'd met a woman who worked for the state's Commission on the Status of Women, a panel created in 1973 to improve health, pay equity, and safety for women.
> "What the hell is that?" she asked.
> "I don't know what the fuck they do," replied her deputy campaign manager, Matt Kennicott.
> "What the hell does a commission on women's cabinet do all day long?" Martinez asked.
> "I think [deputy campaign operations director Matt] Stackpole wants to be the director of that so he can study more women," Kennicott said.

Martinez laughed hysterically in response.

Finally, as she and her campaign manager discussed Ben Lujan, the U.S. representative for New Mexico's 3rd congressional district and a popular figure among Hispanics, Kennicott said, "Somebody told me he's absolutely eloquent in Spanish, but his English? He sounds like a retard." Martinez responded by laughing again. The first Hispanic woman governor in the United States seems challenged in supporting women, women's issues, and minority issues in legislation.

In returning to this concept of bipartisanship, Martinez does not prove with any examples that she works well with others. She simply says, "In New Mexico, I inherited the largest structural deficit in state history, and our legislature is controlled by Democrats. We don't always agree, but we came together in a bipartisan manner and turned that deficit into a surplus." People who have worked with her have said the opposite. According to Terrell (2013):

Listening to Women on the Right

But there also have been bruising legislative fights in which, Democrats say, Martinez has shown little if any willingness to compromise. And the harsh attack ads and mailers Martinez ran against some Democrats during the 2012 election still are fresh on the minds of lawmakers.

The "works-well-with-Democrats" theme is a talking point that Martinez herself has cultivated. With voters around the country getting increasingly fed up with partisan gridlock in Congress, the image of a comprising pragmatist is an appealing one for a politician to try to project....

"It's her way or the highway," Jennings said, adding that while Martinez talks about bipartisanship, "She's got her [political] machine going all the time. She acts like she's lily white, but it's just not true."

"There's a few things where she worked with the Legislature, but they're few and far between," said Sanchez, who frequently has been singled out for criticism by Martinez.

Sanchez also listed education reform as an example of an issue in which Martinez has refused to compromise. "We've sent her good education reform bills that she vetoed," he said.

Martinez has been in her position since 2010 and thus far has not created better paths for women or minorities. She used feminine style to reify the narratives she sees best as a Republican, not as a woman or a Hispanic woman.

Martinez ends her 2012 convention speech with a return to the myth of the American Dream. "It is success and success is the American dream, and that success is not something to be ashamed of or to demonize. There is one candidate in this election who will protect that dream. One leader who will fight hard to keep the promise of America for the next generation. And that's why we must stand up and make Mitt Romney the next president of the United States."

There are a few issues with the conclusion of her speech. First, who is demonizing success? People tend to demonize greed, not success. Second, how does she prove Romney will "keep the promise of America"? Part of feminine style is valuing inclusivity. This is not apparent in the construction of her speech, especially in the conclusion. Inclusivity, especially in the Republican Party, should mean including women and minorities. Third, Mitt Romney is not the American Dream. He came from means; his family was wealthy. Finally, she does not really empower others as is also a part of the feminine style. As WE demonstrated, she has said and/or been a bystander to some terrible statements about women and Hispanics. By applying certain myths about success and American life, and by making reference to guns and religion, she is able to construct a speech that was very popular amongst her constituents at the 2012 Republican National Convention.

Lessons Learned

Does Susana Martinez, aka "Susana Barracuda," employ feminine style to appeal to her audience? The answer is yes and no. To some extent, she tells stories about how her life experiences influenced her political judgments. She guarded the church parking lot. She carried a gun while doing so. Her father was a Marine and a sheriff. These are very specific examples she probably chose given her audience and the fact that it was a conservative political convention. These examples resonated with her audience. Had she spoken extensively about race and gender, she may not have been received in the same way. Additionally, it is the nature of political conventions to tell stories so one cannot be sure how much of her rhetoric is her employing "feminine style" and how much of this is simply convention speech.

As far as "valuing inclusivity and the relational nature of being," this is more of a challenge. As we mentioned, the GOP has issues appealing to women and minorities. Since she is both, some might assume she would include these demographics as least as references throughout her speech but she does not. We argue she covered many of the same things her male counterparts discussed such guns, capitalism, business, the economy, and why Obama is unsuccessful.

The third element of feminine style according to Blankenship and Robson (1995) is "conceptualizing power of the public office as a capacity to 'get things done' and to empower others." We really do not see many elements of this in her speech. She mentions that when she meets young girls who come up to greet her, she feels like she is "paving a path for those little girls to follow." Perhaps this is how she empowers others—rhetorically rather than through governmental policies.

The fourth element of feminine style is "approaching policy

formation holistically." She says she is bipartisan, but there is evidence suggesting she is not. Some people who have worked with her have said she wants things her way and that is it. She does have a relatively good approval rating with the public (Blake, 2012).

Finally, in feminine style, "moving women's issues to the forefront of the public arena" (p. 359) is important. She does not do this much at all. As mentioned, the GOP does not fare well with women. It is surprising Martinez does not do a better job discussing how the party is handling women and women's issues. There certainly is the need to try to prove that the GOP legislates in ways to help those in need.

Campbell's (1989) explanation of feminine style included using "a personal tone," treating "audience members ... as peers, with an emphasis on identification," and inductive argumentation (p. xv). Martinez does not reason with much evidence here (beyond her personal anecdotes and stories). In fact, there is little evidence to support many of the conclusions of her speech. She does use a personal tone because she tells personal stories. Her audience identifies with the stories she selected to tell because many of them may believe in the myth of the American Dream. If they accept this myth as truth, then they believe it is just as easy for any poor person or woman to just pull themselves up out of poverty or the working class and get a better job or start a business or go to college. In fact, Romney made mention of some of these things on the campaign trail. When he spoke at Otterbein University in Columbus, Ohio, in 2012, he told the story of his friend Jimmy John who borrowed $20,000 from his father to start a business. He suggested other students just do that ... just borrow money from your parents to start a business. This is an upper class narrative. The majority of Americans cannot simply borrow $20,000 from their parents to start a business. In short, Martinez does make attempts to unite her audience with Romney and these values while dividing them from Obama's values and ethics. Furthermore, she still holds a party line in that she extends a feminine invitation for voters to vote Republican. She is successful in this way as far as feminine style is concerned.

What can others learn from her? First of all, the use of a personal tone or the ability to tell a story does resonate with audiences. This is not a new concept, really. Second, inviting the audience to a discussion is more effective. As Foss and Griffin (1995) wrote, "rhetors will be able to recognize situations in which they seek not to persuade others but simply to create an environment that facilitates understanding, accords values and respect to others' perspectives and contributes to the development of relationships of equality" (p. 17). Ideally, the rhetor should do these things in order to be effective. We argue this lack of actual empathy is one of the key things lacking in attracting women and minorities to the Republican Party.

♦ SIX ♦

Condoleezza Rice

Karlyn Kohrs Campbell (1989) first made the argument that scholars should study women's rhetoric to challenge the dominant forms of speech with which we are most familiar (i.e., "the classics"). In studies of the classics, this approach left out women, Native Americans, African Americans, etc. (Wander, 1983). Not only were several groups of individuals left out of the canon, but it was also the traditional method that "prevented the critic from estimating the truth of a speaker's statements and the adequacy of the values the speaker assumes or recommends" (Wander, 1983, p. 7). Furthermore, if this classical approach was the only method scholars had, we would be unable to get past the text of the speech itself to understand the surrounding contextual issues. Therefore, one branch of theories that go beyond the text and examine women in context are feminist theories, of which there are several: radical feminism, liberal feminism, Marxist feminism, and Standpoint feminism (which grew out of Marxist theory). Each of these ideologies came alive under the three waves of feminism. The first wave of feminism was comprised of the abolitionists and suffragists. These women fought for the abolition of slavery and the right for women to vote. They also gained the right to own and inherit property and to divorce. The second wave of feminism began in the mid–1960s where we see Betty Freidan's *The Feminine Mystique* begin to raise questions about the standpoint of feminism from a white, upper-class female perspective (and not paying attention to racial minorities, lesbians, and lower-class females, for example). The most obvious gain from this wave was the Equal Rights Amendment. The third wave does not differ too much from the second wave, but these women wanted a more secure voice of their own. The third wave has similar goals to the second wave, but exists in order to push toward a goal of total equality. We are currently in the third wave of feminism.

Certain common elements underlie each of the types of feminist theories. Grant (1993) believes there are three core concepts that bind feminist theories: the concepts of woman, experience, and personal politics. These beliefs are derived from an early feminist notion that women are oppressed simply because they are female, not by virtue of socio-economics or class. The varying feminist ideologies employ different strategies, but the above mentioned characteristics are core to all of them. Last, "there are considerable differences in social theory and political strategy between campaigns to get more women into prominent positions in public life" (Ramazanoglu, 1989, p. 9).

One woman in a prominent position that represents some of these liberal feminist values is Condoleezza Rice. In order to understand the rhetoric of Condoleezza Rice from a feminist orientation, we begin by exploring Rice as a liberal feminist. We will then offer a feminist criticism of Rice's popular culture interviews and videos with Oprah Winfrey because these are where she really defines who she is and where she came from in a way that classifies her as a particular type of feminist.

Liberal Feminism

Liberal feminism argues that the liberal principles of equality, freedom, and equality of opportunity must be fully extended to women. This more conservative form of feminism does not call for specific structural changes to society. Neither patriarchy nor capitalism is identified as the enemy of women; rather, the restricted reach of liberalism is identified as the problem. Several characteristics in the current literature adequately explain this ideology. According to Wendell (1987),

> Liberal feminists usually are ... committed to major economic re-organization and considerable redistribution of wealth, since one of the modern political goals most closely associated with liberal feminism is equality of opportunity, which would undoubtedly require and lead to both.... The liberal feminist

tradition ... has always asserted that the value of women as human beings is not instrumental to the welfare of men and children and that it is equal to the value of men.... Liberal feminists have always promoted equality of legal rights for women, and have more recently demanded an end to de facto discrimination on the basis of sex.... Liberal feminists have the traditional liberal beliefs in the power of education as a means of social reform and its importance to human fulfillment, and since Mary Wollstonecraft, they have demanded education for girls and women equal to that offered to boys and men [p. 66].

Grounded in civil law, liberal feminism is committed to political autonomy for women. It includes working toward moral reform, but also property reform, thus giving more power to own property and then pass it on to a woman's children and grandchildren. For reasons of lineage and inheritance, some men supported this; they wanted their children and grandchildren to inherit their property if they died, and women were instrumental in this process. But just as the Garrisonian women relied on the Bible, so did the liberal feminists. Elizabeth Cady Stanton modeled her declaration of women's rights after the Declaration of Independence, which declared "all men are created equal." Stanton, Stewart, the Grimke sisters, and others modeled and supported their speeches with such documents. According to Wendell (1987), "liberal feminism is not committed to a number of philosophical positions ... including abstract individualism, certain individualistic approaches to morality and society, valuing the mental/rational over the physical/emotional, and the traditional liberal way of drawing the line between the public and private" (p. 65). "The traditional liberal notion of self-ownership is about being the proprietor of one's person and capacities, owing nothing to society for them" (Brace, 2000, p. 447). Liberal feminism advances the ideologies of Wollstonecraft and the Garrisonian women to a greater economic equality such as women can own property or pass on inheritance to her children. Now, we examine how Condoleezza Rice is a liberal feminist—or at least someone who has tenets of liberal feminism in her discourse.

Rice and Liberal Feminism

An examination of Rice's political style and image through the lens of liberal feminism will help rhetorical scholars better understand

Six • *Condoleezza Rice*

how women in politics can advance and more positively represent multiple perspectives in an attempt at equality for women in politics and in other areas. In adopting a liberal feminist approach through discursive means, we discover how she maintains all of the contradictions her various roles demands as well as the benefits and limitations for her and women in politics. We chose liberal feminism as the dominant theory for this inquiry for several reasons. First, liberal feminism is quite conservative and traditional compared to the other feminist movements. This approach makes sense because Condoleezza Rice is a conservative female politician: she identifies as conservative, she has explained many times why she and her family are conservative, and she worked in several conservative political administrations, including that of George W. Bush. In order to earn the positions Rice has, such as secretary of state and national security advisor, she has had to increase her appeal to more traditional audiences. Third, the way she has increased her appeal has been through discursive and nondiscursive means. The verbal elements of her identity and of her feminine style are imbedded within the dominant perspective. Fourth, Elshtain (1993) points out that liberal feminists "share with mainstream defenders of the status quo in political science a set of positivist presumptions which define, delimit, structure and gear their analyses and their conclusions in certain directions and toward particular ends" just as Rice has. Because the dominant narratives on gender are too powerful to resist so boldly, instead of directly resisting, one must conform and then resist slowly. These tactics are what made the suffragists and abolitionists (and Rice) powerful. Just as they conformed to their audiences through religious and Biblical means, Condoleezza Rice has made appeals based on religion and the Bible in several of her speeches. As Elshtain (1993) says, "The best entry into the world of liberal feminism is through an exploration of their terms of discourse: How do they describe and explain public and private phenomena? What motivations, potentialities, and desired outcomes are held out for women?" (p. 242).

Condoleezza Rice was the 66th secretary of state (and first African American female secretary of state) in the George W. Bush administration. She was also Bush's national security advisor during his first term. Before that, she was a political science professor and provost at Stanford University. Rice was born in Birmingham, Alabama, and was raised there during segregation. Her mother was a teacher and her father was a guidance counselor and minister. At a young age, she took up figure skating, ballet, and French. She has said in many interviews that she always wanted to be a professional pianist but lacked the skills. Rice attended the University of Denver earning degrees in political science and inevitably a Ph.D. in the field. Rice was a registered Democrat until 1982 when she changed parties, citing Jimmy Carter's failed foreign policy and her Republican father's influence. She said at the 2000 Republican National Convention that her father was a Republican because the Democrats would not register him to vote in Jim Crow Alabama in 1952 but the Republicans did. She therefore identifies as a conservative, African American woman in American politics.

Interviews with Oprah

We chose to analyze two of Rice's interviews with Oprah Winfrey. One interview was on the show *Master Class* and the other was in Oprah's magazine, *O*. This was a deliberate decision for several reasons. First, Oprah has a way of interviewing people that allows them to tell a story in a way that a speech cannot. Second, Rice was interviewed at two different times, once in 2002 and once in 2011 (nine years apart). We believe that Rice may have had different perspectives when working within the Bush administration (2002) as opposed to after the Bush administration (the 2011 interview). Often people are willing to discuss important issues in different ways once they are no longer in a particular organization. Also, the ongoing Iraq war had been very controversial. Many of the issues that occurred while she was national security advisor and secretary of state are a direct reflection of her political values and as such we want to analyze them. Finally, Oprah is likely more able to discuss issues like race, religion, and gender in ways others cannot since Oprah is also a successful African American, Christian woman who was raised in the South, much like Rice. Both interviews are quite lengthy; the magazine interview is approximately 12 pages long and the TV interview is approximately 40 minutes long. We will first discuss the themes in terms of how she discusses gender and race and then we will analyze these according to liberal feminist ideology.

Race and Gender

Because race and gender are ideologically important to one's identity, in America we have many political problems intertwined with these issues. The Confederate flag has been removed from the capitol in South Carolina after a racially-motivated shooting killed nine African Americans at the Emanuel African Methodist Episcopal Church in downtown Charleston. The white man, Dylann Roof, who killed these nine black church members said, right before he shot them, "No, you've raped our women, and you are taking over the country.... I have to do what I have to do." According to the Southern Poverty Law Center, "The number of Patriot groups, including armed militias, skyrocketed following the election of President Obama in 2008—rising 813 percent, from 149 groups in 2008 to an all-time high of 1,360 in 2012." Quite seriously, there is a racial divide in America and in politics. This was evident in the 2012 election; Scocca (2012) reported that 88 percent of Romney voters were white while "Obama's support was 56 percent white, 24 percent black, 14 percent Latino, 4 percent Asian, and 2 percent other." It is therefore is important to contextualize the problems of race in America, especially as they relate to conservative or liberal politics.

As mentioned, Rice identifies as a conservative woman. She maintains that her childhood presented many challenges but also gave her the necessary leadership skills she has today. Since she grew up in Alabama during segregation, she speaks extensively about how the events of this time influenced her. Rice said in the 2011 interview: "I am the descendant of slaves just a few generations removed. This country has a terrible birth defect of slavery and I don't believe that we are now nor do I think we are ever likely to be, certainly not in my lifetime, race blind. It's just too much to ask given our history but the nice thing is we no longer have preconceptions about who somebody is or what they might do because they look a certain way."

Interestingly, while she suggested that how we look no longer matters, she is a strong proponent of affirmative action. In her book *A Memoir of My Extraordinary, Ordinary Family and Me*, written in 2011, she states,

> Stanford's Political Science Department wanted to hire me. I got a call from Stanford's affirmative action officer. If a department was willing to hire a minority professor, the university would provide half the money for the position. Even with that incentive, departments were reluctant. But this time the department had come to her.
> "How did this happen?" she asked.
> Years later, after having been on the other side of faculty hiring, especially as the provost of Stanford, I understood exactly what had happened. Stanford, in an effort to diversify its faculty, had made it possible to hire minorities without going through the normal processes. The Department of Political Science saw a young, black, female Soviet specialist and decided to make an affirmative action hire.
> Contrary to what has sometimes been written about me, I was and still am a fierce defender of affirmative action of this kind. Why shouldn't universities use every means necessary to diversify their faculty?

Rice was a little less decisive with her response in 2002 when Oprah asked her if she believed in affirmative action. She replied, "When it's practiced well—when you don't tell people you have to have 15 percent of this or 20 percent of that, even if someone's not qualified." That Rice clearly believes in policies that promote equal opportunity employment is interesting because she worked for an administration that did not practice such policies. In fact, the Bush administration fought the University of Michigan's decision to use a system that increased racial diversity. Rice, in splitting from the Bush administration's policies on equal opportunity, is valuing individualism and economic equality—both strong components of liberal feminism. The Bush administration put other policies in place that negatively affected women and minorities, including No Child Left Behind, Personal Responsibility, Work and Family Promotion Act (requiring more work hours for welfare recipients), DOMA (defense of marriage act), and opposition to increasing the minimum wage, just to name a few.

Despite how the administration handled policies affecting women and minorities, Rice's individual experiences as a black woman have shaped how she sees the world. When asked what it is like to be the first black and/or female Secretary of State, National Security Advisor or University Provost, she said in the 2011 *Master Class* interview:

Six • Condoleezza Rice

> Look, I can't go back and recreate myself as a white male and tell you how it would have felt if I would have been a white male.... I am a package. I am Condoleezza Rice. I am 5'7¾". I'm black and I'm female and it all kind of goes together. I am very proud of the fact that our country has come as far as it has so that we are talking about the first black female Secretary of State. Who would have thought it 40 years ago when I was growing up in Birmingham, Alabama.

The personal narratives she presents strongly identify her as a black woman from the South. She continues:

> It's very difficult to separate myself and my evolution from the circumstance of Birmingham—first of all it was a scary place in 1962 and 1963—all of those images that are now pretty far back in our nation's historical memory were very much the memories that shaped who I am. Birmingham was the most segregated big city in America.
>
> This was a place where the public safety commissioner, Bull Connor, along with of course the Governor George Wallace was known just to be hardcore segregationists [*Master Class* interview, 2011].

In fact, one of her school friends was killed in the 16th Street Baptist Church fire in 1963 while she was in attendance at her father's church down the street. It is certainly understandable how these events molded who she is. But it is unclear how she managed issues of race and gender in the Bush administration, a place where policies did more harm than good for women and African Americans. We suspect a large part of her ability to succeed in Washington stems from her childhood. Rice said,

> But Birmingham also had another side which was this side that was a group of people who were determined to overcome a group of people who were determined to prove themselves despite the circumstances. We had ballet lessons— and we had French lessons we even had lessons in etiquette what fork to use so the parents were determined to prepare their kids to be really excellent. It also had extremely high expectations—you were always told you might have to be twice as good and that wasn't actually a matter for debate. It was sort of a fact that was stated and there were no excuses for poor performance in school or for poor performance at anything. So it was a wonderful combination of a community that was in some ways so segregated that they rigorously controlled the messages that we received and that message was it may be a very racist place and you may not be able to control your circumstances but you can sure control how you react to your circumstances and here's how you react—you're twice as good; you work hard; you do everything better than they might do it [*Master Class* interview, 2011].

Listening to Women on the Right

These messages likely contributed to her work ethic and interest in what might typically be considered activities associated with the dominant, white culture (ballet, French, piano, etiquette, figure skating, etc.). These experiences work well with liberal feminism because they individualize her as a Republican woman. Additionally, this training probably helped her as part of the Bush administration especially since she had to learn to compete with and work with mostly white men. She attributes much of her ability to do this to her childhood. She says in the 2011 *Master Class* interview,

> I do think that those of us who grew up in segregation were able to spot at a hundred paces when somebody was underestimating you and when somebody underestimated me, it made me want to prove them wrong—a lot of what goes on in Washington and in the White House is just turfiness and turf consciousness and so you have to try to not take it personally but I knew I was younger by maybe a couple of decades than many of the people with whom I was going to be working especially the second time around when I was National Security Advisor. I wasn't on guard for whether somebody underestimated what I could do. That isn't the way that those lessons come into play. The way that it comes into play is that if someone comes too close or steps on something that you think is your responsibility then you're not at all shy about saying move away get out of my way and I think that toughness in the White House really does come from being a young kid who was always determined that nobody was going to underestimate you and what you were going to do. And I can remember going to President Bush on at least one occasion and saying if that person ever does that to me again then one of us is resigning.

She was keenly aware of her age, her competition, and her overall environment. In order to compete with others in this situation, she likely had to be "twice as good" as the white men she was working with. So perhaps her childhood interest in those typically white activities helped her. But as a woman, she could never really be a part of the club—the men's club. In fact, for as hard as she tried, Dick Cheney still attacked her in his tell-all memoir released in 2011. She felt he attacked her integrity saying she provided misinformation to the president about North Korea and that she "'tearfully' admitted she had been wrong to push for Bush to apologize for inaccurately alleging that Iraq had attempted to obtain yellowcake uranium in Niger" (Mohammed, 2011). All the French and ballet lessons she had taken could not trump

Cheney's power in that context. Cheney framed her as the weak, crying woman who admitted he was really right.

Finally, there is the work ethic as she defines it for herself. Certainly, her lineage of a sharecropper grandfather who traded cotton for tuition at Stillman College, a Presbyterian minister and guidance counselor for a father, and a schoolteacher for a mother were instrumental in her success. But she believes faith and hard work are key. She said in the 2011 interview, "Because of that strong family structure and an intense faith, I've never believed that God would fail me if I'm faithful." Also, when Oprah asked her how she prepared for 9/11, she said, "Since I was a girl I have relied on faith—a belief that I'm never alone, that the bottom will never fall out too far." That faith played a large role in her life and her rhetoric in defining her success. This is again interesting because she worked in an administration that has certainly made attempts to legislate morality (e.g., DOMA). According to Edward Ashbee (2009),

> Commentaries on his presidency record the part played by evangelicals in contributing to his re-election and in turn note his support for the Christian right's political agenda, speaking in forceful terms about building a 'culture of life,' using an executive order to prohibit the use of federal funds for embryonic stem-cell research, boosting federal government funding for abstinence-only sex education, and opposing same-sex marriage, for example.

Rice is known to be pro-choice and in favor of same-sex unions. When *Christianity Today* asked her about these issues, she replied,

> I'm still coming to terms with it [abortion]. I don't like the government involved in these really hard moral decisions. While I don't think the country is ready for legislation to overturn *Roe v. Wade*, certainly I cannot imagine why one would be in favor of partial birth abortion. I also can't imagine why one would take these decisions out of the hands of the family. We all understand that this is not something to be taken lightly.
>
> Regarding gay marriage, she has said, "I have lots of respect for people on both sides of this divide, because there are really hard issues. I don't ever want anybody to be denied rights within our country ... perhaps we will decide that there needs to be some way for people to express their desire to live together through civil union. I think the country, if we can keep the volume down, will come to good answers."

Her faith is seemingly different than George Bush's faith. She believes faith accounts for part of her accomplishments, but hard work is also important. Rice (2011) says,

Listening to Women on the Right

> I have a very strong belief that preparation counts; that you do have to work hard but that it also matters where you are and who you meet and being in the right place at the right time. So you should never ever take for granted what you are given and what you've been able to achieve. You should never assume that it was just through your own smarts and because you were so much better than everybody else that you got there. There were so many people as good as you were, maybe even better, who never quite made it to that place and I try very hard to remember that I've been good but I've been lucky and fortunate and blessed too.

She combines her faith (being blessed) with being hardworking and fortunate. She also understands that one could work so hard and still not make it. Or one could work less than others and still be successful if one comes from the right place.

The ways in which she has defined herself in these interviews is through her upbringing as a black woman in the South who is hardworking and has faith in God. One might be surprised to hear about these narratives for a few reasons. First, she worked in the Bush administration whose legislation often impeded progress for women and minorities. Second, she was the national security advisor and secretary of state so she was most often interviewed about public issues like the War on Terror or Russia or some other international issues. And third, her personal narratives about race and gender were subordinated because it is possible she did not prefer to discuss personal issues or she did not have many opportunities to do so.

Certainly, her personal life helps explain part of why she competed in male-dominated professions that were mostly Caucasian. In so doing, she may have learned that no matter how hard she tried, she still could not be in the good old boy's club, as she received much criticism by Donald Rumsfeld and Dick Cheney after the administration ended. And as important as race and gender are, Rice hardly allowed these factors to play a role in the decisions of the Bush administration (Lusane, 2006). The point is that Rice, while she may not call herself a feminist, was in fact a feminist working in an administration that did not value equal opportunity for women. However, her specific type of rhetoric—individualist and based on a particular view of government—presented as a fairly conservative, traditional type of feminist discourse.

Six • *Condoleezza Rice*

Lessons Learned

Based on the literature, there are a few key topics we want to discuss as we present Rice as a liberal feminist. These topics are redistribution of wealth, equality of opportunity,

value of women not integral to the welfare of men and children, the end of discrimination on the basis of sex, and education leading to social reform (Wendell, 1987). We begin with redistribution of wealth.

The George W. Bush administration reduced taxes significantly through the Economic Growth and Tax Relief Reconciliation Act of 2001, the Job Creation and Worker Assistance Act of 2002, and the Jobs and Growth Tax Relief Reconciliation Act of 2003. All three acts reduced taxes especially for the wealthiest one percent. Rice was a part of this administration and thus a part of these policies. She believes there should be spending cuts instead of higher taxes. And she has been cited as saying that welfare is an entitlement program that "tear[s] apart the fabric of who we are" (Republican National Convention Speech 2012). Given her political positions on taxes and entitlements, she likely does not support the redistribution of wealth.

The next value of liberal feminism is equality of opportunity. She has stated many times that she believes in equal opportunity employment laws and affirmative action. Rice was hired at Stanford because of affirmative action laws. She believes if it is practiced well, then it is a good way to diversify institutions.

The third value we attend to is the value of women as not necessary to the welfare of men and children. This point is interesting because Rice has never been married and has no children. As a result, she does not make the common claims about economic security equating to the family as many Republican women do. But she does connect the role her family played in her education. In short, she does retain this liberal feminist value that disassociates her value as a woman from that of a husband and children.

The fourth value espoused in liberal feminist ideology is the end of discrimination on the basis of sex. Based on her views of affirmative action, it is apparent she believes we should not discriminate based on sex. She has also been quoted as saying her father was a feminist. And her parents always supported her in all of her educational endeavors. Rice has said she would not be the person she is without her parents and their support. Furthermore, Rice experienced severe discrimination under Jim Crow laws growing up in Alabama in the 1960s. She would likely be an advocate (and she is in many ways) of nondiscrimination on the bases of sex and race.

Finally, Rice definitely subscribes to the liberal feminist values of education leading to social reform. According to Koebler (2012),

> "If you look at why [Americans] are here or why their parents are here or their grandparents are here, someone believed that in the United States of America, if you worked hard, you could have a better life. That's what set us apart," she told a group at the Council on Foreign Relations. "It's fragile, and we have to make sure that's [still] true. If it ever becomes not true because the education system can't deliver it, then there's no hope of rebuilding it."

She and former New York City schools superintendent Joel Klein served on a task force with the goal of understanding the role of education and national security. They believe that the lower the quality of education, the more of a threat there is to America's future. She also does not feel standardized tests are accurate and believes education is key to getting out of poverty. She really is a firm believer in education and education reform.

Although Rice's childhood was plagued with racism and discrimination, she does not actively fight these social issues with any political change. In college she said she had a professor "who was preaching about [scientist] William Shockley, who claimed that blacks just didn't have high IQs. And from somewhere deep within myself I said to him, 'Who do you think you are? I'm better at your culture than you are. I'm the one who plays Beethoven. I'm the one who speaks French. So obviously this can be taught.'" Clearly, she is aware that some people are racist. After growing up in Jim Crow Alabama and then having experiences like this in college, it is odd that she participates in a political party that has traditionally been challenged by reaching out to women and minorities. Certainly, race and gender cannot be separated, given how powerful these ideological constructs are in her life. Ideally, if Rice were a different type of feminist she could break the male-driven ideological frames but then she likely would not have survived in her roles

Six • Condoleezza Rice

in the Bush administration. Perhaps with less to lose and many years later, it should be noted that she boldly spoke out against Donald Trump as the Republican nominee, tweeting: "Enough! Donald Trump should not be President. He should withdraw. As a Republican, I hope to support someone who has the dignity and stature to run for the highest office in the greatest democracy on earth." Although Rice has a complicated identity and is a woman of many firsts, her achievements and values should be acknowledged.

♦ SEVEN ♦

Senate Sisters

On October 1, 2013, after months of partisan gridlock, the United States government shut down. During this first government shutdown since 1996, when Newt Gingrich was Speaker of the House and Bill Clinton was president, Congress had stayed in session until the wee hours of September 29, but there was no solution to the budgetary impasse. Given that House Republicans insisted on defunding Obamacare as the price for keeping the government open, while Senate Democrats and President Barack Obama firmly rejected that position, a shutdown seemed inevitable. Indeed, 800,000 federal employees were indefinitely furloughed, and another 1.3 million were required to report to work without known payment dates until the compromise was reached on October 16, 2013. Senate majority and minority leaders announced they had come to a deal that re-opened the government until January 2014. The proposal passed Congress and was quickly signed into law by President Obama on October 17. This gross simplification of the budget shutdown glosses over one key fact about the negotiations—that Republican women were key to reaching an agreement. A headline on the October 20, 2013, *Huffington Post*'s webpage summarized the happenings in Washington, D.C.: "Men Got Us Into the Shutdown, Women Got Us Out" (Bassett). Senator John McCain said that his female colleagues could take most of the credit for driving the budget compromise that reopened the U.S. government and raised the debt ceiling. McCain said, "Leadership, I must fully admit, was provided primarily from women in the Senate." Following weeks of stagnation with the budget, Mark Pryor, a senator from Arkansas, quipped that people like to joke about female leadership but that females in the

Senate are a good thing and "we're all just glad they allowed us to tag along so we could see how it's done" (Bassett). The framework for the debt deal was laid by six women—three of whom are Republican. Susan Collins, who started the group, told the *New York Times* that she did not think it was "a coincidence that women were so heavily involved in trying to end" the stalemate (Weisman and Steinhauer, 2013). Given the significance—and femaleness—of the compromise, it is worthy of analysis and in line with the goals of this book. This chapter studies the words of the three conservative women involved in the deal as well as the media portrayals of those women to understand the rhetorical strategy of "compromise." Taken together, the comments from the female senators and the media coverage yield a text that helps us understand women's and society's thoughts and feelings about compromise, woman's role in politics, and a language for expressing the combination of the two.

In particular, this chapter examines the discourse surrounding the compromise through the lens of Sara Ruddick's idea of maternal thinking. Ruddick's account of mothering in her book *Maternal Thinking: Toward a Politics of Peace* has two central components: (1) the theoretical development of what she calls "maternal thinking," which is grounded in maternal practice and explained by what she calls the "practicalist conception of truth (PCT)," and (2) the case for her claim that maternal thinking can ground a feminist peace politics (Bailey, 1994, p. 189). In recent years, a number of scholars have argued that this distinctive mode of thought should inform our political life. Jean Elshtain (1981) argues that maternal thinkers could radically reform public values and could even create an "ethical polity" devoted to a politics of compassion and citizen involvement (pp. 322, 326–29).

The budget negotiations, then, provide an opportunity to study how maternal thinking can transform our political life. The case study also provides a rhetorical opportunity to link two seemingly irreconcilable positions—conservatism and feminism. Given that coverage of conservative women and feminist thought is often fraught with the perception that the two are incompatible, conservative women and feminism are often seen as polarized but perhaps not in this case (Schreiber, 2010, p. 433). As Ronnee Schreiber (2008) argued in her important book, *Righting Feminism: Conservative Women and American Politics*, conservative women have recognized the opportunity to play with the meanings of feminism for quite some time. In fact, she explained that a growing number of conservative women are successfully using feminist rhetoric to achieve conservative political ends. This chapter lends insight into this growing trend and serves as a test case—a set of generalizable knowledge points—of maternal thinking. As we argue, though, while maternal thinking is demonstrated from Susan Collins and other women involved in the budget negotiations, it may not be a viable strategy for all female politicians because maternal thinking is systematically and subtly devalued throughout history.

This chapter first examines a type of democratic feminist theory—maternal thinking. It then goes on to analyze the budget compromise of 2013 and examines the connection. The chapter concludes that the compromise was talked about in maternally-oriented ways—pragmatic and personal—but we also argue that maternal thinking is still seen a female-centric strategy. Therefore, this rhetorical and political strategy might not be useful for all candidates.

The Democratic Potential of Maternal Thinking

In her book, Ruddick defines the practice of mothering in terms of three activities: (1) preservative love, the interest in preserving and protecting the life of a child; (2) fostering growth; and (3) social training, or training a child to become acceptable to the mother's social group (Ruddick, 1989, p. 15). Preservative love, nurturing, and social training are three nearly universal features that define maternal practice for Ruddick. To be a mother, Ruddick wrote, is to be committed to meeting these demands by works of preservative love, nurturance, and training (1989, p. 17). Her reliance on pragmatism and her idea that truths arise from practices is nothing new. She argued that her practicalism is rooted in the work of writers such as Habermas, Winch, and Rorty. However, she was the first scholar to examine the experience of mothering and to develop a theoretical framework and vocabulary for this analysis (O'Reilly, 2009, p. 296). In defining mothering as a practice, she analyzes the work as distinct from the biological identity of a mother. Indeed, she regards mothers' work as a function of a social practice rather than as a consequence of biological destiny. For Ruddick, "mothering" designates a conscious social practice, which means, then, that mothering is not just a female practice but one that is "distinguished by the aims that identify them and by the consequent demands made on practitioners committed to those aims" (Ruddick, 1989, pp. 13–14). Obviously this book is rooted in an examination of conservative *women*, but we remind readers that maternal thinking is not biological in nature. Similar to what rhetorical critics have argued about feminine style that we pointed out in Chapter Five, maternal thinking is a strategy useful to a variety of people regardless of their sex or gender. The chapter is in line with what Sarah LaChance Adams (2010) noted: "It is the practice of mothering that makes one a mother, not a biological or social imperative. Therefore, the title of 'mother' is not strictly limited to biological mothers, or even women…. True maternal commitment is voluntary and conscious; it is not inevitable nor is it dictated by nature." Thus, the word "mother" needs to be, as Mielle Chandler (1998) has argued, "understood as a verb; something one does, a practice" (273). The practice of mothering is what we investigate in this chapter, to see if it can be understood through the budget compromise.

A huge benefit of the practice of maternal thinking, according to Ruddick and her supporters, is that it gives way to a particular peace politics. And in her original incarnation of the idea, Ruddick talks about peace politics in a way one might assume—the absence of war and the political reasoning it takes to offer a diplomacy rooted in pacifism. Extensions of her work have been iterated to mean peace politics broadly defined. Alison Bailey (1994) argued that peace is not just the absence of violence or the resistance to nuclear war and war machinery but that it is also the freedom from threats of poverty and institutional violence (p. 196; see also Brown 1991). Interestingly, "peace" was often used to describe Washington, D.C., once a budget deal was struck. Kevin Carmichael (2013) argued that Washington neared budget "peace" and was on the "verge of budget peace for the first time in four years." Therefore, we use a language of "peace politics" symbolically.

Certainly we recognize and even partly agree with those who have problematized maternal thinking. As Boling (1991) argued, scholars should be skeptical of any arguments that treat women's monopoly over child rearing as a given (p. 608). Further, Catharine MacKinnon (1987) stated that privileging maternal thinking often overlooks that it is a mode of thought women have learned in response to oppressive social arrangements (pp. 38–39). To be sure, scholars have always made the mistake of valuing aspects of femininity and maternalism without attending to the oppressive social relations that give rise to it. And the dangers and implications of this dubious scholarship could be a book in and of itself. But we posit that the value of treating and testing maternal thinking as a feminist school of thought yields more scholastic benefit than it prohibits.

The Budget Deal

In October 2013, *Time* magazine profiled the "women's club" of Congress under the headline "Women are the only adults left in Washington." The article argued,

> It's quite an irony that the U.S. Senate was once known for having the worst vestiges of a private men's club: unspoken rules, hidden alliances, off-hours socializing and an ethic based at least as much on personal relationships as merit to get things done. That Senate—a fraternal paradise that worked despite all its obvious shortcomings—is long gone. And now the only place the old boys' network seems to function anymore is among the four Republicans and 16 Democrats who happen to be women.

The article touted this new "women's club" as one that offers the same political benefits of the original men's club as well as some updates: mentor lunches and regular dinners, bridal and baby showers, and playdates for children and grandchildren. Indeed, there is a deep sense in Washington that the "sisterhood" unites the women and allows them to get things done.

At first glance, although the budget compromise may not seem a likely case study to test maternal thinking as a school of thought—and one that is interesting given the preconceived idea that conservative women's rhetoric is often devoid of obvious feminist politics—we argue that it at least seems to contain the two basic criteria. Indeed, the dialogue surrounding the budget compromise has a real focus on pragmatism and the politics of care. It is these elements we outline below.

Pragmatism

Amy Gutmann and Dennis Thompson (2010) reflected on political compromise and seemed to argue that compromise is necessarily pragmatic. They write, "little change can happen in democratic politics without some compromise, and almost no major change can happen without major compromises" (p. 1129). Compromise helps to soothe problems and affairs. And in the most basic sense, political compromise is the only way to make progress in political deadlock. In short, ideology is tempered by pragmatic compromise. But pragmatism does not just reference political action. It is also, of course, a philosophical way of thinking that assesses the truth of theories and beliefs in terms of practical applications. Ruddick (1989) speaks of pragmatism as a type of practice. She writes, "to engage in a practice is, by definition, to accept connections that constitute the practice" (p. 14). She argued that this practice often depends on a shared language and actions that arise out of community of participants that have shared and tested their truths. Motherhood, or caregiving, in particular, is pragmatic because it gives way to a particular type of truth. As Ruddick (1989) often claimed, maternal thinking is a philosophical perspective that values the thinking that grows out of the work that mothers do.

This pragmatism is rampant in the discourse used by those involved with the budget compromise and in articles written about their efforts. North Dakota senator Heidi Heitkamp argued, "It is about getting people in a room with different life experiences who will look at things a little differently because they're moms, because they're daughters who've been taking care of senior moms, because they have different life experience than a lot of senior guys in the room" (Newton-Small, 2010, n.p.). The idea that their experience as women, caregivers and nurturers led them to fight for a budget compromise was a prevalent theme in the discourse from and about the women. Sally

Listening to Women on the Right

Steenland (2013), director of the Faith and Progressive Policy Initiative at the Center for American Progress, wrote,

> The women bring first-hand experience with caring for young children and elderly parents, along with figuring out how to balance the demands of family and work. Their life experiences cross party lines and connect them to the lives of everyday Americans who face similar challenges.... It was the everyday experiences of women senators—along with their outsider status in a male-dominated institution—that helped give them the skills and allies they needed to make the government work for the American people [n.p.].

Even Susan Collins herself argued that she sees herself and her female comrades as "bridge builders in the Senate" (Jan, 2013, n.p.). She was able to build that bridge through her "monthly bipartisan dinners with women senators." This bipartisan common ground is repeatedly referred to, by Collins and others, as "common sense." Collins said, "There is a group in the common sense caucus that's willing to lead, take risks and come up with solutions that are bipartisan" (2013, n.p.). Kelly Ayotte of New Hampshire said in an interview that Collins's proposal was a "common sense plan" (Jan, 2013, n.p.) and mused that she really appreciates Collins "as a common sense bipartisan consensus builder, which is what we needed here" (Collins, 2013, n.p.). Collins argued that she enacted the bipartisan compromise because she believes it to be what the country needed and wanted. "I think most people in our country are in the center and want to see common sense pragmatism in Washington," she stated. "They are sick and tired of excessive partisanship that has led to gridlock" (Vucci, 2013, n.p.). President Obama acknowledged the common sense caucus as the "ones who have been able to get things done" because they are the ones who are constructive on the issues (Epstein, 2013, n.p.).

This strategy of compromise was one that the women argued had been successful before. The Maine Republican had "learned from experience" that "you can't solve problems if you're not talking" (Ricker, 2013, n.p.). In an interview on *Morning Joe*, Collins argued that the Senate needed to "be pragmatic." She continued that the previous strategies are not "a winning strategy ... and unacceptable." She stated, "we think the women in the Senate, the six of us, actually seven women that have been working together, do have a good bipartisan solution that works. Let's get to it." And others claimed that she did not have a narrow partisan agenda because Collins has always demonstrated her willingness to stand for principle rather than partisanship. Senator Angus King, also from Maine, argued that Collins had "always been independent-minded, not an insider with the old boys of the Republican establishment in the Senate" (Jan, 2013, n.p.). Collins seemed to agree when she argued, "I don't think it's a coincidence that women were so heavily involved in trying to end this stalemate." She continued, "Although we span the ideological spectrum, we are used to working together in a collaborative way" (Weisman and Steinhauer, 2013, n.p.). Arriving at a bipartisan compromise to solve a two-week-long government shutdown illustrates a level of pragmatism Ruddick seemed to foreshadow. Indeed, Collins, other women, and media accounts of their actions seem to suggest that their ability to compromise was rooted in their pragmatic, practical experiences as women.

Moreover, the strategy, and the bipartisan work to arrive at it, is touted by the women as the key to future governance. In a 2013 Senate session, Collins stated, "It is past time for us to stop fighting. And it is past time for us to reopen government.... Let's proceed with governing rather than continuing to embrace a strategy that will lead us only to a dead end." As we outlined in this chapter, media covering the budget compromise and the women involved seem to claim that their experience as women, mothers, and caregivers gave way to their ability to govern in a way that valued compromise and accord over gridlock and disagreement. This relationship between "mothering" and thinking brings the tenets of practicalism and pragmatism front and center. In the next section we detail the second component of maternal thinking—maternalism. Taken together, these two themes provide purchase for the claim that the discourse used by and about the women involved in the budget compromise illustrates maternal thinking.

Maternalism

Almost as important as the idea that practical experience leads to practical politics is the idea that the type of practical experience is important. Ruddick (1989) calls maternalism the idea that a particular type of reason derives from women's work, experiences, and ideals (p.

9). Whereas traditional political society may make women's culture, experience and ways of knowing invisible, silenced or trivialized, a maternal school of thought gives voice to the work of mothering. It is an intellectual life that has everything to do with mothering—that is, thinking with care and compassion.

As illustrated above, the women working to avoid the debt crisis were quick to point to their position as mothers, caregivers and women as fundamental to their way of governing. What's more is that the women were also quick to reveal they were working from a point of care and compassion for all women and children. When Collins (2013) released a press release about her plan to avoid the budget crisis, she wrote that the implications and consequences of a shutdown were serious and felt more acutely by some than others. She wrote, "Pregnant women and little children who depend on the food provided through the WIC program are at risk." Their gender, then, is important to their larger political responsibility. In a *Time* magazine profile of the women involved in the budget compromise, Newton-Small (2013) argued that most of the senators feel "they speak not just for the voters in their states but for women across America" (n.p.). When Heidi Heitkamp, a senator from North Dakota, voted against tightening gun laws after the Newtown school shooting, she was unprepared for the backlash from women's groups. She reported, "A female friend in the Senate said to me, 'You know, it's because they feel you represent all women, not just the women of North Dakota,'" Heitkamp said. "It just clicked for me for the first time. I was, like, 'Oh, now I get it'" (Newton-Small, 2013, n.p.). These women are thinking and voting from a place of maternal care.

This way of thinking was sharply contrasted to the normal way of doing politics. Collins repeatedly argued that the politics of the situation were irrelevant. She said, "There's a more important issue here than poll numbers, and that is our ability to govern and show the American people we can do what is right and that we care about them" (Kucinich, 2013, n.p.). This ethic of care is shown to be pragmatic, practical. And important. The American people were placed ahead of politicians in Washington. Collins said, "We need to be pragmatic. This is not going to be a Republican solution or a Democratic solution. This is going to be a solution that is good for the country" (Newton-Small, 2013, n.p.). Their dialogue also became about masculine versus feminine way of viewing a situation. Senator Lisa Murkowski, from Alaska, said, after thanking Senator Collins for her "persistence and insistence that we continue this effort to work collegially" in a Senate session:

> We all know that if you're just trying to move the ball to just one person, you don't get anywhere. We do a lot of sports analogies around here and quite honestly, I am really tired of sports analogies. But what I do appreciate is that as a senate, we cannot work together as individuals and expect to accomplish the work that is needed not only for my constituents in Alaska but around the country. And regardless of who's in the majority or who's in the minority, in order to make it work for the country, we've got to be working together.

That same Senate session allowed Senator Collins to say that she wanted her colleagues to "receive the kudos that they deserve for being willing to do what this body does too rarely. Come out of our partisan corners and stop fighting and start legislating." She continued, "I know that my colleagues are tired of hearing about women in the Senate, but the fact is they were the first two to contact me.... It was a wonderful group of people united by our determination to demonstrate that we could compromise, we could govern, we could bring an end to this impasse." And it was the "friendships the Senate women have developed" that helped them craft a long-term budget without the "counterproductive barbs that some politicians throw at each other when they don't agree," Senator Amy Klobuchar of Minnesota stated on MSNBC's *Morning Joe* (Bassett, 2013, n.p.). And while Murkowski recognized the risk of not playing by the normal, political rules, she ultimately concluded, "Politics be damned" (Weisman & Steinhauer, 2013, n.p.). Of course, we would be remiss to not mention that Kelly Ayotte—one of the leaders in the group—was unseated during the 2016 election cycle. In one of the most competitive and closely watched Senate races of 2016, Ayotte lost to her challenger—Governor Maggie Hassan, a Democrat. And even though both women emphasized bipartisanship, Ayotte was ultimately unsuccessful. While many pundits are speculating that it was her "delicate dance around Donald Trump's candidacy" that caused her to lose the faith of the state's independent voters, we do not know for sure (Seelye, 2016, n.p.). Ayotte announced in November of 2016 that she would cast a write-in vote for Mike Pence given that she could not support a candidate "who brags about degrading and assaulting women" (Rogin, 2016, n.p.). Regardless, Ayotte is a rising star in Washington, regarded as "knowledgeable and competent" (Rogin, 2016, n.p.).

Lessons Learned

The above quotation from Murkowski is particularly fitting as she lost the 2010 Republican primary to a Tea Party candidate. She won the general election as a write-in candidate and used the opportunity as a chance to be more independent, more collaborative and less constrained by party politics. This is, of course, a luxury that might not be affordable for all in Washington. In what remains of this chapter, we will work to unpack three key implications from maternal thinking as a rhetorical strategy.

While Collins herself has a high approval rating in Maine—69 percent just after the budget deal—she received attacks from all sides of the aisle (Kucinich, 2013, n.p.). As her fellow Maine senator Angus King reminded, "There's always a risk in these situations. She may get out ahead of her caucus and what she proposed may not end up being the solution" (Jan, 2013, n.p.). Murkowski herself ominously declared that she will "have retribution in her state" but that it did not bother her as "there are people who are really hurting" (Weisman & Steinhauer, 2013, n.p.). Indeed, outsider status is not always well received by the electorate. Collins and others could take a cautionary lesson from Senator Olympia Snow, another moderate Republican from Maine who was forced into retirement because of what she called "corrosive partisanship." Steenland (2013) reminds us that "their cooperative efforts answer the question of whether women make a difference in the institutions where they work and lead: It is a firm yes. But that is not the whole answer; in order for women to make a difference, there must be enough of them in sufficient leadership positions for their diverse voices to be heard. Unfortunately, we still have a long way to go to reach a critical mass of women in Congress." As we discuss in the conclusion, women did pick up more seats in 2014 but women still only make up around 20 percent of Congress. And it is hard to discern if the maternal thinking exhibited in the specific instance of the budget negotiations really led to any real gains by women.

And perhaps that is because at the end of it all, Washington really did return to business as usual. While the efforts by Collins, Murkowski, and four other women were often cited as important by (male) senators, they were just as often cited as a starting point for negotiations rather than the lynchpin. Senator Orrin Hatch argued that "Susan has done us all a great favor by having the courage to come up with the amendments." Senator Mark Pryor said that Collins "deserves a lot of credit for getting us together and moving the ball down the field" (Camia, 2013, n.p.). But ultimately, the measure was not endorsed by Speaker Boehner or President Obama (Kucinich, 2013, n.p.). And while Collins provided an optimistic conclusion, "Before I went to the Senate floor, no one was presenting any way out. I think what our group did was pave the way, and I'm really happy about that," she concedes that maternal thinking did not fully get the job done (Weisman & Steinhauer, 2013, n.p.). Female-led compromise did, however, prompt further negotiations. "Without our charging ahead, I wonder if they would have ever come to a way to bring this unacceptable impasse to an end," Collins questioned (McDermott, 2013, n.p.). But instead of being responsible for the deal, Collins wryly stated that she knew her colleagues were just tired of hearing about women in the Senate (Camia, 2013).

And perhaps that is not only sexism at work. By the headlines and congressional statements, a political observer might think that only women were responsible for starting conversation. And indeed, Collins, Murkowski and Ayotte were the leaders. But the "common sense caucus" was a 14-member group. Senator Joe Manchin, the first Democratic collaborator on the Collins-led committee, said that the gender mix of the committee was great. "It helped tremendously," he said and added, "would it have worked as well if it had been 12 women or 12 men? I can't say for sure, but it worked pretty well with what we had" (Weisman & Steinhauer, 2013, n.p.). Obviously, then, men were a huge portion of this compromise, but they are rarely discussed in media accounts. This absence begs s question. Even though scholars claim maternal thinking is gender neutral, will men ever be associated with the behaviors associated with the philosophical idea? Even the men involved in the compromise seemed to distance themselves from the work. Senator John McCain, who was one of the senators involved in the initial talks, routinely joked that women were taking over Washington when asked about the negotiations (Weisman & Steinhauer, 2013, n.p.).

If compromise is so pragmatic, maternal, and productive, why would men be so eager to distance themselves from the strategy? Moreover, the media and the men in Congress act as though women invented bipartisanship. Those that follow politics closely and have for a long time may be scratching their heads right now. It was not until the early 1990s that Americans really started to see differences between parties. Until then, the American public was loath to admit that partisanship was particularly important (Brewer, 2005, p. 221). While it is hard to say for sure if perception is reality, it is likely, though, that the male dominated Congress of the 1980s was able to disagree without being disagreeable. They may have even had friendships, experiences, and ways of thinking that allowed them to value compromise. That context is missing from the conversation about these female senators. Instead, media favor an overly simplistic story about how women are the ones that play nice, make concessions and work peacefully.

To be sure, we are not minimizing the women's role in this important compromise. We pointed out much evidence above that without them, the debt crisis would have continued indefinitely. And we relish an opportunity for the mainstream media to tout female politicians as important. Just the same, we are not sure the benefits of maternal thinking are actualized in this case study. Long ago Ruddick (1983) warned,

> Men who are able and allow themselves to be mothers enter the truly human world of maternal work and learn its lessons. Although it is undeniable that more maternal work is done by women than by men—and that, accordingly, the work has been shaped, for better or worse, by its connection to women—I look forward to the day when "mothers" are as apt to be male as female. Then preservative love and moral authority, private care and public responsibility will be seamlessly joined [p. 5].

Seven • Senate Sisters

So, while we found evidence that maternal thinking guided the women and media who wrote about them, perhaps this chapter does not illuminate all that we need to know. For evidence that maternal thinking is widespread, and we argue that it should be, perhaps we should be using a test case that does not involve women.

Concluding Thoughts and Ideas

In the introduction, we laid out what we think is the political realty of the 21st century—the inhospitable policies designed to deny women access to medical coverage, equal pay, and protection from violence. True or not, the perception is that much of this "war on women" is coming from the Republican Party. For those of us who care deeply about the political system and are trained in rhetoric, it makes sense that we would want to understand how, then, women within the Republican Party negotiate this tension. This book offered seven case studies that illuminate how some women are existing in this liminal space that could be referred to as "Politicking While Female." It seems particularly difficult for GOP women to follow traditional feminist strategies at a time with their party has a complicated relationship with women's *issues*—at least given the way media frames its policies. We analyzed women who offer us a model of perhaps faux feminist discourse—Terri Lynn Land, Joni Ernst, and Susana Martinez. These women seem to be drawing on feminist presentational styles but ultimately fall short. We argue in these instances that the advertising campaign and snappy campaign slogans suggest a feminist politics but the policy positions could not be called feminist. As we argued in the introduction, women care about reproductive health issues and family-friendly policies such as income equality and job security. As our analyses point out, even the female Republican politicians do not offer much in the way of feminist policies. These analyses were followed by more complex conversations about Carly Fiorina, Nikki Haley, Condaleeza Rice, and the seven women involved in the budget compromise of 2013. In these case studies, we saw breaks in the pattern. With Rice and the women involved in the budget shutdown, we argued that there were actual instances of productive conversations regarding gender, gendered rhetoric and policy making. These instances are limited, though, and really only prove that feminism is a palatable messages if it is the right "brand" of feminism. An individualized, liberal brand of feminism is seen as effective by the party. With Fiorina and Haley, we argue that their feminist rhetoric is specific to their subject positions and does allow them to walk a line between conservative, traditionalist and feminist advocate. In this conclusion, we illuminate lasting lessons and perhaps offer advice to women who may be caught in this same bind. We want to stress that just because we do not understand or agree with the rhetorical choices made does not mean there is no lasting value from them. As this project might suggest, we are probably not the target audience of the politicians featured in this book. Just the same, asking whether there are productive lessons learned is a worthy activity. Here we offer a formalized review of our analysis, offer an extension of the political context we discussed in Chapter One and highlight some lasting lessons. We conclude with some speculation on Elise Stefanik and Cathy McMorris Rodgers, both of whom seem to be rising stars in the Republican Party.

Knowing what we know from these case studies, we feel we must highlight the current political reality of the 114th Congress when it reconvened in January of 2015. The Republicans swept into power "winning nearly every contested race across the country, gaining governor's mansions and adding to their majority in the House of Representatives" (Ball, 2014, para. 1). There were 99 women in the 113th Congress. When the 2014 midterm election was complete, there were 100 female voting members of Congress (Mundy, 2014). The number of female congressional representatives did not rise significantly. True, there was a surge of (Republican) women elected to the U.S. Congress, notably Elise Stefanik of New York, the youngest woman ever elected to Congress who we will discuss later in this chapter, and Mia Love of Utah, the daughter of Haitian immigrants and the first black female Republican to be elected to Congress. Indeed, these women are new

Concluding Thoughts and Ideas

faces in Washington and bring with them new ideas and new rhetorical strategies. But we cannot confuse visibility and productive politics. Bonnie Dow (2001) has argued that critics and society at large cannot mistake the success of an individual for the success of a discourse and politics. And we argue that the 2014 election is a precise illustration of this claim. The personalization of a few female members of Congress' success stories allows society and our field, if we are not careful, to mistake visible women for viable feminist politics.

Of the 11 new female candidates who won election, four are Republicans and seven are Democrats (Friedman, 2014). The Republican sweep did not signal a major shift in female leadership. Moreover, as the *Washington Post* reported soon after the 2014 midterm elections, 20 men will have a leadership gavel and only one woman will. Henderson (2014) wrote that while much as been made about the addition of nonwhite faces and younger members, "the fact remains that the uppermost levels of the Republican Party in the House and in the Senate remain overwhelmingly white and overwhelmingly male. A few historic elections can't change that" (n.p). If we want women in the Senate who philosophize from their subject positions and use maternal thinking and feminine style to adjudicate policy issues, we need to elect a whole lot more of them. We also need them in leadership positions. Skeptics might say that these women are all junior representatives—newly elected—so it makes sense that they are not in powerful positions. And we hope those optimists are correct. What we fear, though, is that women's power in the Congress has been so deeply concentrated in the Democratic Party that the shift to a GOP–controlled Senate might mean women will lose clout. And if what we show in this book is correct, there are very few rhetorical strategies that allow GOP women to navigate their subject position in a way that allows them to be female, use their experiences as females and rise through the ranks.

What actually seems to work in the Republican Party is almost a denial of femininity. And, based on the case studies we examined, female Republican candidates certainly reject policies that explicitly benefit women, children and family. What we have argued in this book is that stating, "I'm a woman. My experience being a woman means I know best" is often minimized or ignored, even as advertisements like

Concluding Thoughts and Ideas

Terri Lynn Land's pay lip service to women's knowledge of women. This female subject position is instead replaced by an identity that values traditional messages of masculinity. So, for example, we have Ernst and Land drawing on their sex but in a comical way. In an advertisement we did not examine, Land likens being a senator to being a mother and claims she will make Washington "mind" like she does her children. And Ernst cheekily proclaims knowing how to make a good biscuit will translate into good policy making. While these analogies are funny, they do not actually translate into a message about how their experience, and even needs, as women will make them good policy makers. That is, the humorous advertisements do not translate into actual strategies or skills that could be put to use in the Senate. We are therefore left to conclude that explicit discussions of one's femaleness is not seen as an asset to the Republican Party. And certainly the female experience and using it as evidence are not valued. In other words, even though femaleness is discussed and visible, we do not see how this female dominant position differs qualitatively from the male form of politicking. Further, since most, if not all, of the women featured in this book deny that there is an actual "war on women," their incentive to use policy making as an opportunity end this war is low. Given that the women in 2014, like Ernst, were elected due to a large turnout of male voters, it seems that the brand of femaleness espoused by these women is palatable to the male voters but not necessarily to the female electorate. This finding bolsters what previous critics have argued about the double bind that female politicians face. While there may be a "female" rhetorical strategy that can be utilized to an individual's advantage, women are still unable to act "too" feminine lest they be perceived as incapable or weak. Instead, the more mainstream female candidates will depend heavily on traditional and masculine myths, icons, and character traits (Parry-Giles & Parry-Giles, 1996, p. 349). Worse, as Parry-Giles and Parry-Giles (1996) wrote, "a 'feminine style' might work to occlude genuine opposition to patriarchy. Its use may only reflect a presentational shift that does not violate patriarchal constructions and that does repress the 'feminine'" (p. 349). Indeed, in the instances we have highlighted in this book, these explicit and bawdy inclusions of one's gender seem to replace substantive conversations

Concluding Thoughts and Ideas

about hegemonic politics. Rather than signal a shift in the conversation, these case studies seem to suggest a shift in the *expression* of the same old conversation.

While speculative, it is worth considering whether male candidates could use the same type of expression. If it is not the actual experience of being a woman that is being stressed, then Republican men could, presumably, engage in maternal thinking and liberal feminist discourse. Like Martinez, could they use invitational rhetoric strategically? Or is it like Fiorina and the way her biological sex allows her to make particular rejections and acceptances regarding femininity? Previous research has indicated that male candidates do not use these types of feminine presentational styles (Johnson, 2005, p.18). There is much to be gleaned for a male, Republican candidate who needs to win the votes of women while maintaining party platforms. These case studies show that it is possible to offer a particular brand of feminism or, at least, a female-friendly message while campaigning. Future research should examine male candidates' use of these strategies. In particular, with the successful use of compromise, liberal feminist tenets, and feminine style, male candidates may turn their attention to those types of rhetorical strategies.

What lessons should be drawn from the Republican victory in 2014, then? Does it mean that those Republican women had a great strategy that really resonated with voters—suggesting that voters, too, do not want an overt discussion about sex, feminism, and gendered issues? The fact that personhood amendments were struck down in Colorado and North Dakota suggests that the electorate does not favor some of the extreme measures offered (McDonough, 2014). In North Dakota, for example, a personhood ballot measure that would have amended the state constitution to say "the inalienable right to life of every human being at any stage of development must be recognized and protected" was defeated by almost 30 percentage points (Bassett, 2014). And Colorado rejected a similar measure for the third time. Voters in Mississippi, South Dakota, and Florida have defeated similar attempts to curb access to a woman's right to choose (Bassett, 2014). Time and time again, Americans have shown that they reject some measures that are part of this "war on women."

Concluding Thoughts and Ideas

Indeed, in 2014, the Democrats were victorious with female voters. Koplowitz (2014) noted that "in the 10 most competitive Senate races in the 2014 midterm elections, GOP candidates won the women vote in just two races, according to exit polling" (para. 1). The two Senate contests in which Republicans were victorious were in Arkansas and Kentucky. Exit polls revealed that female voters broke in favor of the Democrats by 7 percentage points overall, which was better than the 2010 midterm elections, where women favored the GOP by a single percentage point (Brown, 2014). Republicans did win the gender gap in the midterm elections of 2014 by winning male voters by 14 percentage points (Bassett, 2014c).

Perhaps the Democrats running for Senate in 2014 got their strategy wrong. Perhaps the Democrats should have sought strategies to appeal to female voters while also appealing to more male voters. Or maybe the Democrats should have focused on winning women voters by a greater margin. Finally, the wins could be primarily an issue of getting out the vote. It is true that Democrats normally fare better in years when there is a presidential election because it is easier to attract the more diverse voters they depend upon (such as women, young voters, and minority voters) when the president is on the ticket.

Pundits have long expounded on what strategies Democrats might have pursue in order to be more successful. Indeed, as the months and weeks and days ticked down to the midterm election, countless hours of attack advertisements hammered home a simple Republican message: "You should hate the president. Vote accordingly." Jeff Schweitzer (2014), former White House policy advisor, argued, "the far right has been able to convince the public that everything bad is Obama's fault, but that Obama is responsible for nothing that is good. When that does not work, they create the illusion that what is good is bad; healthcare comes to mind" (para. 4). Indeed, the president's approval rating hovered around 40 percent during the 2014 midterm elections (Newton-Small, 2014).

With the president's popularity in question, Democrats sought to run away from President Obama and his record. For example, Alison Lundergan Grimes, who challenged incumbent senator Mitch McConnell in Kentucky, refused to say that she had voted for President

Concluding Thoughts and Ideas

Obama, even though she was an Obama delegate (Acosta, 2014; Weisman & Parker, 2014). Democrats also refused offers to have the president campaign with them, preferring instead to call on other surrogates, such as Michelle Obama. Running away from their party might have made the Democrats appear to think there was something wrong with their values or their record. It certainly meant that no one was making the case that President Obama had a record for which to vote. Weisman and Parker (2014) explained that "Democrats tried to distance themselves from the president's health care law and economic policies, despite signs that both may be working" (para. 32). With unemployment below 6 percent, the dollar the strongest it had been in years, the stock market at record highs, and gas prices at record lows, it was unfathomable to many that Obama was seen as a weakness rather than an asset. As David Letterman quipped in early November 2014, "This is what happens when we have midterm elections. The Republicans, of course, have turned against Obama, and the Democrats have also turned against Obama. That's a lonely, lonely gig being president, ladies and gentleman. Take a look at this: Gas under $3 a gallon—under $3 a gallon. Unemployment under 6 percent, whoever thought? Stock market breaking records every day. No wonder the guy is so unpopular" (Benen, 2014a, n.p.). Letterman was not wrong. Dr. Matthew Dickinson (2014), a professor at Middlebury College, argued that the economy "continues to improve. Unemployment has dropped almost 2 percent, from 7.8 percent to 5.8 percent since Obama's re-election. The annualized gross domestic product grew by 4.6 percent in the second quarter of 2014—the highest growth rate in 2.5 years. The stock market has hit record highs" (para. 2).

Indeed, voters who had the economy foremost in their mind voted to oust the Democrats. A third of voters felt the economy was doing worse. Fifty-five percent of those voters voted "in opposition to the president. Health care played a similar role: 47 percent of voters said that the health care law went too far, among these voters 57 percent were voting, at least in part, as a gesture against Mr. Obama" (McDermott and Feldman, 2014, para.10). According to Stanley Feldman, professor of political science at Stony Brook University, and Monika L. McDermott (2014), an associate professor of political science at Fordham University:

Concluding Thoughts and Ideas

Voters going to the polls today were very pessimistic about the state of the U.S. economy according to the exit poll results. Seventy-one percent of voters in the exit poll said that economy is not so good or poor. And 78 percent were very or somewhat worried about the future direction of the economy. Despite improving unemployment statistics and recent evidence of economic growth, only 33 percent of voters believe that the economy is getting better.

Kotkin (2014) reported that "despite the economic recovery, it is precisely these voters, particularly the white middle and working classes, who, for now, have deserted the Democrats for the GOP, the assumed party of plutocracy" (para. 2). Therefore, voters were unaware of the nation's economic gains, they simply could not yet feel those gains. Nearly 80 percent stated that the recession had not ended for them and their families (Kotkin, 2014).

Some scholars may find it befuddling that middle-class American families who could not feel the economic gains of the recovery sought to vote for the party that voted against increasing the minimum wage, against providing health care benefits to families who were long without them, against jobs bills, and forgiving tax breaks to the rich "job creators." But to Americans, the 2008 recession likely appeared to have gone on forever. This situation was probably exacerbated by the fact that President Obama could not tell the American people in 2008 that we stood at the brink of the great depression. Americans might have had no choice but to believe the story that president Obama and the Democrats left them no choice but to turn to the Republicans for help, because the Democrats offered no counter-narrative. They simply pretended not to be Democrats.

And this game of make believe could have been the true reason for the 2014 midterm election results. For example, "Rob Collins, executive director of the National Republican Senatorial Committee, said Senate Democrats hurt themselves by not using President Obama more on the campaign trail. 'They sidelined their best messenger,' he said" (Sarlin and Seitz-Wald, 2014, para. 5). Jim Manley, a former spokesman for Senate Majority Leader Harry Reid, concurred, and added, "How is the base supposed to get excited when elected Democrats are going to such great length to put as much distance as they can between them and a president that was elected twice by the American people?"

Concluding Thoughts and Ideas

(Acosta, 2014). Additionally, Sarlin and Seitz-Wald (2014) explained that by not defending President Obama's record, the party quietly accepted the Republicans' premise that he had failed. Finally, an anonymous Democratic strategist put it in straightforward terms: "Running away from the president is never smart. You look like chicken s—" (Acosta, 2014, para. 3).

Unfortunately, the economy was not the only fear midterm election voters had. According to Hurlburt (2014),

> A Walmart-funded bipartisan series of monthly focus groups of married women—so-called "Walmart Moms"—captures this floating angst clearly. September anxiety around ISIL, they noted, "has almost completely been replaced by Ebola" in October. The pollsters interpreted subjects' anxiety about these issues, as well as border security, as "emblematic of anxiety they feel regarding other issues, including national security, job security, and people "getting stuff they aren't entitled to," such as healthcare and other government benefits. Trust in government competence is at or near an all-time low. Economic pessimism and anxiety are stubbornly high [para. 9].

These fears are not rational, as anxiety filled the nation in response to Ebola, a disease that killed one person in America (Talbot, 2014). But this would not be the first time a large block of female voters were thought to be motivated by fear. Between 2000 and 2004, security moms voted for George W. Bush (Hurlburt, 2014) so we could fight the terrorists abroad instead of at home. Indeed, Hurlburt (2014) pointed to the "Daisy Girl ad" that Lyndon Johnson used in the 1964 election as evidence that fear tactics persuade women, because although 45 percent of men believed that Barry Goldwater would involve America in a war, 53 percent of women were found to be persuaded. We argue that the fear Americans felt heading into the midterm election was irrational and that strong rhetorical leadership by the Democrats could likely have eased the fear and reassure Americans that we were on the right path. While a number of factors likely came together to ensure the election outcomes, there are powerful forces other than the rhetorical attempts analyzed in this book that were at work.

We now turn our attention back to the most recent election—the 2016 presidential election and the Republican Party proving itself incredibly electable despite the contextual elements we have outlined

Concluding Thoughts and Ideas

in this book. As we have mentioned, 2016 threw many political pundits, rhetorical critics and politicians for a loop. It is hard to say with certainty that these women will rise to more prominence or that they will engage in the strategies covered in this book. But we feel they are worthy of mention. We chose to highlight Elise Stefanik and Cathy McMorris Rodgers for a couple of different reasons. First, they are women who both successfully negotiated their re-elections bids in 2016 though they had different approaches to the Trump candidacy. Second, they are Republicans who were elected in typically Democrat- leaning areas and districts. Third, and related, they often talk about themselves as independent or nonpartisan voices. Finally, both women are often talked about as the future of the Republican Party. In fact, both were listed on *NewsMax*'s list of 50 most influential Republican women (Blosser, 2016). We hope that these profiles, as well as the women discussed above, will encourage future scholarship to continue the investigation of how Republican women navigate this current political climate.

Elise Stefanik, 32 years old, educated at Harvard and moderate, worked in Washington for ten years before she ran in New York's 21st District in 2014 making her the youngest women ever to be elected to Congress. Despite being a staffer in the George W. Bush administration and a campaign aide for Mitt Romney in 2012, Stefanik touts her willingness to break rank with her party as a strength. She even lists it on her website. According to a *Congressional Quarterly* analysis, Stefanik has voted against her party on divisive issues 15 percent of the time (Akin, 2016). Her district, known as "the North Country" by locals, is rural and old mill towns. While most voters are registered Republicans, they chose Barack Obama in his two presidential races and a former Republican representative from the district, John McHugh, served in the Obama administration. Many in the area are progressive when it comes to social issues (Akin, 2016). Despite being seen by some as an outsider, given the many years she spent in Albany and other more cosmopolitan places in New York, Stefanik won all 12 counties in her district in 2016 (Adirondack Daily Enterprise, 2016). In an effort reminiscent of Joni Ernst, her strategy of logging hundreds of miles in her Ford pickup through her largely rural district propelled her to victory

Concluding Thoughts and Ideas

in a district where more than 88 percent of the population does not have a college degree (Akin, 2016). In addition, she participated in a Republican initiative called The Women2Women Conversations Tour, which was launched in 2014 as a place for women across the country to discuss issues during election cycles (Gangitano, 2016). Indeed, her margin of victory in 2016 was higher than 2014 despite the complicated presidential landscape (Adirondack Daily Enterprise, 2016). Stefanik's position on Trump was "I'm supporting my party's nominee. But I'll continue being an independent voice for the district." Her campaign spokesperson elaborating by defining her stance as "I'm going to support the nominee of my party, but when I disagree with him I'm going to stand up and talk about it, and she's done so." Indeed, Stefanik has condemned some of Trump's most egregious missteps including his attack on the Kahn family, his proposed ban on Muslims and his promise to build a wall along the border with Mexico (Akin, 2016). Some experts say that her lack of a disavowal of Trump may hurt her if she needs to win a statewide election, but that hers was a "very clever strategy" and one that faced every member of Congress (Akin, 2016).

Cathy McMorris Rodgers kept her seat representing Washington's 5th District making her the fourth-highest-ranking House Republican and the highest-ranking female (Ryals, 2016). McMorris Rodgers is known as an effective member of Congress. Over her previous four-year tenure, three bills that she sponsored or co-sponsored have been signed into law (Ryals, 2016). She has been the leader of the House Republican Conference and plans to seek a third term in that capacity. The chair is tasked with setting legislative priorities for the party, facilitating the election of party leaders, and has been a springboard for more prominent roles in the GOP (Hill, 2016).

Like Stefanik, she won every county in her district. And she ran on a platform of being a middle-ground Republican who is committed to being a "government of the people, by the people and for the people" (Ryals, 2016). Also like Stefanik, she was a reluctant supporter of Donald Trump and vowed to hold him accountable. After the primary election, she wrote on her Facebook page:

> Did I cast my ballot with enthusiasm? Not exactly—I'm still getting to know Mr. Trump like so many others. We had a positive first meeting last week. Since

Concluding Thoughts and Ideas

then, I've continued the conversation with his team to better understand how he plans to lead moving forward and unite the country around a forward-looking, conservative policy agenda. I'm encouraged so far and look forward to learning more. Do I have concerns about the comments he made in the past and on the campaign trail this year about women; people with disabilities; and those from different backgrounds? Absolutely—I vehemently disagree with such statements. They are wrong in a Presidential campaign; in our workplaces; in our homes; and anywhere else. I've called him out before, and I won't be shy if he does it again because he owes it to our party and our country to treat everyone respectfully and to build an inclusive coalition [McMorris Rodgers, 2016].

After Trump's November 8 victory, McMorris Rodgers said that she was "encouraged to hear his call for unity" (Hill, 2016, n.p.). Another similarity between Stefanik and McMorris Rodgers is that they were both 2016 beneficiaries of the annual Republicans Inspiring Success and Empowerment (RISE) event. The money raised at RISE is used to help women incumbents. The event began with a Women Leaders fundraiser series kicked off by McMorris Rodgers (McPherson, 2016).

We feel compelled, too, to mention Ivanka Trump. While she probably will not be appointed to a cabinet position or elected position, obviously, she was an important woman in the Trump transition team. And, of course, she took an important role throughout his campaign. Donald Trump's first-born daughter gave a major primetime address during the convention and was a visible symbol throughout the election. Feminist commentator Jessica Valenti wrote, "for most of the presidential campaign, Ivanka functioned as a telegenic, articulate shield against accusations of misogyny leveled against Trump. She touted his female-friendly bonafides by talking about all the women he had hired over the years, mentioned the way he supported her career—she even called him a feminist" (Valenti, 2016, n.p.). Ivanka Trump's strategy of basing her "feminism" on empowerment rather than policy change could work very well (Valenti, 2016). And it is, as we have noted in other chapters, a strategy the party has used before. Ronnee Schreiber, author of *Righting Feminism: Conservative Women and American Politics*, who we referenced in the Joni Ernst chapter to help discuss faux maternalism, stated after the election that "using gender as an outreach strategy is an identity politics angle that they often criticize but often invoke." As Valenti extrapolates, "feminism is bad unless someone who

Concluding Thoughts and Ideas

doesn't' actually believe in feminist is touting it" (2016, n.p.). Valenti hypothesizes and we agree that Ivanaka, and, by proxy, her father's message to women, is likely to continue to be something that we have already seen—the polite (and incorrect) belief that women's rights are a bipartisan affair, that so long as it has the appearance and language of women's empowerment, it's good for women. Ivanka is someone worth watching and someone who is and will continue to be a very powerful weapon in Trump's war *for* women.

The review of these women and the breakdown of the 2014 election cycle invite two important considerations. First, the GOP has no shortage of qualified, successful women who are in office and running for office. So even if what we wrote in the prologue is true—that women and Donald Trump have negotiating to do—several women are already off to a good start. These well-educated, moderate Republican women who voted for Donald Trump but did so reluctantly will find a way to navigate their relationship with the president. Second, both Stefanik and McMorris Rodger's victories in 2016 reveal a party that is committed to bolstering female candidates and incumbents. So, while we argue that these female candidates still have the same problem—negotiating their female identity within a party that has a complicated, at best, and problematic, at worst, relationship with women's issues—the party does seem to be making strides to include more female voices. Or, at the very least, support the voices already there. As a reader may have already guessed based on the literature reviewed in this book, we think government and democracy works best when diverse voices are heard and involved in policy-making. We do not envy the government officials who have to navigate the murky reality of getting those voices involved. But we have provided a variety of people and case studies that may be the blueprint for getting it done.

References

Abdullah, H. (2012, November 8). How women ruled the 2012 election and where the GOP went wrong. *CNN*. Retrieved on July 14, 2014, from http://www.cnn.com/2012/11/08/politics/women-election/.

Acosta, J. (2014, November 4). Let the second-guessing begin: Some Dems question "avoid Obama" strategy. Retrieved from *CNN Politics*. http://www.cnn.com/2014/11/03/politics/obama-strategy-democrats-questioning-acosta/.

Adams, S. (2010). "Maternal Thinking." In O'Reilly, A. (Ed.), *Encyclopedia of Motherhood*. Thousand Oaks: Sage.

Adirondack Daily Enterprise. Stefanik surges to re-election: Incumbent wins all 12 counties in northern NY district. Accessed http://www.adirondackdailyenterprise.com/news/local-news/2016/11/stefanik-surges-to-re-election/.

Akin, S. (2016, October 25). Elisa Stefanik's cautious dance with Trump. *RollCall*. Retrieved from https://www.rollcall.com/news/elise-stefanik-trump-tightrope-new-york-donald-trump-cautious-dance.

Alter, C. (2014, March 10). "Bossy" women: 16 leaders who've overcome that label (and worse). *Time*. Retrieved from http://time.com/16382/16-successful-women-who-were-once-called-bossy-or-worse/.

Ashbee, E. (2009). The Bush administration and the politics of sexual morality. In Wroe, A., & Herbert, J. (Eds.), *Assessing the George W. Bush Presidency*. Edinburgh: Edinburgh University Press. doi:10.3366/edinburgh/9780748627400.003.0013.

Associated Press. (2014, July 7). House GOP to D.C. residents: Guns OK, marijuana dangerous. Retrieved July 14, 2014, from http://www.wjla.com/articles/2014/07/house-gop-to-d-c-residents-guns-ok-marijuana-dangerous-105165.html.

Bailey, A. (1994). Mother, diversity and peace politics. *Hypatia, 9*, 188–198.

Ball, M. (2014, November 5). The Republican wave sweeps the midterm elections. *The Atlantic*. Retrieved from http://www.theatlantic.com/politics/archive/2014/11/republicans-sweep-the-midterm-elections/382394/.

Ball, M. (2014, October 14). Did Republicans blow the Michigan Senate race? *The Atlantic*. Retrieved from http://www.theatlantic.com/politics/archive/2014/10/did-republicans-blow-the-michigan-senate-race/381399/.

Bassett, L. (2014, November 6). Democrats actually gained women's support

References

since last midterm election. *Huffington Post.* Retrieved from http://www.huffingtonpost.com/2014/11/06/democrats-gained-womens-support_n_6116540.html.

Bassett, L. (2014, November 4). Colorado and North Dakota voters reject fetal personhood measures. *The Huffington Post.* Retrieved from http://www.huffingtonpost.com/2014/11/04/personhood-colorado_n_6104120.html.

Bassett, L. (2014, October 20). Men got us into the shutdown, women got us out. *The Huffington Post.* Retrieved from http://www.huffingtonpost.com/2013/10/16/shutdown-women_n_4110268.html.

Bassett, L. (2014, October 16). Senate candidate Joni Ernst endorses federal personhood bill for fetuses. *The Huffington Post.* Retrieved from http://www.huffingtonpost.com/2014/10/16/senate-candidate-endorses_n_5997126.html.

Bassett, L. (2012, November 6). Todd Akin election results: Claire McCaskill defeats GOP challenger. *The Huffington Post.* Retrieved from http://www.huffingtonpost.com/2012/11/06/todd-akin-election-results-2012_n_2049695.html.

Bassett, L., & Jamieson, D. (2013, June 17). Dems rebrand minimum wage, sick leave as women's issues to pressure GOP. *The Huffington Post.* Retrieved from http://www.huffingtonpost.com/2013/06/17/women-minimum-wage_n_3441754.html.

Batley, M. (2014, May 6). Republicans develop strategy to win over women. *Newsmax.* Retrieved from http://www.newsmax.com/Politics/Republicans-women-voters-equal-pay/2014/05/06/id/569769/.

Baucus, M. (2012, March 19). Work is not done to combat domestic violence. *U.S. News & World Report.* Retrieved from http://www.usnews.com/debate-club/should-the-violence-against-women-act-be-reauthorized/max-baucus-work-is-not-done-to-combat-domestic-violence

Bauer, S. (2014, October 27). Obama goes to Wisconsin in bid to oust Scott Walker. *The Huffington Post.* Retrieved from http://www.huffingtonpost.com/2014/10/27/obama-wisconsin_n_6055968.html.

Beckwith, R. T. (2015, September 16). Transcript: Read the Full Text of the Second Republican Debate. Time. Retrieved from http://time.com/4037239/second-republican-debate-transcript-cnn/.

Behuniak-Long, S. (1992). Justice Sandra Day O'Connor and the power of maternal legal thinking. *The review of politics, 54,* 417–444. doi: 147.226.170.251.

Bendery, J. (2013, March 7). Violence Against Women Act now touted by Republicans who voted against bill. *The Huffington Post.* Retrieved from http://www.huffingtonpost.com/ 2013/03/07/violence-against-women-act_n_2832014.html.

Bendery, J. (2012, December 18). Violence Against Women Act: House Republican women emerge as key to possible action. *The Huffington Post.* Retrieved from http://www.huffingtonpost.com/2012/12/18/violence-against-women-act-house-republican-women_n_2322572.html.

Benen, S. (2014a, November 4). "No wonder the guy is so unpopular." *The Mad-*

References

dow Blog: MSNBC. Retrieved from http://www.msnbc.com/rachel-maddow-show/no-wonder-the-guy-so-unpopular.

Benen, S. (2014b, September 3). Violence against women act trips up another GOP lawmaker. *The Maddow Blog: MSNBC*. Retrieved from http://www.msnbc.com/rachel-maddow-show/violence-against-women-act-trips-another-gop-lawmaker.

Benen, S. (2014c, January 30). The Rachel Maddow show/equality: The GOP case against pay equity. *MSNBC*. Retrieved from http://www.msnbc.com/rachel-maddow-show/the-gop-case-against-pay-equity.

Blake, A. (2014, November 6). The GOP won, but the gender gap just got bigger. *Washington Post*. Retrieved from http://www.washingtonpost.com/blogs/the-fix/wp/2014/11/06/the-gop-won-but-the-gender-gap-just-got-bigger/.

Blake, A. (2014, January 22). GOP Congressman's book: "The wife is to voluntarily submit" to her husband. *Washington Post*. Retrieved from http://www.washingtonpost.com/blogs/post-politics/wp/2014/01/22/gop-congressmans-book-the-wife-is-to-voluntarily-submit-to-her-husband/.

Blake, A. (2012, April 12). "The nation's 10 most popular governors—and why." *Washington Post*. Retrieved from http://www.washingtonpost.com/blogs/the-fix/post/the-nations-10-most-popular-governors—and-why/2012/04/11/gIQA9dlzAT_blog.html.

Blankenship, J., & Robson, D.C. (1995). A "feminine style" in women's exploratory discourse: An exploratory essay. *Communication Quarterly, 43*(3), 353–366. doi: 10.1080/01463379509369982.

Blosser, J. (2016, May). Newsmax's 50 most influential female republicans. *Newsmax*. Retrieved from http://www.newsmax.com/TheWire/female-republicans-influential-gop/2016/05/04/id/727129/.

Bobic, I. (2014, October 14). Wisconsin Gov. Scott Walker doesn't think the minimum wage "serves a purpose." *The Huffington Post*. Retrieved from http://www.huffingtonpost.com/.2014/10/14/scott-walker-minimum-wage_n_5985284.html.

Boling, P. (1991). The democratic potential of mothering. *Political Theory, 19*, 606–625. doi: 10.1177/0090591791019004005.

Booker, B. (2014, April 22). In TV ad, GOP Senate candidate mocks "War on women" rhetoric. *National Public Radio*. Retrieved from http://www.npr.org/blogs/itsallpolitics/.2014/04/22/30588260/in-tv-ad-gop-senate-candidate-mocks-war-on-women-rhetoric

Brace, L. (2000). "Not empire but equality": Mary Wollstonecraft, the marriage state and the sexual contract. *The Journal of Political Philosophy, 8*(4), 433–455. doi: 10.1111/1467-9760.00111.

Bradner, E. (2015, September 21). Poll: Fiorina rockets to No. 2 behind Trump in GOP field. *CNN Politics*. Retrieved from http://www.cnn.com/2015/09/20/politics/carly-fiorina-donald-trump-republican-2016-poll/.

Brewer, M.D. The rise of partisanship and the expansion of partisan conflict within the American electorate. *Political Research Quarterly, 58*, 219–229.

Brown, E.N. (2014, November 5). Democrats couldn't count on women for victories

References

in midterm 2014 elections. Will they learn? *Reason*. Retrieved from http://reason.com/blog/2014/11/05/female-voter-turnout-midterms-2014.

Brummett, B. (1979). A pentadic analysis of ideologies in two gay rights controversies. *Central States Speech Journal, 30,* 250–261.

Burke, K. (1989). *On symbols and society* (J. R. Gusfield, Ed.). Chicago: University of Chicago Press.

Burke, K. (1984). *Attitudes toward history*. Berkeley: University of California Press.

Burke, K. (1975). *The philosophy of literary form*. Berkeley: University of California Press.

Burke, K. (1969). *A grammar of motives*. Berkeley: University of California Press.

Bush, B. (1990, June 1). Commencement address at Wellesley College. *American Rhetoric: Top 100 Speeches*. Retrieved from http://www.americanrhetoric.com/speeches/barbara bushwellesley commencement.htm.

Butterfield, F. (1990, May 4). At Wellesley, a furor over Barbara Bush. *New York Times*. Retrieved from http://www.nytimes.com/1990/05/04/us/at-wellesley-a-furor-over-barbara-bush.html.

Camia, C. (2013, October 16). Collins leads Senate sisters in shaping deal. *USAToday*. Retrieved from http://www.usatoday.com/story/news/politics/2013/10/16/collins-government-shutdown-women-senate-deal/2994803/.

Campbell, K.K. (1999). The rhetoric of women's liberation: An oxymoron. *Communication Studies, 50,* 125–137.

Campbell, K.K. (1998). The discursive performance of femininity: Hating Hillary. *Rhetoric & Public Affairs, 1,* 1–19.

Campbell, K.K. (1989). *Man cannot speak for her: A critical study of early feminist rhetoric* (volumes 1–2). New York: Greenwood Press.

Campbell, K.K. (1973). The rhetoric of women's liberation: An oxymoron. *Quarterly Journal of Speech, 59,* 4–86. doi: 10.1080/00335637309383155.

Caputo, M. (2014, September 12). Paging Dr. Freud: Rep. Steve Southerland opens mouth, inserts "lingerie shower." *Miami Herald*. Retrieved from http://miamiherald.typepad. com/nakedpolitics/2014/09/paging-dr-freud-rep-steve-southerland-opens-mouth-inserts-lingerie-shower-.html.

Carmichael, K. (2013, December 15). Washington nears budget peace. *The Globe and Mail*. Retrieved from http://www.theglobeandmail.com/news/world/washington-nears-budget-peace/article15974950/.

Carmon, I. (2013, December 12). Republicans think they can win on abortion. So do Democrats. *MSNBC*. Retrieved from http://www.msnbc.com/msnbc/which-party-can-win-abortion.

Catanese, D. (2014, October 9). Wisconsin's amazing race: The governor's contest is one of the closest in the country, and its outcome could have White House ramifications. *U.S. News & World Report*. Retrieved from http://www.usnews.com/news/articles/2014/10/09/wisconsins-amazing-governors-race-pits-scott-walker-against-mary-burke.

Catanese, D. (2014, April 16). The secret recordings of Susana Martinez: The New Mexico governor is caught on tape denigrating teachers and cursing her opponent. *U.S. News & World Report*. Retrieved July 14, 2014, from

References

http://www.usnews.com/news/blogs/run-2016/2014/04/16/the-secret-recordings-of-susana-martinez.

Chandler, L. (2015, December 21). I Admire Fiorina as a Woman, I Detest Her as a Politician. *New York Times*. Retrieved from http://www.nytimes.com/roomfordebate/2015/10/01/is-carly-fiorina-a-feminist/i-admire-fiorina-as-a-woman-i-detest-her-as-a-politician.

Chandler, M. (1998). "Emancipated subjectives and the subjugation of mothering Practices." In Abbey, S., & O'Reilly, A. (Eds.), *Redefining motherhood: Changing identities and patterns*. Toronto: Second Story Press.

Chappell, M. (2012). Reagan's "gender gap" strategy and the limitations of free market feminism. *The Journal of Policy History, 44*, 115–134.

Charen, M. (2014, April 22). GOP, answer the "war on women" charges. *National Review Online*. Retrieved from http://www.nationalreview.com/article/376213/gop-answer-war-women-charges-mona-charen.

Charland, M. (1987). Constitutive rhetoric: The case of the *"Peuple Quebecois."* *Quarterly Journal of Speech, 73*, 133–150.

Chavez, L. (2015, December 21). We need a new feminism that celebrates self-reliance. *New York Times*. Retrieved from http://www.nytimes.com/roomfordebate/2015/10/01/is-carly-fiorina-a-feminist/we-need-a-new-feminism-that-celebrates-self-reliance.

Chozick, A., & Gabriel, T. (2015, April 12). Carly Fiorina emerges as a G.O.P. weapon against "war on women" charge. *New York Times*. Retrieved from http://www.nytimes.com/2015/08/13/us/politics/carly-fiorina-emerges-as-a-gop-weapon-against-war-on-women-charge.html.

Clark, C., & Clark, J.M. (2008). The Reemergence of the gender gap in 2004. In Whitaker, L.D. (Ed.), *Voting the gender gap* (50–74). Urbana: University of Illinois Press.

Clawson, L. (2014, May 29). Terri Lynn Land dodges on auto bailout and equal pay. *Daily Kos*. Retrieved from http://www.dailykos.com/story/2014/05/29/1302794/-Terri-Lynn-Land-ducks-and-dodges-on-auto-bailout-and-equal-pay#.

Clinton, B. (2012, August 5). 2012 Democratic National Convention speech. Retrieved July 14, 2014, from https://www.youtube.com/watch?v=uzDhk3BHi6Q.

Cohen, K. (2014, November 4). Republican Steve Daines wins Montana Senate race. *Washington Examiner*. Retrieved from http://www.washingtonexaminer.com/republican-steve-daines-wins-montana-senate-race/article/2555736.

Cohen, T. (2013, February 28). House passes Violence Against Women Act after GOP version defeated. *CNN*. Retrieved from http://www.cnn.com/2013/02/28/politics/violence-against-women/.

Cohn, L. (2016, November 15). Meet the women who could end up in Donald Trump's cabinet. Fortunewww. Retrieved from http://fortune.com/2016/11/15/donald-trump-cabinet-women/.

Collins, G. (2014, May 9). Where the girls Are. *New York Times*. Retrieved from http://www.nytimes.com/2014/05/10/opinion/collins-where-the-girls-are.html?_r=0.

References

Collins, P.H. (2000). *Black feminist thought: Knowledge, consciousness, and the politics of empowerment* (2nd Ed.). New York: Routledge.

Creamer, R. (2012). Why the Bain capital controversy is so damaging to GOP chances this fall. *Huffington Post*. Retrieved from http://www.huffingtonpost.com/robert-creamer/why-the-bain-capital-cont_b_1208678.html.

Culp-Ressler, T. (2014, August 15). Candidate can't explain his position on women's health, forgets what birth control is. *Think Progress*. Retrieved from http://thinkprogress.org/ health/2014/08/15/3471777/candidate-colorado-birth-control/.

Davis, J. (2012, March 14). Republicans losing on birth control as 77% in poll spurn debate. *Bloomberg Business*. Retrieved from http://www.bloomberg.com/news/articles/2012-03-14/republicans-losing-on-birth-control-as-77-in-poll-spurn-debate.

Decker, C. (2014, January 29). Seeking support from women, GOP changes messenger but not message. *Los Angeles Times*. Retrieved from http://articles.latimes.com/2014/jan/29/news/la-pn-state-of-the-union-women-analysis-20140129.

Democratic Senatorial Campaign Committee (DSCC). (2014, January 24). Mike Huckabee & Terri Lynn Land show disregard for women's healthcare. *Democratic Senatorial Campaign Committee Webpage*. Retrieved from http://www.dscc.org/pressrelease/whos-yo?page=16.

Dickinson, M. (2014, November 7). Why the economy couldn't save the Democrats. *U.S. News & World Report*. Retrieved from http://www.usnews.com/opinion/blogs/opinion-blog/2014/11/07/why-the-economy-couldnt-save-democrats-in-2014-midterm-election.

Dickerson, B. (2014, October 4). Terri Lynn Land comes out of hiding, but not into focus. *Detroit Free Press*. Retrieved from http://www.freep.com/story/opinion/columnists/brian-dickerson/2014/10/04/land-senate-michigan/16673985/.

Dickerson, B. (2014, June 2). For Terri Lynn Land, happiness is escaping from Mackinac. *Detroit Free Press*. Retrieved from http://archive.freep.com/article/20140601/COL04/306010049/terri-lynn-land-senate-gary-peters.

Dow, B.J. (2001). Ellen, television, and the politics of gay and lesbian visibility. *Critical Studies in Media Communication, 18*, 123–140.

Dow, B.J. (1996). *Prime-time feminism: Television, media culture, and the women's Movement since 1970*. Philadelphia: University of Pennsylvania Press.

Dow, B.J. & Tonn, M.B. (1993). "Feminine Style" and political judgment in the rhetoric of Ann Richards. *Quarterly Journal of Speech, 79*, 286–302. doi: 10.1080/00335639309384036.

The Economist (2016, January 16). Haley's Comet. Retrieved from http://www.economist.com/news/united-states/21688410-governor-South-carolina-auditions-republican-ticket-haleys-comet.

The Economist. (2014, February 8). Barack Obama, deporter-in-chief. Retrieved from http://www.economist.com/news/leaders/21595902-expelling-record-numbers-immigrants-costly-way-make-america-less-dynamic-barack-obama.

Eckholm, E. (2011, October 25). Push for "personhood" amendment represents

References

new tack in abortion fight. *New York Times.* Retrieved from http://www.nytimes.com/2011/10/26/us/politics/personhood-amendments-would-ban-nearly-all-abortions.html.

Eckholm, E., & Severson, K. (2012, February 28). Virginia Senate Passes Ultrasound Bill as Other States Take Notice. *New York Times.* Retrieved from http://www.nytimes.com/2012/02/29/us/virginia-senate-passes-revised-ultrasound-bill.html?pagewanted=all&_r=0.

Edwards-Levy, A. (2014, February 7). Most women say the GOP doesn't understand their problems, poll finds. *The Huffington Post.* Retrieved from http://www.huffingtonpost.com/2014/02/07/women-gop-poll_n_4748200.html.

Eeggert, D. (2013, August 6). Michigan GOP Senate candidate Terri Lynn has deep pockets. *Mlive.* Retrieved from http://www.mlive.com/politics/index.ssf/2013/08/michigan_gop_senate_candidate.html.

Egan, P. (2014, July 17). Schauer closes on Snyder; Peters expands lead over Land for U.S. Senate. *Detroit Free Press.* Retrieved from http://www.freep.com/article/20140717/NEWS06/307170177/.

Electablog. (2014, May 3). Videos: Terri Lynn Land gets mocked, parodied, and skewered for her "Really" ad. *Electablog: Progressive news and commentary.* Retrieved from http://www.eclectablog.com/2014/05/videos-terri-lynn-land-gets-mocked-parodied-and-skewered-for-her-really-ad.html.

Elshtain, J. B. (1993). *Public man private woman: Women in social and political thought* (2nd Ed.). Princeton: Princeton University Press.

Epstein, J. (2013, April 23). Obama pushes big budget deal at dinner with Senate women. Politicowww. Retrieved from http://www.politico.com/politico44/2013/04/obama-pushes-big-budget-deal-at-dinner-with-senate-162478.html.

Ernst, J. (2014, September 15). *About* [Video file]. Retrieved from https://www.youtube.com/watch?v=F_JqmuNkZ30.

Ernst, J. (2014, May 4). *Shot* [Video file]. Retrieved from https://www.youtube.com/watch?v=I3mG9fNOZp4.

Ernst, J. (2014, March 24). *Squeal* [Video file]. Retrieved from https://www.youtube.com/watch?v=p9Y24MFOfFU.

Fard, M. F. (2012, March 2). Sandra Fluke, Georgetown student called a "slut" by Rush Limbaugh, speaks out. *Washington Post.* Retrieved from http://www.washingtonpost.com/blogs/the-buzz/post/rush-limbaugh-calls-georgetown-student-sandra-fluke-a-slut-for-advocating-contraception/2012/03/02/gIQAvjfSmR_blog.html.

Fay, B. (n.d.). Economic demographics of Republicans. *Debt.org.* Retrieved July 14, 2014, from http://www.debt.org/faqs/americans-in-debt/economic-demographics-republicans.

Fiorina, C. (2006). *Tough choices: A memoir.* New York: Penguin.

Fiorina, C. (2015a). *Rising to the challenge: My leadership Journey.* New York: Penguin.

Fiorina, C. (2015b, July 16). If Men Were Treated Like Women in the Office with Carly Fiorina. [Video file]. Retrieved from https://www.youtube.com/watch?v=Tq5OQafDVxc.

Fiorina, C. (2015c, June 24). Redefining Feminism: The state of women in America.

References

Medium. Retrieved from https://medium.com/@CarlyFiorina/redefining-feminism-19d25d8d8dfc#.kn511wxd5.

Fisher, W.R. (1984). Narrative as a human communication paradigm: The case of public moral argument. *Communication Monographs, 51,* 1–22.

Flores, R. (2015, August 9). Fiorina: Women "horrified" by Trump's Megyn Kelly comments. *CBS News: Face the Nation.* Retrieved from http://www.cbsnews.com/news/carly-fiorina-women-horrified-donald-trump-megyn-kelly-comments/.

Foreman, Ann. (1977). *Femininity as alienation: Women and the family in Marxism and Psychoanalysis.* London: Pluto.

Foss, S. K. (2004). *Rhetorical criticism: Exploration and practice.* Long Grove, IL: Waveland Press.

Foss, K.A. (1989). Feminist scholarship in speech communication: Contributions and obstacles. *Women's studies in Communication, 12,* 1–10.

Foss, K. A., & Foss, S. K. (1994). Personal experience as evidence in feminist scholarship. *Western Journal of Communication, 58*(1), 39. doi: 10.1080/10570319409374482.

Foss, K. A., & Foss, S. K. (1991). *Women speak: The eloquence of women's lives.* Prospect Heights, IL: Waveland Press.

Foss, K.A., Foss, S. K., & Griffin, C. (1999). *Feminist rhetorical theories.* Thousand Oaks: Sage.

Foss, S. K., & Griffin, C. L. (1995). Beyond persuasion: A proposal for an invitational rhetoric. *Communication Monographs, 62,* 2–18. doi: 10.1080/03637759509376345.

Foss, S.K., & Griffin, C. L. (November, 1993). *Beyond persuasion: A proposal for an invitational rhetoric.* Paper presented at Speech Communication Association 1993, Miami, FL.

Foss, S. K. & Griffin, C. L. (1992). A feminist perspective on rhetorical theory: Toward a clarification of boundaries. *Western Journal of Communication, 56,* 330–349. doi: 10.1080/10570319209374422.

Foust, C. R. (2004). A return to feminine public virtue: Judge Judy and the myth of the tough mother. *Women's studies in communication, 27,* 269–293.

Fox, E.J. (2016, November 10). Why Hillary Clinton couldn't win over female voters. *Vanity Fair.* Retrieved from http://www.vanityfair.com/news/2016/11/hillary-clinton-female-voters.

Freedman, J. (2012, September 27). U.S. leaves working families in the lurch. *CNN.* Retrieved from http://www.cnn.com/2012/09/27/opinion/freedman-american-families/index.html.

Friedman, A. (2014, November 6). Why the midterms were bad news for women. *New York Magazine.* Retrieved from http://nymag.com/thecut/2014/11/why-the-midterms-were-bad-news-for-women.html.

Frum, D. (2011, July 11). Candid and frank, Betty Ford helped define her times. CNN.com. Retrieved from http://www.cnn.com/2011/OPINION/07/11/frum.betty.ford/.

Frye, N. (1957). *Anatomy of criticism: Four essays.* Princeton: Princeton University Press.

References

Gangitano, A. (2016, October 18). GOP women are listening, and they're talking. *RollCall*. Retrieved from http://www.rollcall.com/news/hoh/gop-women-listening-theyre-talking-elise-stefanik-republican-main-street-partnership.

Gearan, A. (2014, April 29). Women candidates, voters could decide Senate. *Washington Post*. Retrieved from http://www.washingtonpost.com/politics/why-the-senate-gop-takeover-might-actually-help-hillary-clinton/2014/11/05/d39ca90e-6442-11e4-9fdc-d43b053ecb4d_story.html.

Gerald R. Ford Foundation. (n.d.). Betty Ford timeline. Retrieved from http://geraldrfordfoundation.org/betty-ford-timeline/.

Gibson, K.L., & Heyse, A.L. (2014). Depoliticizing feminism: Frontier mythology and Sarah Palin's "the rise of the Mama Grizzlies." *Western Journal of Communication, 78,* 97–117. doi: 10.1080/10570314.2013.812744.

Gibson, K.L., & Heyse, A.L. (2010). "The difference between a hockey mom and a pit bull": Sarah Palin's faux maternal personal and performance of hegemonic masculinity at the 2008 Republican national convention. *Communication Quarterly, 58,* 235–256. doi: 10.1080/0`463373.2010.503151.

Gibson, M. (2012, March 8). After Limbaugh, maybe it's finally time to ignore the "slut" slur. *Time*. Retrieved from http://newsfeed.time.com/2012/03/08/in-rush-limbaughs-wake-women-are-reclaiming-the-word-slut/.

Gizzi, J. (2014, August 5). Michigan Senate race tightens. *Newsmax*. Retrieved from http://www.newsmax.com/Politics/gary-peters-terri-lynn-land-michigan-senate/2014/08/05/id/587101/.

Gold, M. (2014, November 4). Republican Scott Walker wins hard fought Wisconsin gubernatorial race. *Washington Post*. Retrieved from http://www.factcheck.org/2014/05/abortion-attack-goes-too-far-in-montana/.

Goldmacher, S. (2014, October 13). This is Joni Ernst's closing argument: Iowa Republican uses her military background to hit Bruce Braley on defense, foreign policy issues. *The National Journal*. Retrieved from http://www.nationaljournal.com/politics/joni-ernst-s-closing-salvo-centers-on-military-service-20141013.

Goldman, E. 1969. *Anarchism and other essays*. New York: Dover.

Graham, D. A. (2015, October 20). What happened to Fiorina? *The Atlantic*. Retrieved from http://www.theatlantic.com/politics/archive/2015/10/what-happened-to-carly-fiorina/411451/.

Grant, J. (1993). *Fundamental feminism: Contesting the core concepts of feminist theory*. New York: Routledge.

Gray, K. (2014, May 28). Mackinac notebook: Land falters amid media; Rich Chicks have stickers with zing. *Detroit Free Press*. Retrieved from https://web.archive.org/web/20140530045200/http://www.freep.com/article/20140528/NEWS06/305280175/mackinaw-land-peters-rick-chicks.

Gray, K., & Helms, M. (2014, May 28). Peters, Land take it to the stage at Mackinac in race for U.S. Senate. *Detroit Free Press*. Retrieved from https://web.archive.org/web/20140528232409/http://www.freep.com/article/20140528/NEWS06/305280141/senate-peters-land-mackinac-conference.

Greenberg, J. (2012). Nikki Haley ties Obama to Boeing labor dispute. Retrieved

References

from http://www.politifact.com/truth-o-meter/statements/2012/aug/30/nikki-haley/haley-ties-obama-boeing-labor-dispute/.

Griffin, C. L. (1993). Women as communicators: Mary Daly's hagiography as rhetoric. *Communication Monographs, 60*(2), 158–177. doi: 10.1080/03637759309376306.

Gutgold, N. (2001). Managing rhetorical roles: Elizabeth Hanford Dole: From spouse to candidate 1996–1999. *Women & Language, 24*(1), 29–37.

Gutmann, A., & Thompson, D. (2010). The mindsets of political compromise. *Perspectives on Politics, 8,* 1125–1143. doi 147.226.133.74.

Haberman, M. (2014, October 21). Scott Brown gains on Shaheen in N.H. *Politico.* Retrieved from http://www.politico.com/story/2014/10/scott-brown-jeanne-shaheen-senate-new-hampshire-elections-112086.html.

Haley, N. (2016, February 20). *Full Text, Video: S.C. Gov. Nikki Haley's Republican State of the Union Response.* Speech presented at State of the Union Address Response. Retrieved February 20, 2016, from http://www.wbur.org/2016/01/12/watch-live-nikki-haley-sotu-response.

Haley, N. (2016, February 15). *Nikki Haley RNC speech (text and video).* Speech presented at Republican National Convention in Florida, Tampa. Retrieved February 15, 2016, from http://www.politico.com/story/2012/08/nikki-haley-rnc-speech-transcript-080376.

Haley, N. (2012). *Can't is not an option.* New York: Sentinel.

Hargreaves, S. (2013). The new American Dream—The myth of the American dream. *CNN.* Retrieved July 14, 2014, from http://money.cnn.com/2013/12/09/news/economy/america- economic-mobility/.

Hariman, R. (1995). *Political style: The artistry of power.* Chicago: University of Chicago Press.

Harris, B. (2014, January 15). Obama, Nobel Laureates urge rise in U.S. minimum wage. *Inter Press Service (IPS).* Retrieved from http://www.ipsnews.net/2014/01/obama-nobel-laureates-urge-rise-u-s-minimum-wage/.

Hart, R. (1997). *Modern rhetorical criticism.* Boston: Allyn & Bacon.

Hayden, S. (2003). Family metaphors and the nation: Promoting a politics of care through the Million Mom March. *Quarterly Journal of Speech, 89,* 196–215. doi: 10:80/0033563032000125313.

Hayes, H. (2005). Sandra Day O'Connor: The center vote that counted. *Perspectives Magazine, 14*(2). Retrieved from http://www.americanbar.org/content/dam/aba/publishing/perspectives_magazine/women_perspectives_SandraDayOconnorFall2005.authcheckdam.pdf.

Hee Lee, M. (2015, September 25). Carly Fiorina's "secretary to CEO" career trajectory (fact checker biography). *Washington Post.* Retrieved from Retrieved from https://www.washingtonpost.com/news/fact-checker/wp/2015/09/25/carly-fiorinas-bogus-secretary-to-ceo-career-trajectory-fact-checker-biography/http://www.bloomberg.com/politics/features/2015-04-30/what-brought-carly-fiorina-down-at-hp-is-her-greatest-2016-asset.

Heller, N. (2015, January 13). Barbara Boxer's California. *The New Yorker.* Retrieved from http://www.newyorker.com/news/news-desk/barbara-boxers-california.

References

Henderson, N-M. (2014, November 19). In the 114th Congress, men will chair 20 house committees. A woman will chair 1. *Washington Post*. Retrieved from http://www.washingtonpost.com/blogs/the-fix/wp/2014/11/19/in-the-114th-congress-men-will-chair-20-house-committees-a-woman-will-chair-1/.

Henderson, N-M. (2014, July 15). Land's clever anti-"war on women" ad didn't do much to close the gender gap in Michigan. *Washington Post*. Retrieved from http://www.washingtonpost.com/blogs/she-the-people/wp/2014/07/15/lands-clever-anti-war-on-women-ad-didnt-do-much-to-close-the-gender-gap-in-michigan/.

Hennebergert, M. (2015, April 30). What brought Carly Fiorina down at HP is her greatest 2016 asset. *Bloomberg Politics*.

Hill, K. (2016, November 9). McMorris Rodgers sets sights on House leadership, praises Trump's call for unity. *The Spokesman Review*. Retrieved from http://www.spokesman.com/stories/2016/nov/09/mcmorris-rodgers-sets-sights-on-house-leadership-p/.

Hohmann, J. (2014, October 5). GOP's midterm mantra: No to domestic violence. *Politico*. Retrieved from http://www.politico.com/story/2014/10/republicans-women-2014-elections-domestic-violence-111608.html.

Hurlburt, H. (2014, November 4). The fear playbook. *Politico*. Retrieved from http://www.politico.com/magazine/story/2014/11/the-fear-playbook-112489.html#.VI9KrtLF92A.

Illing, S. (2016, June 4). The GOP's women problem: Report shows the party of Trump is struggling to elect women to Congress. *Salon*. Retrieved from http://www.pewresearch.org/fact-tank/2016/11/09/why-2016-election-polls-missed-their-mark/.

Isquith, E. (2014, January 22). GOP Congressman: Wives should "voluntarily submit" to their husbands. *Salon*. Retrieved from http://www.salon.com/2014/01/22/gop_congressman_wives_should_voluntarily_submit_to_their_husbands/.

Jacobs, J. (2014a, November 6). 10 reasons Joni Ernst won Iowa's open U.S. Senate seat. *Des Moines Register*. Retrieved from http://www.desmoinesregister.com/story/news/elections/2014/11/05/this-is-why-joni-ernst-won-iowa/18525295/.

Jacobs, J. (2014b, May 8). Sarah Palin lends star power to Joni Ernst. *Des Moines Register*. Retrieved from http://www.desmoinesregister.com/story/news/politics/elections/2014/04/27/sarah-palin-joni-ernst-iowa/8311707/.

Jaffe, A. (2014, October 22). Southerland says he still hasn't read VAWA. *The Hill*. Retrieved from http://thehill.com/blogs/ballot-box/house-races/221604-southerland-says-he-still-hasnt-read-vawa-it-doesnt-matterits.

Jamieson, K.H. (1995). *Beyond the double bind*. New York: Oxford University Press.

Jamieson, K.H. (1988). *Eloquence in an electronic age*. New York: Oxford University Press.

Jan, T. (2013, October 12). Main's Collins suddenly the moderate in the middle. *Boston Globe*. Accessed at http://www.bostonglobe.com/news/nation/2013/10/12/maine-collins-suddenly-moderate-middle/OUmh8v3mJZ30sn4mhzUDvO/story.html.

References

Jarrett, V. (2010, September 17). Closing the wage gap: It's a matter of survival for working families. *Washington Post.* Retrieved from http://www.washingtonpost.com/wp-dyn/content/article/2010/09/16/AR2010091605115.html.

Johnson, D. I. (2005). Feminine style in presidential debate discourse, 1960–2000. *Communication Quarterly, 53,* 3–20. doi: 10.1080/01463370500055814.

Jones, J.M. (2012, November 9). Gender gap in 2012 vote is largest in Gallup's history. *Gallup.* Retrieved from http://www.gallup.com/poll/158588/gender-gap-2012-vote-largest-gallup-history.aspx.

Jones, T. (2014, October 27). Wisconsin voters know Scott Walker—and that's his problem. *Bloomberg News.* Retrieved from http://www.bloomberg.com/news/2014-10-27/wisconsin-voters-know-walker-and-that-s-his-problem.html.

Kaufmann, K.M. (2002). Culture wars, secular realignment, and the gender gap in party identification. *Political Behavior, 24,* 283–307.

Kiefer, F. (2014, October 17). Joni Ernst faces big problem in Iowa Senate race: Women voters. *Christian Science Monitor.* Retrieved from http://www.csmonitor.com/USA/Politics/DC-Decoder/2014/1017/Joni-Ernst-faces-big-problem-in-Iowa-Senate-race-women-voters-video.

Kiley, J. (2014, November 5). As GOP celebrates win, no sign of narrowing gender, age gaps. Pew Research.org. http://www.pewresearch.org/fact-tank/2014/11/05/as-gop-celebrates-win-no-sign-of-narrowing-gender-age-gaps/.

Kilgore, E. (2014a, October 7). NRSC bails on Terri Lynn Land. *Washington Monthly.* Retrieved from http://www.washingtonmonthly.com/political-animal-a/2014_10/nrsc_bails_on_terri_lynn_land052374.php/

Kilgore, E. (2014b, February 26). Playing the green tambourine. *Washington Monthly.* Retrieved from http://www.washingtonmonthly.com/political-animal/2014_02/playing_the_green_tambourine049226.php.

King, L. (2016, November 11). Donald Trump and the Republican women who spurned him face challenges. *USAToday.* Retrieved from http://www.usatoday.com/story/news/politics/2016/11/09/donald-trump-and-republican-women-who-repudiated-him-face-challenges/93562266/.

Koba, M. (2013, July 8). 38 Percent of U.S. workers have no paid sick leave: CNBC. *The Huffington Post.* Retrieved from http://www.huffingtonpost.com/2013/07/08/paid-sick-leave-us-workers-_n_3562419.html.

Koebler, J. (2012, March 20). Condoleeza Rice on education: American Dream on verge of collapse. *U.S. News & World Report.* Retrieved on July 14, 2014, from http://www.usnews.com/news/articles/2012/03/20/condoleezza-rice-on-education-american-dream-on-verge-of-collapse.

Koplowitz, H. (2015, May 4). Who is Carly Fiorina's husband? *International Business Times.* Retrieved from http://www.ibtimes.com/who-carly-fiorinas-husband-meet-frank-fiorina-2016-candidates-biggest-booster-1907199.

Koplowitz, H. (2014, November 5). Midterm 2014 election results: Republicans still have a women problem, exit polling shows. *International Business Times.* Retrieved from http://www.ibtimes.com/midterm-2014-election-results-republicans-still-have-women-problem-exit-polling-shows-1719233.

References

Koplowitz, H. (2014, October 7). Midterm elections 2014: Republicans fight back against "war on women" with domestic violence campaign ads. *International Business Times.* Retrieved from http://www.ibtimes.com/midterm-elections-2014-republicans-fight-back-against-war-women-domestic-violence-campaign-1700521.

Kotkin, J. (2014, November 5). The demographics that sank the Democrats in the midterm elections. *Forbes.* Retrieved from http://www.forbes.com/sites/joelkotkin/2014/11/05/the-demographics-that-sank-the-democrats-in-the-mid-term-elections/.

Kroll, A. (2014). Is New Mexico Gov. Susana Martinez the next Sarah Palin? Petty. Vindictive. Weak on policy. And yet she's being hailed as the Republican Party's great new hope. *Mother Jones.* Retrieved on July 14, 2014, from http://www.motherjones.com/politics/2014/04/governor-susana-martinez-new-mexico-2016.

Kruse, M. (2015, November 1). "I have buried a child": How Carly Fiorina has made the death of her addicted stepdaughter a central story in her campaign. *Politico.* Retrieved from http://www.politico.com/magazine/story/2015/10/gop-debate-carly-fiorina-2016-i-buried-a-child-213306.

Kumar, A., & Vozella, L. (2012, February 22). McDonnell, Virginia Republicans back off mandatory invasive ultrasounds. *Washington Post.* Retrieved from http://www.washingtonpost.com/local/dc-politics/mcdonnell-virginia-republicans-back-off-mandatory-invasive-ultrasounds/2012/02/22/gIQAUmzEUR_story.html.

Kucinich, J. (2013, October 11). Rara avis—a moderate—suggests way out of crisis. *Washington Post.* Retrieved from http://www.washingtonpost.com/politics/2013/10/11/ff2d29e0-32c0-11e3-8627-c5d7de0a046b_story.html.

Lakoff, G. (1996). *Moral Politics: What conservatives know that liberals don't.* Chicago: University of Chicago Press.

Land, T. L. (2014, April 23). The real war on women [Blog post]. *Terri Lynn Land's Blog.* Retrieved from http://terrilynnland.com.

Landsbaum, C. (2016, October 19). The debate audience literally laughed when Donald Trump says he respects women. *New York Magazine.* Retrieved from http://nymag.com/thecut/2016/10/the-debate-crowd-laughed-when-trump-said-he-respected-women.html.

Larsen, C. (2001). *Persuasion: Reception and responsibility.* Belmont, CA: Wadsworth.

Lavender, P. (2014, September 12). Rep. Steve Southerland wonders if his female opponent has "ever been to a lingerie shower." *The Huffington Post.* Retrieved from http://www.huffingtonpost.com/2014/09/12/steve-southerland-lingerie_n_5812378.html.

Lazar, A. (2014, July 10). Wealthy Senate candidate paid very low tax rate. *The Huffington Post.* Retrieved from http://www.huffingtonpost.com/2014/07/10/terri-lynn-land-tax_n_5574438.html.

Leibovich. M. (2014, November 2). If pigs could vote. *New York Times Magazine* 11.

Levy, G. (2016, January 21). Fiorina campaign denied "ambush" of pre-schoolers.

References

US News & World Report. Retrieved from http://www.usnews.com/news/articles/2016-01-21/fiorina-campaign-denies-ambush-of-pre-schoolers.

Lewis, T. (2011). Winning woman suffrage in the masculine west: Abigail Scott Duniway's frontier myth. *Western Journal of Communication, 75,* 127–147. doi: 10.1080/10570314.2011.553877.

Liptak, K. (2012, September 27). Akin: McCaskill more "ladylike" in last election. *CNN Politics.* Retrieved from http://politicalticker.blogs.cnn.com/2012/09/27/akin-mccaskill-more-ladylike-in-last-election/.

Lithwick, D. (2012, July 17). Virginia Republicans try to shut down abortion clinics once again. *Slate.* Retrieved from http://www.huffingtonpost.com/2013/07/15/virginia-abortion-clinic_n_3599262.html.

Louden, A., & McCauliff, K. (2004). The "authentic candidate": Extending candidate image assessment. In Hacker, K., (Ed.), *Presidential Candidate Images* (85–103). Lanham, MD: Rowman & Littlefield.

Lusane, C. (2006). *Colin Powell and Condoleezza Rice: Foreign policy, race, and the new American century.* Westport, CT: Praeger.

Lynch, J.Q. (2016, July). Ernst says she declined to be Trump's running mate. *The Gazette.* Retrieved from http://www.thegazette.com/subject/news/government/elections/ernst-says-trump-invited-her-to-be-running-mate-20161110.

MacGillis, A. (2014, November 4). Joni Ernst is one of 2014's most extreme candidates—but you wouldn't know it from Iowa's press coverage. *The New Republic.* Retrieved from http://www.newrepublic.com/article/120118/joni-ernst-capitalized-broken-media-landscape-iowa.

MacKinnon, C. (1987). *Feminism unmodified.* Cambridge: Harvard University Press.

Manchester, J. (2016, March 9). Ex-rival Fiorina endorses Cruz, "horrified" by Trump. *CNN Politics.* Retrieved from http://www.cnn.com/2016/03/09/politics/ted-cruz-carly-fiorina-endorsement-florida/.

Manza, J., & Brooks, C. (1998). The gender gap in U.S. presidential elections: When? Why? Implications? *American Journal of Sociology, 103,* 1235–66.

Marcotte, A. (2014, January 31). The GOP's latest ploy: Flatter married women. *The Daily Beast.* Retrieved from http://www.thedailybeast.com/articles/2014/01/31/the-gop-s-latest-ploy-flatter-married-women.html.

Marcotte, A. (2014, July 29). A female candidate in Michigan won't help Republicans win women voters. *Slate.* Retrieved from http://www.slate.com/blogs/xx_factor/2014/07/29/terri_lynn_land_s_michigan_senate_race_republicans_can_t_beat_the_war_on.html.

Marilley, S.M. (1996). *Woman suffrage and the origins of liberal feminism in the United States, 1820–1920.* Cambridge: Harvard University Press. doi: 10.4159/harvard.9780674431331.

Martinez, S. (2012, August 29). 2012 Republican National Convention speech. Tampa, FL. Retrieved July 14, 2014, from https://www.youtube.com/watch?v=NEewz5v04mU.

McCarver, V. (2012). The new oxymoron: Socially conservative feminism. *Women & Language, 35,* 57–77.

McDermott, D. (2013, October 16). Maine Sen. Collins takes charge in shutdown

References

compromise. Seacoastonlinewww. Retrieved from http://www.seacoastonline.com/article/20131016/News/310160356.

McDermott, M., & Feldman, S. (2014, November 5). 2014 Midterm elections: Why Republicans may have had an edge. *CBS News*. Retrieved from http://www.cbsnews.com/news/2014-midterm-elections-why-republicans-may-have-had-an-edge/.

McDonough, K. (2014, November 5). Debbie Downer's official guide to women and the 2014 elections. *Salon*. Retrieved from http://www.salon.com/2014/11/05/debbie_downers_official_guide_to_women_and_the_2014_elections/.

McDonough, K. (2014, April 17). GOP's new class of jokers: Meet the "rising stars" of the dumbest rebrand ever. *Salon*. Retrieved from http://www.salon.com/2014/04/17/gops_new_class_of_jokers_meet_the_rising_stars_of_the_dumbest_rebrand_ever/.

McGee, M. C. (1975). In search of "The People": A rhetorical alternative. *Quarterly Journal of Speech, 61*, 235–249.

McMorris Rodgers, C. (2016, May 18). Why I voted for Donald Trump. *Facebook*. Retrieved from https://www.facebook.com/cathyforcongress/posts/10156957539010323.

McPherson, L. (2016, September 21). McMorris Rodgers to host Carly Fiorina and fundraiser Wednesday. *RollCall*. Retrieved from https://www.rollcall.com/news/mcmorris-rodgers-host-carly-fiorina-fundraiser-Wednesday.

McVeigh, K. (2012, February 21). Virginia pre-abortion ultrasound could constitute sex crime, Democrats warn. *The Guardian*. Retrieved from http://www.theguardian.com/world/2012/feb/21/virginia-abortion-bill-could-constitute-rape.

Mercer, A., Deane, C., & McGeeney, K. (2016, November 9). Why 2016 election polls missed their mark. *Pew Research Center*. Retrieved from http://www.pewresearch.org/fact-tank/2016/11/09/why-2016-election-polls-missed-their-mark/.

Messina-Dysert, G. (2014, April 29). Why we still need a feminist agenda. *The Huffington Post*. Retrieved from http://www.huffingtonpost.com/gina-messinadysert/why-we-still-need-a-femin_b_5232359.html.

Miller, C.C. (2016, November 12). Why women did not unite to vote against Donald Trump. *New York Times*. Retrieved from http://www.nytimes.com/2016/11/13/upshot/why-women-did-not-unite-to-vote-against-donald-trump.html.

Miller, J. (2014, October 7). Ad is offensive, false, Scott Brown tells Jeanne Shaheen. *Boston Globe*. Retrieved from http://www.bostonglobe.com/metro/2014/10/07/tough-new-jeanne-shaheen-questions-scott-brown-abortion-rights-credentials/fdpPaJKJcDImUFNX2YQD0K/story.html.

Miller, Z. J. (2014, January 23). Huckabee: GOP waging a "war for women." *Time*. Retrieved from http://swampland.time.com/2014/01/23/huckabee-gop-waging-war-for-women/.

Mohammed, A. (2011, August 31). Exclusive: Condoleezza Rice fires back at Cheney memoir. *Reuters*. Retrieved from http://www.reuters.com/article/2011/08/31/us-usa-rice-cheney-idUSTRE77U6GN20110831.

References

Moorhead, M. (2012). Mitt Romney says achievement gap in Massachusetts improved on his watch. Politifactwww. Retrieved from April 10, 2016: http://www.politifact.com/truth-o-meter/statements/2012/jul/18/mitt-romney/romney-says-achievement-gap-massachusetts-improved/.

Mundy, L. (2014, November 6). 100 women in Congress? So what? *Politico*. Retrieved from http://www.politico.com/magazine/story/2014/11/100-women-in-congress-so-what-112663.html.

Murphy, P. (2014, December 10). Surprise! the GOP closed the gender gap. *The Daily Beast*. http://www.thedailybeast.com/articles/2014/12/10/how-republicans-won-the-war-on-women.html.

Murray, S. (2015, October 20). Carly Fiorina's fall. *CNN Politics*. Retrieved from http://www.cnn.com/2015/10/17/politics/carly-fiorina-poll-numbers/.

National Organization for Women. (2015). Our issues. Retrieved from http://now.org/about/our-issues/.

National Partnership on Working Families (2013, April). *Working women need paid sick days: Fact sheet*. Retrieved from http://www.nationalpartnership.org/research-library/work-family/psd/working-women-need-paid-sick-days.pdf.

National Republican Senate Committee (NRSC). (2014, August 19). Duty, Honor, Iowa [Video file]. Retrieved from https://www.youtube.com/watch?v=PcYLVcungss.

Newton-Small, J. (2014, October 14). Vulnerable Democrats run away from Obama. *Time*. Retrieved from http://time.com/3507165/alison-grimes-barack-obama-midterm-elections/.

Newton-Small, J. (2014, August 17). Why Joni Ernst isn't "Iowa's Sarah Palin." *Time*. Retrieved from http://time.com/3132793/why-joni-ernst-isnt-iowas-sarah-palin/.

Newton-Small, J. (2013, October 16). Women are the only adults left in Washington. *Time*. Retrieved from http://swampland.time.com/2013/10/16/women-are-the-only-adults-left-in-washington/.

Noble, J. (2016, July 19). Ernst expands profile in convention speech. *Des Moines Register*. Retrieved from http://www.desmoinesregister.com/story/news/politics/2016/07/19/ernst-expands-profile-convention-speech/87270186/.

Nocera, J. (2014, May 10). Where the girls are. *New York Times*. Retrieved from http://www.nytimes.com/2014/05/10/opinion/collins-where-the-girls-are.html.

Norrander, B. (2008). The history of the gender gap. In Whitaker, L.D. (Ed.), *Voting the gender gap* (9–32). Urbana: University of Illinois Press.

Okin, S. M. (1989). *Gender, justice and the family*. New York: Basic Books.

Olasky, M. (1992). *The tragedy of American compassion*. Wheaton, Illinois: Crossway.

Ontheissues.org (2014, March 15). Republican Party on gun control. Retrieved on July 14, 2014, from http://www.ontheissues.org/celeb/republican_party_gun_control.htm.

O'Reilly, A. (2009). "I envision a future in which maternal thinkers are respected and self-respecting": The legacy of Sara Ruddick's "Maternal Thinking." *Women's Studies Quarterly, 37*, 295–298.

Palmer, A. (2014). GOP solution to "war on women": Women. *Politico*. Retrieved

References

from http://www.politico.com/story/2014/04/gop-war-on-women-105453_Page2.html.
Panama City News Herald [Staff]. (2014, October 29). Letter: Send Southerland packing. *Panama City News Herald*. Retrieved from http://www.newsherald.com/opinions/letters-to-the-editor/letter-send-southerland-packing-1.393375.
Parker, A. (2013, February 28). House renews Violence Against Women measure. *New York Times*. Retrieved from http://www.nytimes.com/2013/03/01/us/politics/congress-passes-reauthorization-of-violence-against-women-act.html?pagewanted=all.
Parker, K. (2014, January 15). Parker: Republicans continue their war on women. *Houston Chronicle*. Retrieved from http://www.chron.com/opinion/outlook/article/Parker-Republicans-continue-their-war-on-women-5174990.php.
Parry-Giles, S.J., and Parry-Giles, T. (1996, December). Gendered politics and presidential image construction: A reassessment of the "feminine style." *Communication Monographs, 63*, 337–353.
Parry-Giles, T. (2010). Resisting a "treacherous piety": Issues, images, and public policy deliberation in presidential campaigns, *Rhetoric & Public Affairs, 13*, 37–64.
Parti, T. (2014, November 4). Gwen Graham squeaks by Steve Southerland in Florida. *Politico*. Retrieved from http://www.politico.com/story/2014/11/election-results-gwen-graham-steve-southerland-florida-112525.html.
Pateman, C. (1988). *The sexual contract*. Stanford: Stanford University Press.
Peeples, J. A., & DeLuca, K.M. (2006). Gendered politics and presidential image construction: A reassessment of the "feminine style." *Communication Monographs, 63*, 337–353.
Peters, G. (2014, January 29). U.S. Rep. Gary Peters: Congress' next steps in the fight for equal pay. *Detroit Free Press*. Retrieved from http://archive.freep.com/article/20140129/.OPINION05/301290046/gary-peters-equal-pay-women-rights-gender-equality-michigan-congress
Peters, J., and Haberman, M. (2016, July 6). Senator Joni Ernst is given prime speaking slot at GOP convention. *New York Times*. Retrieved from http://nyti.ms/29y9kJG.
Phillip, A. (2015, December 14). What happened to Carly Fiorina? *Washington Post*, December 14, 2015 Retrieved from https://www.washingtonpost.com/politics/what-happened-to-carly-fiorina/2015/12/14/78bf2da8-a0e2-11e5-8728-1af6af208198_story.html.
Pratto, F., & Stallworth, L.M., & Sidanius, J. (1997). The gender gap: Differences in political attitudes and social dominance orientation. *British Journal of Social Psychology, 36*, 49–68.
Przybyla, H.M. (2015, September 23). Carly Fiorina's gender may not be asset in 2016 race. *USA Today*. Retrieved from http://www.usatoday.com/story/news/politics/elections/2015/09/23/carly-fiorina-women-voters-2016/72625346/
Quindlen, A. (2008, September). Can you say "sexist"? *Newsweek*. Retrieved from www.newsweek.com/id/157543.
Ramazanoglu, C. (1989). *Feminism and the contradictions of oppression*. New York: Routledge.

References

Rankin, L. (2014, May 2). The lie of the GOP's response to the "war on women." *Talking Points Memo*. Retrieved from http://talkingpointsmemo.com/cafe/the-lie-of-the-gop-s-response-to-the-war-on-women.

Reeve, E. (2013, May 6). The ghost of Sandra Fluke is haunting Rush Limbaugh's mega-deal. *The Wire*. Retrieved from http://www.thewire.com/politics/2013/05/rush-limbaugh-contract-sandra-fluke/64904/.

Reilly, K. (2016, October 8). Carly Fiorina: Donald Trump Should "Step Aside" as Presidential Nominee. *Time*. Retrieved from http://time.com/4523922/carly-fiorina-donald-trump-mike-pence/.

Reinhard, B., & Peterson, K. (2014, April 18). GOP seeks to erase "war on women" label. *Wall Street Journal*. Retrieved from http://online.wsj.com/articles/SB10001424052702304626304579510031992699894.

Reston, M. (2014, November 7). In Iowa, GOP's Joni Ernst broke a gender barrier on her own terms. *Los Angeles Times*. Retrieved from http://www.latimes.com/nation/politics/la-na-joni-ernst-women-20141108-story.html.

Reston, M. (2014, January 30). Democratic women push President Obama's increase in minimum wage. *Los Angeles Times*. Retrieved from http://articles.latimes.com/2014/jan/30/news/la-pn-democratic-women-push-minimum-wage-20140130.

Rice, C. (2010). Condoleezza Rice: A memoir of my extraordinary, ordinary family and me. New York: Delacorte Press.

Ridge, S. (2015, January 23). Meet the intriguing Republican women taking on Hillary Clinton. *The Telegraph*. Retrieved from http://www.telegraph.co.uk/women/womens-life/11362262/Republican-women-taking-on-Hillary-Clinton-for-female-vote.html.

Rodino-Colocina, M. (2012). Man up, woman down: Mama Grizzlies and anti-feminism during the year of the (conservative) woman and beyond. *Women and Language*, 35(1), 79–95.

Rogan, J. (2016, November 11). Trump team discussion Ayotte for defense secretary. *Washington Post*. Retrieved from https://www.washingtonpost.com/news/josh-rogin/wp/2016/11/11/trump-team-discussing-ayotte-for-defense-secretary/?utm_term=.027d1a42c9b8.

Rogers, E. (2015, January 20). The Insiders: Why Democrats are so frightened of Joni Ernst. *Washington Post*. Retrieved from http://www.washingtonpost.com/blogs/post-partisan/wp/2015/01/20/the-insiders-why-democrats-are-so-frightened-of-joni-ernst/.

Rosin, H. (2014, April 30). The war on women has lost its purpose. *Miami Herald*. Retrieved from http://article.wn.com/view/2014/04/30/Rosin_War_on_women_has_lost_its_purpose/.

Rountree, III, J. C. (1998). Coming to terms with Kenneth Burke's pentad. *American Communication Journal*, 1(3). Retrieved April 15, 2007, from http://www.acjournal.org/holdings/vol1/iss3/burke/rountree.html.

Rubin, J. (2014, May 22). How is Ernst doing it? *Washington Post*. Retrieved from http://www.washingtonpost.com/blogs/right-turn/wp/2014/05/22/how-is-ernst-doing-it/.

Rucker, P., & Balz, D. (2014, May 11). How Joni Ernst's ad about "castrating hogs"

References

transformed Iowa's U.S. Senate race. *Washington Post.* Retrieved from http://www.washingtonpost.com/politics/how-joni-ernsts-ad-about-castrating-hogs-transformed-iowas-us-senate-race/2014/05/11/c02d1804-d85b-11e3-95d3-3bcd77cd4e11_story.html.

Ruddick, S. (1989). *Maternal thinking: Toward a practice of peace.* Boston: Beacon Press.

Ryals, M. (2016, November 8). U.S. Rep. Cathy McMorris Rodgers retrains 5th district seat. *Inlander.* Retrieved from http://www.inlander.com/Bloglander/archives/2016/11/08/us-rep-cathy-mcmorris-rodgers-retains-5th-district-seat.

Saleton, W. (2013, January 14). The party of rape. *Slate.* Retrieved from http://www.slate.com/articles/health_and_science/human_nature/2013/01/phil_gingrey_todd_akin_and_richard_mourdock_the_gop_s_rape_problem_is_spreading.html.

Sanchez, L. (2013). Role models: Winning the Hispanic Vote: What Republicans can learn from Chris Christie and Susana Martinez. *The Ripon Forum.* Retrieved on July 14, 2014, from http://www.riponsociety.org/article/role-models/.

Sargent, G. (2014, May 19). The GOP Senate candidates: Climate skeptics and believers in personhood. *Washington Post.* Retrieved from http://www.washingtonpost.com/blogs/plum-line/wp/2014/05/19/the-gop-senate-candidates-climate-skeptics-and-believers-in-personhood/.

Sarlin, B. (2014, July 28). Michigan Senate race a rare bright spot for Democrats. *MSNBC.* Retrieved from http://www.msnbc.com/msnbc/michigan-senate-race-rare-bright-spot-democrats.

Sarlin, B. & Seitz-Wald, A. (2014, November 7). Why the Democrats lost, according to everyone. *Reuters.* Retrieved from http://www.msnbc.com/msnbc/why-the-democrats-lost-midterms-according-everyone.

Scher, A. The new face of Republican women in congress. *The Progressive.* Retrieved from http://www.progressive.org/news/2015/03/188022/new-face-republican-women-congress.

Schlesinger, R. (2012, August 20). Todd Akin, what is "legitimate rape"? *U.S. News & World Report.* Retrieved from http://www.usnews.com/opinion/blogs/robert-schlesinger/ 2012/08/20/todd-akin-what-is-legitimate-rape.

Schow, A. (2014, April 23). GOP senate candidate Terri Lynn Land describes "the real war on women" in America. *Washington Examiner.* Retrieved from http://www.washingtonexaminer.com/gop-senate-candidate-terri-lynn-land-describes-the-real-war-on-women-in-america/article/2547625.

Schow, A. (2014, October 16). A Republican plan to combat the "war on women" narrative that might actually work. *Washington Examiner.* Retrieved from http://www.washingtonexaminer.com/a-republican-plan-to-combat-the-war-on-women-narrative-that-might-actually-work/article/2554889.

Schreiber, R. *Righting Feminism: Conservative women and American politics.* New York: Oxford University Press, 2008. doi: 10.1093/acprof:oso/9780195 331813.001.0001.

Schultheis, E. (2014, August 21). Policy statements complicate Joni Ernst's

References

personality-driven Iowa Senate run. *The National Journal*. Retrieved from http://www.nationaljournal.com/politics/policy-statements-threaten-joni-ernst-s-personality-driven-iowa-senate-run-20140821.

Schultz, M. (2014, May 6). Dem ad accuses GOP Senate candidate Land of moving women backward. *Detroit News*. Retrieved from http://article.wn.com/view/2014/05/06/Dem_ad_accuses_GOP_Senate_candidate_Land_of_moving_women_bac/.

Schwartz, I. (2014, November 3). Joni Ernst: Democrats "believe you can't be a real woman if you're conservative." *Real Clear Politics*. Retrieved from http://www.realclearpolitics.com/video/2014/11/03/joni_ernst_democrats_believe_you_cant_be_a_real_woman_if_youre_conservative.html.

Schweitzer, J. (2014, November 4). The price of failure and rise of extremism: How Democrats blew it. *Huffington Post*. Retrieved from http://www.huffingtonpost.com/jeff-schweitzer/the-price-of-failure-and_b_6099752.html.

Scocca, T. (2012, November 7). Eighty-eight percent of Romney voters were white. Retrieved from http://www.slate.com/articles/news_and_politics/scocca/2012/11/mitt_romney_white_voters_the_gop_candidate_s_race_based_monochromatic_campaign.html.

Seelye, S. (2016, November 9). Maggie Hassan unseats Kelly Ayotte in New Hampshire Senate race. *New York Times*. Retrieved from http://www.nytimes.com/2016/11/09/us/politics/new-hampshire-senate-hassan-ayotte.html.

Sen. Collins: "There is a group in the common sense caucus that's willing to lead." (2013, October 18). *CBSlocal*. Retrieved from http://washington.cbslocal.com/2013/10/18/sen-collins-there-is-a-group-in-the-common-sense-caucus-thats-willing-to-lead/.

Serwer, A. (2012, March 20). Republicans are blocking the Violence Against Women Act. *Mother Jones*. Retrieved from http://www.motherjones.com/politics/2012/03/republicans-violence-against-women-act.

Sheinin, D., Thompson, K., & McDonals, S.N. (2016, Jan 27). Betty Friedan to Beyonce: Today's generation embraces feministm on its own terms. *Washington Post*. Retrieved from https://www.washingtonpost.com/national/feminism/betty-friedan-to-beyonce-todays-generation-embraces-feminism-on-its-own-terms/2016/01/27/ab480e74-8e19-11e5-ae1f-af46b7df8483_story.html.

Shen, A. (2014, March 29). Inside the GOP's attempt to change its "war on women" image. *Think Progress*. http://thinkprogress.org/election/2014/03/29/3419593/inside-the-gops-attempt-to-change-its-war-on-women-image/.

Shepardson, D. (2014, April 10). Obama rips Terri Lynn Land on pay issue. *Detroit News*. Retrieved from http://www.detroitnews.com/story/news/politics/politics/2014/09/23/land-mutal-funds-senate/16107677/.

Shreiber, R. (2008). *Righting feminism: Conservative women and American politics*. Oxford: Oxford University Press.

Sigelman, L., Sigelman, C.K., & Fowler, C. A bird of a different feather? An experimental investigation of physical attractiveness and the electability of female candidates. *Social Psychology Quarterly, 50*, 32–45. doi: 147.226.190.79.

References

Silver, N. (2016, April 27) Can Carly Fiorina Save Ted Cruz's Candidacy? *A FiveThirtyEight Chat*. Retrieved from http://fivethirtyeight.com/features/can-carly-fiorina-save-ted-cruzs-candidacy/.

Sims, J. (2011, December 5). Obama administration reverses Bush policy on affirmative action. *Peoplesworld.org*. Retrieved from http://peoplesworld.org/obama-administration-reverses-bush-policy-on-affirmative-action/.

Sioux City Journal. (2014, October 17). Joni Ernst meets with SCJ Editorial Board [Video file]. *Sioux City Journal*. Retrieved from http://siouxcityjournal.com/news/video-joni-ernst-meets-with-scj-editorial-board/youtube_236a7a58-8d9c-5370-bf72-031cb8ea99fb.html.

Snowdon, Q. (2014, November 5). After wildly expensive race, Coffman wins re-election to 4th term in Congress. *Aurora Sentinel*. Retrieved from http://www.aurorasentinel.com/news/coffman-wins-re-election-2014/.

Solomon, M. (1988). Ideology as rhetorical constraint: The anarchist agitation of "Red Emma" Goldman. *Quarterly Journal of Speech, 74*, 184–200. doi: 10.1080/00335638809383836.

Soltis-Anderson, K. (April 15, 2014). Win women, win the midterms. *The Daily Beast*. Retrieved from http://www.thedailybeast.com/articles/2014/04/15/win-women-win-the-midterms.html.

Sommers, C.H., and Rosen, C. (2015, October 28). How Carly Fiorina is redefining feminism step one: Less whining. *Politico*. Retrieved from http://www.politico.com/magazine/story/2015/10/carly-fiorina-feminism-213304.

Sonmez, Felicia. (2012, April 27). Romney to college students: Pursue your dreams, even if you have to borrow to do so. *Washington Post*. Retrieved on July 14, 2014, from http://www.washingtonpost.com/blogs/post-politics/post/romney-to-college-students-pursue-your-dreams-even-if-you-have-to-borrow-to-do-so/2012/04/27/gIQAFGM8lT_blog.html.

Southerland for Congress. (2014). *Advocate* [Television commercial]. Retrieved from http://youtu.be/fnqFSB77OMk.

Southern Poverty Law Center (2015, July 16). Hate & Extremism. Retrieved from http://www.splcenter.org/what-we-do/hate-and-extremism

Spangler, T. (2014, July 17). Where did Senate candidate Terri Lynn Land's $3 million come from? *Detroit Free Press*. Retrieved from http://www.freep.com/article/20140717/NEWS06/307170034/.

Starr, A. (2004, September). Dixie Chicks: A new kind of Democrat is in the South and she's no shrinking violet. *Atlantic Monthly, 294*, 34–37.

Steenland, S. (2013, October 23). Faith in values: Women senators prove collaboration is better than conflict. *Americanprogress.org*. Retrieved from https://www.americanprogress.org/issues/religion/news/2013/10/23/77836/women-senators-prove-collaboration-is-better-than-conflict/.

Stelter, B. (2016, November 10). "The polls clearly got it wrong": The autopsy will take months. *CNNMoney*. Retrieved from http://money.cnn.com/2016/11/10/media/election-day-polls/.

Stob, P. (2008, May 1). "Terministic screens," social constructionism, and the language of experience: Kenneth Burke's utilization of William James." *Philosophy and Rhetoric, 42* (2), 131–152.

References

Stokols, E. (2013, February 27). Democrats take issue with Mike Coffman's move to the middle. *Fox 31 Denver*. Retrieved from http://kdvr.com/2013/02/27/democrats-take-issue-with-mike-coffmans-move-to-the-middle/.

Stolberg, S. G. (2014, October 28). Joni Ernst's playbook, for women to win men's vote. *New York Times*. Retrieved from http://www.nytimes.com/2014/10/29/us/iowans-playbook-for-women-to-win-mens-vote.html?_r=0.

Sullivan, D. (1998). Images of a breakthrough women candidate: Dianne Feinstein's 1990, 1992, and 1994 campaign television advertisements. *Women's Studies in Communication, 21*(1), 7–26.

Sullivan, P. (1989). The 1984 Vice-Presidential Debate: A case study of female and male framing in political campaigns. *Communication Quarterly, 37*(4), 329–343. doi: 10.1080/01463378909385554.

Susanna Martinez. (n.d.). *Susanna Martinez Bio*. Retrieved from http://www.susanamartinez.com/bio/.

Taibbi, M. (2012). Greed and debt: The true story of Mitt Romney and Bain Capital. *Rolling Stone Magazine*. Retreieved from http://www.rollingstone.com/politics/news/greed-and-debt-the-true- story-of-mitt-romney-and-bain-capital-20120829#ixzz45T4uwWix.

Talbot, M. (2014, November 10). Midterm anxieties. *The New Yorker*. Retrieved from http://www.newyorker.com/magazine/2014/11/10/midterm-anxieties.

Terkel, A. (2012, April 6). Scott Walker quietly repeals Wisconsin equal pay law. *The Huffington Post*. Retrieved from http://www.huffingtonpost.com/2012/04/06/scott-walker-wisconsin-equal-pay-law_n_1407329.html.

Terrell, S. (2013). Governor's bipartisan portrayal riles some state Democrats. *Santa Fe New Mexican*. Retrieved on July 14, 2014, from http://www.santafenewmexican.com/news/legislature/governor-s-bipartisan-portrayal-riles-some-state-democrats/article_963f1218–8fd1–53c3-b1aa-f9054bc47fbd.html.

Trevor, M.C. (1999). Political socialization, party identification, and the gender gap. *Public Opinion Quarterly, 63*, 62–89.

Tumulty, K. (2014, November 10). Republicans make inroads with women voters. *Washington Post*. Retrieved from http://www.washingtonpost.com/politics/republicans-make-inroads-with-women-voters/2014/11/10/5bb42052-6695-11e4-836c-83bc4f26eb67_story.html.

Unlocking Potential Project. Accessed June 22, 2015, from http://www.up-project.org/strategy.html.

Valenti, J. (2016, November 15). The empowerment trap: Ivanka Trump and the art of co-opting feminism. *The Guardian*. Retrieved from https://www.theguardian.com/world/2016/nov/15/ivanka-trump-feminism-us-election.

Valenti, J. (2014, November 6). 2014 was an election of firsts for Republican women. But it wasn't a "win" for women at all. *The Guardian*. Retrieved from http://www.theguardian.com/commentisfree/2014/nov/06/2014-election-republican-women-record-numbers.

Vasby-Anderson, K., & Horn Sheeler, K. (2005). *Governing codes: Gender, metaphor, and political identity*. New York: Lexington Books.

Vitali, A. (2015, September 22). Carly Fiorina talks Trump and religion, rocks

References

for Fallon on "Tonight Show." NBCNewswww. Retrieved from http://www.nbcnews.com/politics/politics-news/carly-fiorina-talks-trump-religion-rocks-fallon-tonight-show-n431346.

Vorhees, J. (2014, November 5). Joni makes 'em squeal: The country's most conservative Senate candidate scores a huge victory for the GOP. What she'll do in Washington is anyone's guess. *Slate.* Retrieved from http://www.slate.com/articles/news_and_politics/politics/2014/11/joni_ernst_iowa_senate_the_country_s_most_conservative_senate_candidate.html.

Vorhees, J. (2012, October 24). Slatest PM: The as-God-intended edition. *Slate.* Retrieved from http://www.slate.com/blogs/the_slatest/2012/10/24/slatest_pm_the_as_god_intended_edition.html.

Vozzella, L. (2013, January 23). Cuccinelli backed failed bill to ease ultrasound rule. *Washington Post.* Retrieved from http://www.washingtonpost.com/local/va-politics/cuccinelli-backed-failed-bill-to-ease-ultrasound-rule/2013/01/28/fa47f5b8-698f-11e2-ada3-d86a4806d5ee_story.html.

Wadley, W. (2014, October 17). Candidates tout distinctions in turbulent Senate race. *NBC Montana.* Retrieved from http://www.nbcmontana.com/news/candidates-tout-distinctions-in-turbulent-senate-race/29208714.

Walsh, J. (2013, September 25). GOP's economic war on women about to explode. *Salon.* Retrieved from http://www.salon.com/2013/09/25/gop%E2%80%99s_economic_war_on_women_about_to_explode/.

Walsh, K. T. (2014, November 5). Obama's unpopularity affected Democrats in midterm elections. *U.S. News & World Report.* Retrieved from http://www.usnews.com/news/articles/2014/11/05/obamas-unpopularity-affected-democrats-in-mid-term-elections.

Wander, P. (1983). The ideological turn in criticism. *Central States Speech Journal, 34,* 1–18. doi: 10.1080/10510978309368110.

The Week (Staff). (2012, March 9). Rush Limbaugh vs. Sandra Fluke: A timeline. *The Week.* Retrieved from http://theweek.com/article/index/225214/rush-limbaugh-vs-sandra-fluke-a-timeline.

Weisman, J. (2014, April 8). Democrats use pay issue in bid for women's vote. *New York Times.* Retrieved from http://www.nytimes.com/2014/04/09/us/politics/democrats-use-pay-issue-in-bid-for-womens-vote.html.

Weisman, J., & Parker, A. (2014, November 4). Riding wave of discontent, G.O.P. takes Senate. *New York Times.* Retrieved from http://www.nytimes.com/2014/11/05/us/politics/midterm-elections.html?_r=0.

Weisman, J., & Steinhauer, J. (2013, October 14). Senate women lead in effort to find accord. *New York Times.* Retrieved from http://www.nytimes.com/2013/10/15/us/senate-women-lead-in-effort-to-find-accord.html?pagewanted=all&_r=0.

Wendell, S. (1987). A (qualified) defense of liberal feminism. *Hypatia, 2*(2), 65–93. doi: 10.1111/j.1527-2001.1987.tb01066.x.

Whelehan, I. (1995). *Modern Feminist Thought.* New York: New York University Press.

Whitaker, L.D. (2008). Introduction. In Whitaker, L.D. (Ed.), *Voting the gender gap* (1–7). Urbana: University of Illinois Press.

References

The White House, Office of the Press Secretary. (2012, July 13). Remarks by the President at a campaign event in Roanoke, Virginia [Press release]. Retrieved from http://www.whitehouse.gov/the-press-office/2012/07/13/remarks-president-campaign-event-roanoke-virginia.

Wicks, B. (2013, June 21). Why the GOP has lost the women's vote for 2014 and beyond. *The Daily Beast.* Retrieved from http://www.thedailybeast.com/witw/articles/2013/06/21/why-the-gop-has-lost-the-women-s-vote-for-2014-and-beyond.html.

Will, G. F. (2014, September 26). Joni Ernst's Iowa campaign makes quick work of the "war on women." *Washington Post.* Retrieved from http://www.washingtonpost.com/opinions/george-will-joni-ernst-and-bruce-braley-battle-in-iowa-senate-race/2014/09/26/fdeefde0-44e1-11e4-b47c-f5889e061e5f_story.html.

Will, G. F. (2014, April 13). A counter for Michigan hysterics. *Sentinel & Enterprise.* Retrieved from http://www.sentinelandenterprise.com/columnists/ci_25558073/george-will-counter-michigan-hysterics.

Winfrey, O. (2011). Oprah presents: Master Class: Condoleezza Rice. Chicago, IL. Retrieved from http://www.youtube.com/watch?v=0MLcfFEFRqs, http://www.youtube.com/watch?v=_UB9xpnHrM4, & http://www.youtube.com/watch?v=QMwhp600aqE

Winfrey, O. (2002, February). Oprah talks to Condoleezza Rice. *Oprah Magazine.* Retrieved from http://www.oprah.com/omagazine/Oprah-Interviews-Condoleezza-Rice.

Wood, C. (2014, April 1). Will women buy the "War on women" Obama lie? *The New American.* Retrieved from http://www.thenewamerican.com/reviews/opinion/item/18084-will-womend-buy-this-obama-lie.

Woods, A. (2014a, April 8). Female GOP Senate candidate said women want job flexibility more than equal pay. *The Huffington Post.* Retrieved from http://www.huffingtonpost.com/2014/04/08/terri-lynn-land-equal-pay_n_5113386.html.

Woods, A. (2014b, April 22). GOP Senate candidate argues she isn't waging a war on women because she's a woman. *The Huffington Post.* Retrieved from http://www.huffingtonpost.com/2014/04/22/terri-lynn-land_n_5191636.html.

Zornick, G. (2013, May 7). The GOP's new outreach to women: It's a trap. *The Nation.* Retrieved from http://www.thenation.com/blog/174210/gops-new-outreach-women-its-tra.

Zremski, J. (2014, May 31). GOP wages war on "war on women." *Buffalo News.* Retrieved from http://www.buffalonews.com/city-region/washington-politics/gop-wages-war-on-war-on-women-20140531.

Index

abortion 2, 8, 11, 14–16, 21, 32, 35–36, 38–40, 71, 125, 148
Akin, Todd 14–15
american dream 35, 69, 82, 91–92, 94, 98, 105–108, 112, 114, 166, 168
authenticity 29, 31, 42, 45, 49, 56, 71

Ballenger, Bill 31
bipartisanship 136
Burke, Kenneth 82–85, 87–90, 93, 96, 98–99, 160, 174, 177
Bush, Barbara 7–8

Cheney, Dick 124–126, 171
civic republicanism 85, 87
Clinton, Hillary 3
compromise 131, 135, 136, 139–142, 148
Confederate 84, 93, 121
Coulter, Ann 93, 97
Cuccinelli, Ken 15
double bind 24, 61, 64, 66, 79–80, 147

dramatism 82–83, 87, 91

economy 150–152

feminine style 58, 61, 65, 67, 102, 104–107, 110, 112–114, 133, 146–148, 159, 162, 168, 173
Fluke, Sandra 13–14, 17
friendship 134, 139

gender gap 9, 10–12, 22–23, 29–30, 106, 149

Haley, Nikki 24, 144, 162, 166
Hariman, R. 83–87
hegemonic masculinity 52–55
Huckabee, Mike 16–17

individualism 52

Kelly, Megyn 72

Lakoff, George 68, 74–75, 77
Levin, Carl 23, 27–28
liberal feminism 117–119, 122, 124, 127, 170, 179
Limbaugh, Rush 13–14, 17

Martinez, Susana 25, 101
maternal persona 63
maternal thinking 49, 131, 132–134, 137, 142–143
McCain, John 49, 130, 142
McMorris Rogers, Cathy 154–155
minimum wage 12, 18–19, 32–33, 36, 51, 122, 151
Mourdock, Richard 15

National Organization for Women 32

Palin, Sarah 44, 48–49
patriarchy 147
Paycheck Fairness Act 18–19, 33, 39

Index

Pelosi, Nancy 13, 17
Pentad 82–83, 86–89, 160, 174
Peters, Gary 27–29, 36, 38, 42
pragmatism 135
private sphere 29–30, 58, 61
public sphere 58–59, 61

realist style 83–84
Republican National Convention 57, 85–86, 91–92, 94, 103, 105, 109, 120, 127, 165–166, 170
Rice, Condoleezza 12, 25–26, 99, 144–145, 150, 168, 170–171, 174–175, 180
Romney, Mitt 1, 10, 14, 22, 91, 95–96, 101, 105–106, 108–109, 112, 114, 121, 153, 172, 176–178

sick leave 19–20
Sikh 81–82
Snow, Olympia 140
Stefanik, Elise 153–154
strict father 68, 75
tough love 38, 69, 75, 78, 102
tough mother 63, 67–78

Trueman, Laura 34
Trump, Ivanka 155–156

Violence Against Women Act 20

war on women 28–29, 147
whiteness 146
Will, George 39–40, 42
Winfrey, Oprah 117, 120, 122, 125, 180

www.ingramcontent.com/pod-product-compliance
Ingram Content Group UK Ltd.
Pitfield, Milton Keynes, MK11 3LW, UK
UKHW042014140426
5217IPUK00015B/1176